DOCK ELLIS

In the Country of Baseball

DOCK ELLIS
IN THE COUNTRY OF BASEBALL

by Donald Hall

with Dock Ellis

Coward, McCann & Geoghegan, Inc.
New York

Copyright © 1976 by Donald Hall

SBN: 698-10658-X

Library of Congress Cataloging in Publication Data

Hall, Donald, 1928-
   Dock Ellis in the country of baseball.

   1. Ellis, Dock. 2. Baseball. I. Ellis, Dock, joint author. II. Title.
GV865.E44H34   796.357′092′4 [B]   74-30602

PRINTED IN THE UNITED STATES OF AMERICA

DOCK ELLIS

In the Country of Baseball

One: The Country of Baseball

1. *The Country of Baseball*

Baseball is a country all to itself. It is an old country, like Ruritania, northwest of Bohemia and its seacoast. Steam locomotives puff across trestles and through tunnels. It is a wrong-end-of-the-telescope country, like the landscape people build for model trains, miniature with distance and old age. The citizens wear baggy pinstripes, knickers, and caps. Seasons and teams shift, blur into each other, change radically or appear to change, and restore themselves to old ways again. Citizens retire to farms, in the country of baseball, smoke cigars and reminisce, and all at once they are young players again, lean and intense, running the base paths with filed spikes.

Or they stay in the city, in the capital of the country of baseball. At the mouth of the river, in the city of baseball, young black men wear purple leather maxicoats when they leave the ball park. Slick dressers of the twenties part their hair in the middle and drive roadsters. In old *barrios* everyone speaks Spanish. Kids playing stickball, and kids running away from cops, change into fierce adults rounding third base in front of fifty thousand people, and change again into old men in their undershirts on front stoops.

Though the grass transforms itself into a plastic rug, though the players speak Arkansas or Japanese, though the radio adds itself to the newspaper, and the television to the radio, though salaries grow from workingmen's wages to lawyers' compensations, the country remains the same; everything changes, and everything stays the same.

The players are white and black, Cuban and Welsh and Mississippi

9

farmers. The country of baseball is polyglot. They wear great mustaches and swing bottle-shaped bats, and some of them dress eccentrically. John McGraw's Giants play two World Series wearing black uniforms. Now the citizens' hair shortens, their loose uniforms turn white, their faces turn white also, and the white world cheers—while on the other side of town, black crowds cheer black ballplayers. Now the hair returns—beards, handlebar mustaches, long locks hanging beside the catcher's mask; now brightly colored knickers cling close to thick legs; now bats are scooped out at the thick end; now black and white play together again.

In the country of baseball the magistrates are austere and plain-spoken. Many of its citizens are decent and law-abiding, obedient to their elders and to the rules of the community.

But there have always been others—the mavericks, the eccentrics, the citizens of independent mind. They thrive in the country of baseball. Some of them display with Lucifer the motto, "I will not serve." Some of them are known as flakes, and unless they are especially talented bounce from club to club, to retire from the active life sooner than the others. Left-handed pitchers are reputed to be craziest of all, followed by pitchers in general, and left-handers in general. Maybe forty percent of the population in the country of baseball is flaky, at least in the opinion of the other sixty percent.

When Al Hrabosky meditates hate, in his public solitude behind the St. Louis mound, he perpetuates a great tradition.

The country of baseball begins to take shape at the age of six. Earlier, sometimes. Dock Ellis's cousin gave him a baseball to hold when Dock was in his crib. But Little League starts at six and stickball and cowpastureball at about the same age. At seven and eight and nine, the players begin to reside wholly in the country of baseball. For the people who will live there forever, the long summers take on form—time and space shaped by the sharp lozenge of the base paths. Then high school, maybe college, maybe rookie league, Class A, Double A, Triple A—the major leagues. In the brief season of maturity, the citizens of this country live in hotels, watch movies, pick up women who lurk for them in lobbies, sign autographs for kids, and climb onto the team bus for the ride to the ball park at five in the afternoon.

In their brief season, they sit for a thousand afternoons in front of their lockers, pull on archaic stockings, set their knickers at the height they affect, and josh and tease their teammates. Tony the trainer measures a tender elbow, tapes an ankle. Then the citizens saunter without urgency onto the field, gloves under arms, and pick up a ball.

Richie Hebner sees Richie Zisk. "Hey," he says, "want to play catch?"

Baseball, they tell us, is part of the entertainment industry.

Well, money changes hands; lawyers make big money; television people and their sponsors make big money. Even the citizens make big money for a while. But like actors and magicians and country singers and poets and ballet dancers, when the citizens claim to be in it for the money, they are only trying to be normal Americans. Nothing is further from the country of baseball than the business life. Although salaries grow and contract clauses multiply, the business of baseball like the business of art is dream.

In the cardboard box business, a boss's expectations rise like a plateau gradually elevated, an infinite ramp leading to retirement on the ghost plains of Arizona. And in the country of cardboard boxes, the manners of Rotary proliferate: the false laughter, the bonhomie of contracts, the golf played with boss's boss. Few flakes survive, in the country of cardboard boxes.

But in the country of baseball, men rise to glory in their twenties and their early thirties—a garland briefer than a girl's, or at least briefer than a young woman's—with an abrupt rise, like scaling a cliff, and then the long meadow slopes downward. Citizens of the country of baseball retire and yet they never retire. At first it may seem that they lose everything—the attention of crowds, the bustle of airplanes and hotels, the kids and the girls—but as they wake from their first shock, they discover that they live in the same place, but that they live in continual twilight, paler and fainter than the noon of games.

Dock visits an old friend, Alvin O'Neal McBean, retired to his home in the Virgin Islands. In the major leagues, McBean was *bad*. The language of Rotary does not flourish in locker rooms or dugouts; the citizens' speech does not resemble the honey tongued *Reader's Digest;* eccentricity breeds with outrage. "McBean would as soon curse you as look at you," Dock says—even if you were his manager or his general manager; and he could *scream*. He was therefore not long for the major leagues. Now Alvin O'Neal McBean supervises playgrounds, the old ballplayer teaching the kids old tricks, far from reporters, umpires, and Cadillacs. "He's made the Adjustment," says Dock. "He doesn't *like* it, but he's made the Adjustment."

The years on the diamond are fantasy. The citizens *know* they live in fantasy, that the custom cars and the stewardesses and the two-inch-thick steaks belong to the world of glass slippers and golden coaches drawn by unicorns. There fathers were farmers and one day they will be farmers also. Or their fathers loaded crates on boxcars for a hundred dollars a week and one day they too will load crates on boxcars for a hundred dollars a week. Just now, they are pulling down two thousand.

But for them, the fantasy does not end like waking from a dream or like a transformation on the stroke of midnight. They make the Adjustment, and gradually they understand that even at a hundred dollars a week, or even on top of a tractor, they live in a crepuscular duplicate of their old country.

And most of them, whatever they thought, never do just what their fathers did. When they make the Adjustment, they sell insurance or real estate to their former fans, or they open a bar in the Missouri town they came from. They buy a restaurant next to a bowling alley in their old Oakland neighborhood, and they turn paunchy, and tilt a chair back behind the cash register, remembering—while they compute insurance, while they pull draft beer—the afternoons of August and the cold September nights under the blue lights, the pennant race at the end of the dying season.

The country of baseball never wholly vanishes for anyone once a citizen of that country. On porches in the country of baseball old men are talking. Scouts, coaches, managers; car salesmen, manufacturers' representatives, bartenders. No one would let them exile themselves from that country if they wanted to. For the kids with their skateboards, for the men at the Elks, they remain figures of youth and indolent energy, alert at the plate while the pitcher fidgets at the mound—a young body always glimpsed like a shadow within the heavy shape of the old body.

The old first baseman, making the final out of the inning, in the last year he will play, underhands the ball casually toward the mound, as he has done ten thousand times. The ball bounces over the lip of the grass, climbs the crushed red brick of the mound for a foot or two, and then rolls back until it catches in the green verge. The ball has done this ten thousand times.

Basketball is not a country. It's a show, a circus, a miracle continually demonstrating the Newtonian heresy that muscle is lighter than air, bodies suspended like photographs of bodies, the ball turning at right angles. When the game is over, basketball does not continue; basketball waits poised and immobile in the locked equipment room, like the mechanical toy waiting for a hand to wind it.

Football is not a country. It's a psychodrama, brothers beating up on brothers, murderous, bitter, tender, homosexual, ending with the incest of brotherly love, and in the wounds Americans carry all over their bodies. When the game is done, football dragasses itself to a bar and drinks blended whiskey, maybe seven and seven, brooding, its mouth sour, turned down, its belly flowing over its angry belt.

In the country of baseball days are always the same.

The pitchers hit. Bunting, slapping weakly at fat pitches, hitting line drives that collapse in front of the pitching machine, they tease each other. Ken Brett, with the fireplug body, lifts one over the center-field fence, as the big hitters emerge from the dugout for the honest BP. "Did you see *that*?" he asks Wilver Stargell. "Did you see *that*?" he asks Al Oliver.

The pitcher who won the ball game last night lifts fungoes to a crowd in left field—outfielders, utility infielders, even pitchers who pause to shag flies in the midst of running. When they catch a ball, they throw it back to the infield by stages, lazy arcs linking outfielders to young relief pitchers to coaches. Everyone is light and goofy, hitting fungoes or shagging flies or relaying the ball. Everyone is relaxed and slightly self-conscious, repeating the motions that became rote before they were ten. Some citizens make catches behind their backs, or throw the ball from between their legs. Behind the mound, where a coach begins to throw BP to the regulars, Paul Popovich and Bob Moose pick up loose baseballs rolled toward the mound, and stack them in the basket where the BP pitcher retrieves three at a time. Now they bounce baseballs on the cement-hard turf, dribbling them like basketballs. Moose dribbles, fakes left, darts right, jumps, and over Popovich's jumping body sinks a baseball in a wire basket for a quick two points.

Coaches slap grounders to infielders, two deep at every position. Third, short, second, first, a bunt for the catcher. The ball snarls around the horn. Third, short, second, first, catcher. At the same time, the rubber arm of the BP pitcher stretches toward the plate, where Bob Robertson takes his turn at bat. Two balls at once bounce toward Rennie Stennett at second. A rookie up from Charleston takes his cuts, and a shortstop jabs at a grounder from Bob Skinner, and Manny Sanguillen leaps to capture a bunt, and the ball hums across the infield, and Willie Stargell lofts an immense fly to center field. Behind the cage, Bill

Robinson yells at Stargell, "Buggy-whipping, man! Buggy-whipping!"
Stargell looks up while the pitcher loads himself with balls, and sees
that Joe Garagiola is watching him. Tonight is Monday night. "Hey,
man," he says slowly. "What are the rules of this bubble gum contest?"
He whips his bat forward, takes a cut, tops the ball, grimaces. Willie has
two fractured ribs from a ball thrown by a forty-one-year-old Philadelphia relief pitcher. Philadelphia is trying to catch Pittsburgh and lead
the Eastern Division.

"What rules?" says Garagiola. "I don't have them with me."
Willie whips his bat forward with accelerating force. "How many
pieces?" He hits a line drive off the right-field wall.

Garagiola shrugs. "Four or five," he says. "Something like that." He
laughs, his laugh a little forced, as if he felt suddenly foolish. "Got to
have a little fun in this game."

Nearer to game time, with the pitchers running in the outfield, the
screens gone from the infield, five Pirates are playing pepper between
the dugout and the first-base line. Dave Giusti holds the bat, and
fielding are Ramon Hernandez, John Morlan, and Daryl Patterson.
Giusti hits miniature line drives back at the other relief pitchers.
Everyone laughs, taunts, teases. Giusti hits one harder than usual at
Hernandez. Another. The ambidextrous Puerto Rican—who tried
pitching with both arms in the same inning until they stopped him; who
pitches from the left side now, and strikes out the left-handed pinch
hitter in the ninth inning—Ramon drops his glove, picks up a baseball in
each hand, winds up both arms as he faces Giusti head on, and fires two
baseballs simultaneously. Giusti swings laughing and misses them both.

In the outfield, big number seventeen lopes with long strides, then
idles talking to fans near the bullpen for ten minutes, then fields
grounders at second base, says something to make Willie Stargell laugh,
and walks toward the dugout. Seeing Manny Sanguillen talk with Dave
Concepcion and Pedro Borbon, soft Spanish fraternization with the
enemy, he throws a baseball medium fast to hit Manny in the flesh of his
thigh. Manny jumps, looks around, sees who it is, laughs, and runs with
gentle menace toward him. But Dock has turned his back, and leans on
his folded arms at the top of the dugout, scanning the crowd for friends
and for ladies, his high ass angled up like a dragster, his big handsome
head solemnly swiveling over the box seats—bad Dock Ellis, black,
famous for his big mouth, suspended in 1975 for a month without pay,

the suspension rescinded and pay restored, Dock, famous for his Bad Attitude, maverick citizen in the country of baseball.

At Old Timer's Day in Cincinnati, Edd Roush is an honorary captain, who hit .325 in the Federal League in 1914, .352 in the National League in 1921, and played eighteen years. Lou Boudreau plays shortstop. His gut is huge, but he breaks quickly to his left and scoops a grounder from the bat of Pee Wee Reese, and throws to Mickey Vernon at first. I saw Lou Boudreau, player-manager for Cleveland, hit two fly balls into the left-field screen at Fenway Park in the one-game American League pennant play off in 1948. I discovered Pee Wee Reese eight years earlier, when I was twelve, and the soft voice of Red Barber on WOR chatted about the new shortstop up from the Louisville Colonels. Joe Nuxhall pitches, who pitched in the major leagues when he was fifteen years old, and still pitches batting practice for the Cincinnati Reds. And Carl Erskine pitches, and Harvey Haddix. Harvey Kuenn comes to the plate, and then Dixie Walker—who played right field for the Brooklyn Dodgers, and confessed to Mr. Rickey in the spring of 1947 that he could not play with a black man. Dixie Walker flies out to a citizen who retired last year, still limber as a squirrel, playing center field again—Willie Mays.

In the country of baseball, time is the air we breathe, and the wind swirls us backward and forward, until we seem so reckoned in time and seasons that all time and all seasons become the same. Ted Williams goes fishing, never to return to the ball park, and falls asleep at night in the Maine summers listening to the Red Sox on radio from Fenway Park; and a ghostly Ted Williams continues to play the left-field wall, and his flat swing meets the ball in 1939, in 1948, in 1960. In the country of baseball the bat swings in its level swoop, the ball arcs upward into the twilight, the center fielder gathers himself beneath it, and *Dixie Walker flies out to Willie Mays*.

2. *Pitching and Poetry*

I met Dock Ellis and the Pittsburgh Pirates for the first time in 1973. With my literary agent Gerard McCauley and four other unathletic and sedentary men, I had contracted to put on a uniform and participate in spring training—as Paul Gallico and John Kieran and George Plimpton had done before us. While an equipment man was searching for a uniform big enough, I meandered into a team meeting in center field. Everyone wore a uniform except me. The big man wearing number seventeen turned to me and patted me on the stomach. "*Say,* you better do some *laps!*"

I had met Dock Ellis, and this book began.

In a sense, I had met him twenty minutes earlier. Walking through the parking lot on the way to the clubhouse, we had passed a remarkable automobile. It was a long Cadillac with red vinyl trim on the *out*side, and a spectacular grille. ("It ain't nothing," Dock used to say, "but a seven oh seven.") The license plate read DOCK.

I found out later how Dock happened to own it: One day Wilver Stargell, Dock's old roomie and closest Pirate friend, drove Dock to the suburban car agency where Dock's ordinary Cadillac was undergoing treatment. They saw this custom job in the lot. "Man," said Stargell, "this is *your car.*" From the dealer they discovered that the car had been ordered by a nattily dressed young man, a pimp by trade, whose altered circumstances had rendered him incapable of accepting delivery. Dock accepted Stargell's advice, made a trade on the spot, and drove home the Dockmobile.

While we admired the car that morning, I assembled fragments of memory about Dock Ellis. There was the All-Star Game he started in 1971 against Vida Blue, when he had prophesied that they would never start a brother against a brother. There was the time he complained that the Pirates were too cheap to rent him a long enough bed. There was the time he was fined for not signing autographs. The newspapers called him crybaby and troublemaker. I remembered stories that went with his name, but I didn't know his face. When he recommended my exercise program, I didn't know I'd met him. For sixteen years I had lived an hour from Detroit, and my baseball was parochially American League.

Then manager Bill Virdon told the players to do their laps, and I ran with them. When I puffed to the end, dead last, and number seventeen saw me, he seemed surprised—one of the few times I have ever seen him surprised. "You really did it!" he said.

"You told me to," I said proudly, and we chatted a few minutes. He asked me if I was a sportswriter and I told him no, I was a poet. He thought I was pulling his leg at first. Then he decided I wasn't. "Do your thing," he said.

Dock took me on as a pupil, and counseled me on hitting, on running, on back pains, and on other tribulations of the professional athlete. Whenever I was engaged in some futile exercise, I would turn exhausted to find Dock's eyes—amused and oddly respectful—watching me. Every now and then he asked me something about writing. Finally he conceived the idea that he would like to pitch to me. We were never able to achieve this confrontation, although it was something we both wanted. "I'd like to pitch to you," he kept saying.

I was awash with foolhardy courage. "I'd *hit* you," I told him.

"You wouldn't hit me," he said. "It'd be just like BP, only you wouldn't hit nothing."

"Of course I'd hit you."

Dock made a little shrug of pretended resignation. "You hit me," he said, "I hit you."

In the season that followed, Dock was twelve and fourteen, with a 3.05 ERA. He was out with a sore elbow late in the season, or the Pirates might have won their division. The Mets edged past them at the end.

That summer I went to night games at Tiger Stadium, and by day I wrote a number of things, including an account of my week of spring training. That autumn, Dock tape-recorded an introduction to *Playing Around*, the book that collected our humiliations in the sun. He wrote about "one guy that had a gut and a beard," and recorded, among other observations, my triumph over a pitching machine:

> So then the poet—the frustrated ballplayer, I can't recall his name—you could tell this guy wanted to play ball all his life and he just knew he could hit the ball so he got in there and he swung about ten times, and I said, "Oh, the bat is getting heavy, huh?" Because, normally, if you keep swinging the bat it will get heavy. So I said, "Turn the machine down," so then he fouled one off and he was so happy he jumped out of the cage and everyone cracked up.

Actually, it wasn't like that at all.

In March of 1974, during spring vacation from the University of Michigan where I teach, I was invited to read my poems at Rollins College in Winter Park, Florida.

For a poet, the poetry reading is the main source of income connected with writing. Magazines pay little; you may sell a poem for $17.50, or give it away, since many poetry magazines pay nothing. And when you do a book, even if it sells moderately well, you will find yourself with only a few hundred dollars in royalties. But then, as if in obedience to Emerson's notion of compensation, some college will ask you to read your poems for an hour, and maybe spend another hour talking poetry with students—and pay you a thousand dollars. The same college has a library unable to afford $4.95 for one of your books.

Nobody would write poems to make a living anyway. But the poetry reading has brought a touch of comfort to the life of the poet. Especially when the reading occurs at the beginning of March, in Winter Park, at the lotus-eating campus of Rollins College—and baseball camps are busy in every nook and cranny of the peninsula.

I spent ten days in Florida, two of them at Rollins College, and eight at Pirate City.

Ostensibly I went to Pirate City to publicize *Playing Around.* Really, I felt nostalgic about the country of baseball, which I had visited so briefly the year before. I wanted to hang around baseball further, and writing about it seemed the only way. I tried to think of things to write.

Meantime, I enjoyed myself. Each morning I hung around the training diamonds, and Dock came over to gossip between doing laps and other tasks. He suggested that he pitch to me *this* year. I told him I couldn't even swing a bat. In fact, I had barely crawled from the bed in our motel on the Gulf; my back was out, lower back muscle spasms, and I feared that my playing days were over. Dock put on a shrewd look. "I know just where to pitch you," he said. "Low and outside."

He told me how he had dictated his introduction, how he had tape recorders rigged up all over his apartment; with them he practiced being a disc jockey, one of the professions he considered taking up when he finishes playing. He spoke all sorts of things into those tape recorders; maybe sometime he'd be doing a *book.*

For a moment I wondered if I was listening to a hint. Then Dock left to join the other pitchers at practice in catching pop-ups, so we didn't carry the question further. The pitchers gathered on one of the four infields at Pirate City, where the compressed-air howitzer pitching machine— which doubles as a fly-ball or pop-fly machine—occupied home plate. One after another, pitchers lay facedown on the grass next to the pitcher's mound. Don Leppert would pull the lanyard—or whatever you call it—and boom the baseball high into the dazzling blue air of the Gulf. When the ball went up, Leppert yelled to the pitcher to stand up and catch it. Since he had been lying facedown, he had no idea where in the sky to look. His fellow pitchers yelled confusing instructions at him: "Left! Left!" "Behind you!" "Watch out!" "Right!" "No! No!"

Most of the pitchers never found the ball at all. Two were beaned. The crowd of colleagues—each of them doomed to suffer the same indignity—hooted and howled as pitcher after pitcher zigzagged crazily across the infield, jerking this way and that like a lizard cornered by a cat, and searched out the white speck against the bright sky, only to have it crash to the grass beside him. After each round of laughter, bad advice, and catcalls, the new victim would emerge from the chorus, the old one return to its ranks.

"Dock Ellis," yelled Don Leppert. "Dock!" He came forth, hooted at already, sauntering, elegant, and took his prone position. When the howitzer fired, he leaped to his feet and circled the mound. He obviously heard nothing of the misdirections of the others—this was his tenth spring training—and wholly concentrated on distinguishing the little ball. At the last moment, as it fell to the side of him, he flicked out his left hand and caught the ball. He was the only pitcher that morning to catch the pop fly.

Later in the day, going back to the locker room to shower and go home, he was tired and moved slowly. "You were the only one to catch the pop-up," I told him. "Congratulations."

He shrugged. "It just fell in my glove," he said. "I was just protecting my *face*."

Then he looked more serious, perhaps grieved. "I don't *like* the ordeal of catching the ball like that. It's nothing but *killing time*. In a game, the pitcher will *never* catch a ball like that. In a game? *No way!* Third baseman, catcher, *any* infielder. No way they're going to let us catch that ball. It's not practice, even for rookies.

"It's a psychology thing. 'If one of your *infielders* misses a ball like that'—this is manager Danny Murtaugh talking—'we're letting you know how difficult it is.' Oh, *difficult*."

Dock's speech is emphatic. Trying to render his speech, I use so much italic that his conversation looks like Queen Victoria's letters. It is difficult to render anyone's speech in print; Dock's is impossible. He is emphatic, he mimics, he uses grand gesture and subtle intonation and eloquent facial expression. He also varies swiftly from black vocabulary and syntax to academic or legal white, with stops at all stations on the way. His language is so varied that, if he were a fictional character, he would be inconsistent and unrealistic. Sometimes, maybe, Dock *is* unrealistic. But Dock is real.

I thought about wanting to hang around baseball. I thought about the enigma of Dock himself—here was this supposedly bad man, this hostile screaming crybaby of the sports pages; and yet he seemed to me funny, sophisticated, and friendly. I decided to do a little hinting of my own.

"You know that book you might do?" I said the next morning. "If you ever want anybody to read it for you, you know, to help you revise it or anything, I'd be happy to do it."

Dock turned it back, with one of his apparent changes of mind. "Oh, I won't *write* a book," he said. He might *do* a book; he wouldn't *write* one. "You're a writer, aren't you?"

We had smoked each other out.

We stood together in the Florida sun, watching an intrasquad game together, and talked without joking for two hours; we talked about basketball—like so many pitchers, Dock was a great high-school basketball player—and about his daughter, and his wife from whom he was separated, and his boyhood in California, and even about writing poetry. Dock made a tentative analogy between the writer using words to influence the reader, and the pitcher's devices to outsmart the batter. I said I'd think that one over.

Then Dock said good-bye and strolled down the foul line toward the bullpen, where he warmed up to pitch his two innings. It was his first *live* pitching of the year. As he left, he told me pitchers today were not supposed to throw curves or sliders, only fastballs and change-ups; straight pitches. "*No way!*" he said. "I'm going to stand out there"—his voice rose in pitch—"and throw straight pitches, and get my head knocked off? *No way!*"

When Dock came to the mound, Manny Sanguillen grounded out to third base on the first pitch. I heard Manny laugh as he came back to the bench. "Dock, he *curves* me!" he announced to everybody. "He no suppose to do that!"

3. *Fans and the Militant*

Dock Phillip Ellis, Jr., exercises his life in the pursuit of freedom. By freedom Dock means speaking his mind and doing what he needs to do without regard for consequence. This independence has not endeared him to fans. In the spring of 1975—to pick an example at random—a Pittsburgh newspaper printed a photograph of Dock running laps in Florida; his midriff was bare in the heat, and a dog was running after him. The photograph seems inoffensive, but someone in Pittsburgh took the trouble to cut it out of the paper, letter "No Good Black Rat" along the top, and mail it to Dock in Bradenton.

Of course when he makes the papers by screaming about the All-Star Game, or when he gets suspended, or when Commissioner Bowie Kuhn orders him to stop wearing hair curlers in uniform, then the hate mail piles up like slag. Some fans prefer their athletes docile, humble, grateful, clean-cut, and white.

So Dock—being proud, being black, and being his own man; possibly being eccentric—has more than his share of detractors. He can also count on some of the most devoted fans in the world, including most young black people in Pittsburgh, where he played his major league baseball until 1976.

All over the country, Dock is a roguish and spirited celebrity among black people, even among those indifferent to sports. *Jet* has so often printed photographs and news stories about Dock that it seems to have a Dock Ellis Division. *Ebony* has featured him. He is popular because he upsets white racists. He is popular like Muhammad Ali because he does what he pleases and gets away with it. He is popular because he is brave and stylish at the same time. He is also popular because he is loyal to black brothers and sisters everywhere, and spends his leisure in projects for black people—working at the rehabilitation of convicts, fighting sickle-cell anemia, and working with black youth. In these pursuits, he has avoided publicity. Readers of white sports pages know little of this side of him. He combines, in a way known only to himself, pizzaz with dignity.

Much of the public does not *wish* to accord dignity to men who pitch, field, and hit baseballs for a living.

I remember June 8, 1974. Dock was scheduled to pitch against the

San Francisco Giants at Candlestick Park. It was a Saturday afternoon game, and the sun was bright, but high winds from the Bay made it cold. Candlestick is the worst park in the major leagues. Made for football, it suffers a baseball diamond—awkwardly tucked on acres of green plastic—the way a circus horse tolerates a monkey. And no one comes to the games, not since Oakland arrived, across the Bay.

This Saturday was Camera Day. For nearly an hour before the game, fans crowded along the rails of the lower deck with Nikons and Polaroids, Leicas, Instamatics, Hasselblads, and antique box Brownies. The Giants strolled on the dirt at the edges of the field, offering themselves for photographs. One of them led a llama on a rein, another a pony, another a dog, another a camel. A young man not in uniform led a huge tiger. Ballplayers strayed close, but not too close, to the tiger.

Which were the animals, and which the athletes? At the zoo, every day is Camera Day. At Candlestick, only once a year do the visitors come close enough to the animal-athletes to fill camera frames with head and shoulders. The creatures behind the rail, camel or outfielder, gradually melted into each other.

Dock would never have taken part in such a show. In 1971—the year after his no-hitter, the year he started the All-Star Game for the National League, and won nineteen games—Dock was bannered in a Pittsburgh paper, ELLIS PROBABLY MOST UNPOPULAR BUC OF ALL TIME. Sportswriters all over the country had already censured his Bad Attitude. In Pittsburgh, he made people angriest when he refused to sign autographs. That's not exactly what he did, but that's what he was accused of.

Before every Sunday home game at Three Rivers Stadium, selected Pirate players hand out autographed photographs of themselves. In 1971, the players were sitting inside little cages to hand them out. The cage was there, presumably, to protect the players from the fans.

But the metaphor of the cage did not suit Dock. "I went up there and looked at it, so I said, 'I'm not going to be in a cage. I'm no monkey in a cage.' So they said, 'Well, if you don't do it, we're going to fine you.' I said, 'I don't care.' "

He cared enough to pay two sequential one-hundred-dollar fines.

Newspapers and television stations throbbed with indignation. One TV commentator, calling Dock "an egotistical pop-off," rehearsed earlier incidents and mounted to this climax: "Now the Pittsburgh prima donna is refusing to take part in . . . signing autographs in special

booths before game time. . . . This past weekend my eleven-year-old
son got the autographs of Bill Mazeroski and Bob Veale at just such a
booth. He was thrilled. . . . By his action, Ellis has labeled himself as
too big or too important to be bothered with the kids who hold him as
something to look up to, with the fans who pay his salary. I intend to
teach my son that that is not the behavior of a champion . . ."

This one quote can stand in for a hundred others.

A year later, the Pirates changed the system.

Other players felt as Dock did, but did not speak out until he had
provoked the usual abuse. Now the players sit at long tables while fans
file by, and hand out photographs and sign yearbooks. A security guard
stands by the table to protect them. Dock takes his turn.

Tomorrow he will sit at gate C. "I wish they would have me at gate B,"
he tells me. "I can sell more yearbooks there. Can I sell them! I must
have sold at least fifty or seventy-five yearbooks. We don't sign
*any*thing, but . . . let me see, what do we sign? . . . We sign *yearbooks*, that's all we sign is *yearbooks*. They'll throw a piece of paper at
you, or a ball, and I'll say, 'We can't sign that. You've got to get a
yearbook. Go get your yearbook!' " Dock is helping to support his
employers.

"But you *are* handing out autographed pictures?" I ask him.

"Oh, yeah, I'll hand them out."

"Already signed?"

"We don't sign them. Somebody else signs them."

After I have digested this information, I ask Dock to elaborate.

"They tried to get us to sign the autographs beforehand. Like if I'm
signing autographs tomorrow, I should have signed all those pictures
two and a half weeks ago. But a lot of guys wouldn't do it, so they just
said, 'Forget about it,' and they hired a girl to write the names. She does
it *close!*"

With his own right hand, Dock Ellis signed more autographs than
anyone else on the Pirates.

Before almost every game, in every park, Dock loiters along the box
seats, walking from the outfield where he has been running, or from the
bullpen where he has been throwing. People yell at him. He sees old
friends. He chatters and makes new ones. Kids lean out, holding their
pads and pencils. He will sign ten or twenty, move on, sign ten or twenty
more. Frequently, he will make conversation with rapid questions: "Is

that your sister? What you doing up so late? You go to school? Where?
What's your daddy's name? Don't you like the *Pirates?*"

It takes forty minutes, some days, to walk from right field to the
dugout.

Dock complains about the new parks. "You're just not as close to the
fans as you used to be. If you don't have the fans, what're you doing out
there playing ball?"

I ask him if he's aware—if ballplayers are aware—of old fans who have
been coming to the park for fifty years, who watch the players change
while the team remains the same.

"The DIEHARD fans," says Dock, with new heights of emphasis. "They
sit out there in the rain, snow, everything. They won't *leave,* unless
they've got bad health. They'll be *right there.* Today, I saw—" we were
talking after a game with Cincinnati at Pittsburgh "—it was two guys,
their wives. They said, 'Do you remember West Mound Street,
Columbus?' " Dock spent two years at Columbus in the minor leagues.
"I say, *'Yeah!'* That's where the ball park was. I remembered the guy's
voice, and I remember his wife from her glasses.

"Oh, you should have seen me out there today, after the game. I must
have signed a hundred autographs. Of course I was trying to get close to
that girl. I made sure I signed all their autographs, so they would *get
away!* Of course they were Cincinnati fans, hundreds of them— They
went *crazy.* She just happened to be blonde."

All over the league there are fans that a ballplayer knows only at the
ball park. When you go into San Diego, you know you will see the fat
woman on the third-base line whose husband arrives in the fifth inning.
In Philadelphia there is a black family named Eustace always in left-field
boxes. "Take Chicago. I have a lot of friends in Chicago, I don't know
their names but I know their faces; I could see them anywhere and I'd
know them. They got this Japanese family there. She takes pictures, and
she took a picture, an *original* picture of me in curlers."

It must be unpleasant, though, to be yelled at by obnoxious fans.

Dock's face gets serious. This notion touches a principle he lives by.
"The fan's *privilege* is to say what he wants to say. That's the same
privilege I want, to say what I want to say and to do what I want to do."

Of course there is abuse from the fans. "Ellis, you stink!" "Hey, Ellis, crybaby!" "Ellis, where your curlers?" "You suck!"

Once in Chicago he had a quarrel going with the bleacher bums, as they called themselves. "I even had a grown man crying. I was just wolfing. I was getting on them *bad*. A man just shut up, and started crying. Then they apologize. They say, 'We didn't *mean* it.' I say, 'Well, okay, then, don't *say* nothing.'

"That particular time, that's when they *challenged* me to come to the bleacher bums' bar. They was the only ones they let *in*, there. Behind the scoreboard in Chicago. I stayed about an hour and a half. They all wanted to buy me drinks. They were just *amazed* that I came in there."

Not all the abuse is so open. Besides anonymous hate mail, there is the telephone.

"You get a lot of crank calls. You see in the papers, guys saying that people want to kill them? They've been trying to kill me ever since they started writing about me in the papers. If I *told* them, every time somebody called to say he was going to kill me, they'd have to put a man with me every day. They call me and say, 'If you peek your head above that dugout again, we're gonna blow it off!' "

Loitering along the rails signing autographs, Dock mostly talks to the kids. "Well, what's happening, my man?" When he gets abuse from white adults, sometimes he counterattacks through their children, setting young against old to make his point.

"Ellis, you stink! Ellis, if you're going to wear curlers, why don't you get out of baseball?"

Dock searches for the source of the taunts, and finds a pair of white adults with their children, sitting near the field. "I *charge* them. I run over to them, and say, 'What's your phone number? What's your address? Because I'm coming to dinner.' "

While the parents gawk, Dock levels his finger at a child and says, "Is that all right? Am I coming?

"The child is excited anyway, by the fact of me being over there talking to them, because I'm a major league ballplayer. The kid is all happy about it and says, 'Yeah! Dock's coming to dinner.' The parents look like fools. What can the parents say? 'No?' "

And Dock telephones, and comes to dinner, and "They tell me they were booing only because they were going on what they'd read about me."

"How many dinners have you invited yourself to?"

"Three. It's a warm welcome. From there, we sort of become friends. They all still come to the ball park. It just tickles the hell out of me! . . ."

Years ago, newspapers started to call Dock a "militant," short for "black militant." The word annoys him, because it does not mean what it says.

In some ways, Dock is indeed a black militant, and wishes to be. When he was younger, during junior college, he read *Elijah Speaks*; in the minor leagues he went into "a heavy black thing" and isolated himself from whites. More relaxed now, he gets along as easily with whites as with blacks, travels in mixed company, and does not allow himself to be limited by any of the categories to which he belongs, "black," or "athlete," or "Californian." But he is alert to prejudice, he takes pride in his blackness, and he has been a particular friend to the young brothers on the team.

It irritates him that the press calls him "militant" when the term is inappropriate. When he complains about short beds or crowded airplanes, when he wears curlers or refuses to pitch relief, he is characterized as militant. If he complains about anything, he shows a Bad Attitude. If Dock Ellis returned a steak to the chef at Bonanza, complaining that it was too rare, a wire service would report: BLACK MILITANT DOCK ELLIS REFUSES STEAK. When Richie Zisk started screaming to the press about the way the Pirates were treating him, Dock—who regarded Zisk proudly as his pupil in public relations— called him a "white militant."

When someone calls Dock Ellis "militant" because he complains that his hotel bed is too short, he is calling him "an uppity nigger."

4. *Hitting Batters*

In the country of baseball, pitchers are always throwing baseballs at batters. Some pitchers are better known for it than others.

If the pitcher has acquired a certain reputation, the batter may have other matters on his mind besides his batting average, his ribbies, his slugging average, and his team's place in the standings. As Sandy Koufax has remarked, "Pitching is the art of instilling fear."

Dock Ellis is moderately famous for throwing at batters. On May 1, 1974, he tied a major league record by hitting three batters in a row.

They were the first three batters up, in the first inning. They were
Cincinnati Reds batters. Dock's control was just fine.

Four days earlier, I had seen him at a party in Pittsburgh. I wandered
around, talking to various people. Dock's attorney and friend Tom Reich
was there, shaking his head in disapproval of a plan of Dock's. I met
Dock in the kitchen fixing a drink. I asked him with some awe, "Are you
really going to hit every Cincinnati ballplayer Wednesday night?"

He returned the awe. "How you know that?" he said.

We must now consider the history, philosophy, and psychology of
hitting batters.

In the challenge between mound and plate, which is the center of the
game, a reputation can be as effective as an extra pitch. Dock: "The
hitter will try to take *advantage* of you. Like if you are a pitcher who
throws a lot of breaking balls, a lot of sliding fast balls, or if you pitch
away, the hitter will have a tendency to lean across the plate. Quite
naturally, if they know that this is your routine, they'll be trying to go *at*
the ball, to get a better swing at it. They'll be moving up closer on the
plate. Therefore, when you throw *in* on them, you don't throw to hit
them, you throw to brush them back. That means: 'Give me some of the
plate. Let me have my part, and you take yours! Get away! Give me
some room to pitch with!'

"As far as *hitting* a batter, there are situations when it is called for, like
sometimes a pitcher might intentionally or unintentionally hit a batter,
or throw two balls near a hitter. The other team, to retaliate, will either
knock someone down or hit a batter."

Not all pitchers will throw at batters. If you are a batter, you want *your*
pitchers to throw at *their* hitters, to protect *you*.

Bob Veale was the Pirates' best pitcher for years. Between 1962 and
1972, he won a hundred and sixteen games. But he had a flaw. Gene
Clines, a Pirate outfielder at the time, talked to me after Veale was
traded to Boston: "He can throw the ball through a brick wall, but
everybody knew that he was a *gentle* giant. If Veale would knock you
down, it had to be a mistake. He didn't want to hurt anybody." Clines
shook his head in bewildered melancholy. "Who's going to challenge
him? Nobody on the *baseball field* is going to say, 'I'm going to go out
and *get* Bob Veale.' . . . Take a left-handed hitter. Take Willie. They
going to be going up to the plate, and digging in, knowing that Veale is
not going to knock them down. . . ." He shakes his head again, at the
waste of it all.

"Blass was the same way." Steve Blass announced in 1973 that he would *not* throw at batters, even if management fined him for disobeying orders. "Now he was one guy that personally I really didn't like to play behind," Clines told me. "If they knock me down two or three times . . . well, if *he* throws at a batter, he's gonna say, 'Watch out!' . . . and I don't want that, because they never told *me* to watch out! They trying to knock my *head* off! Why go out there and play behind a guy that's not going to protect you?"

Manny Sanguillen: "I tell you about Veale. The only player Veale used to knock down was Willie McCovey. The only one. I was catching. Because McCovey hurt him so much." McCovey hurt Veale by hitting long balls off him. "You remember when McCovey had the operation here?" Manny, whose hands are as quick as the expressions on his face, jabs at his right knee. "Veale used to throw down at the knee!"

When Bruce Kison came up to the Pirates, Dock took to him immediately. Although Kison was six feet six inches and weighed only 155 pounds when he first reported (in the locker room, Dock says, when Kison breathed and filled his frail chest with air, he looked like a greyhound who could walk on his hind legs), he had acquired a reputation for hitting batters. If you hit batters, it is sensible to weigh 230 and look *mean* at all times.

"I was wild," says Bruce Kison, sprawled and smiling. "I've always had a reputation . . . I have a fastball that runs *in*, on a right-handed hitter. In the minor leagues in one game I hit seven batters." Kison laughs, as if he were telling about a time in high school when he attempted a foolish escapade, like chaining a cow in the women's gym, and the cow kicked him, but nobody got hurt. "I was just completely wild. I hit three guys in a row. There were two outs. The manager came out of the dugout and said, 'Bruce, I know you're not trying to hit these guys, but we'll have the whole stands out on the field pretty soon!'

"The next guy up was a big catcher. *No*, he was an *outfielder*, but he came up to the plate with catcher's gear on . . ."

I want to make sure I understand. "But you do, on occasion, throw at batters?"

"Certainly." Kison is no longer smiling. He sounds almost pedantic. "That is part of pitching."

A pitcher establishes his reputation early. Dock came up to Pittsburgh in 1968, and in 1969 was a regular starter. He quickly established himself as mean and strong. "Cepeda is the *biggest*," says

Dock. So it was necessary for Dock to hit Cepeda. "He was trying to take *advantage* of me because I was a rookie. He was trying to *scare* me. I let him know, then, that I was not the type dude to fuck around with. It was a *big thing*, because who would be hitting Cepeda? If you went for the biggest guy, it meant you would go for *anybody*. You weren't scared of *anybody*. I hit McCovey, and I really got *up* on McCovey that year. But he's not so big. Cepeda is the biggest. The rest of the season, from that point on, I had no trouble with the hitters. They were all *running*."

Sometimes one courts trouble, hitting batters.

In 1969, in Montreal, "I hit Mack Jones in the head, but I wasn't trying to hit him in the head. I was trying to hit him in the *side*.

"They had hit Clemente in the chest. So I said, 'The first batter up, I'm going to try to *kill* him. Mack Jones was the first batter. I threw at him. I missed him. I threw at him again. He ducked, and it hit him in the head. He came out to the mound, like he was coming at me." Players rushed out on the field. Enormous Dick Radatz, relief pitcher recently traded from Detroit to Montreal, ran in from the bullpen toward the mound. Dock addressed Radatz, "Hey, man, I'll turn you into a *piece* . . . of . . . *meat!*" Radatz stopped in his tracks.

The umpire behind home plate looked as if he planned to interfere, possibly even to throw Dock out of the game. "But Clemente," Dock remembers, "he intervened, and he told the umpire, 'You leave Dock alone. The motherfuckers hit me twice! Don't mess with Dock!' "

On Wednesday night, May 1, 1974, the Reds were in Pittsburgh. Dock was starting against Cincinnati for the first time that year. As it developed, he was also starting against Cincinnati for the last time that year.

Beginning in spring training, among the palm trees and breezes and gas shortages of Bradenton on the Gulf Coast of Florida, Dock had planned to hit as many Cincinnati batters as possible, when he first pitched against them. He had told some of his teammates, but they were not sure he meant it. Dock loves to sell wolf tickets ("Wolf tickets? Some people are always selling them, some people are always buying them . . . ") and the Pirate ball club had learned not always to take him literally.

Manny knew he meant it. At the regular team meeting before the game—the Pirates meet at the start of each series, to discuss the ball club they are about to engage—Dock said there was no need to go over

Cincinnati batters, their strengths and weaknesses. "I'm just going to *mow* the lineup down," he said. To Manny (who later claimed to the press that he had never seen anybody so wild), Dock said, "Don't even give me no signal. Just try to catch the ball. If you can't catch it, forget it."

Taking his usual warm-up pitches, Dock noticed Pete Rose standing at one side of the batter's box, leaning on his bat, studying his delivery. On his next-to-last warm-up, Dock let fly at Rose and almost hit him.

A distant early warning.

In fact, he had considered not hitting Pete Rose at all. He and Rose are friends, but of course friendship, as the commissioner of baseball would insist, must never prevent even-handed treatment. No, Dock had considered not hitting Pete Rose because Rose would *take it so well*. He predicted that Rose, once hit, would make no acknowledgment of pain—no grimace, no rubbing the afflicted shoulder—but would run at top speed for first base, indicating clearly to his teammates that there was nothing to fear. "He's going to *charge* first base, and make it look like nothing." Having weighed the whole matter, Dock decided to hit him anyway.

It was a pleasant evening in Pittsburgh, the weather beginning to get warmer, perhaps 55 degrees, when Dock threw the first pitch. "The first pitch to Pete Rose was directed toward his head," as Dock expresses it, "not actually to *hit* him," but as "the *message*, to let him know that he was going to get hit. More or less to *press his lips*. I knew if I could get close to the head that I could get them in the body. Because they're looking to protect their head, they'll give me the body." The next pitch was behind him. "The next one, I hit him in the side."

Pete Rose's response was even more devastating than Dock had anticipated. He smiled. Then he picked the ball up, where it had fallen beside him, and gently, underhand, tossed it back to Dock. Then he lit for first as if trying out for the Olympics.

As Dock says, with huge approval, "You have to be *good*, to be a hot dog."

As Rose bent down to pick up the ball, he had exchanged a word with Joe Morgan who was batting next. Morgan and Rose are close friends, called "pepper and salt" by some of the ballplayers. Morgan taunted Rose, "He doesn't like you, anyway. You're a white guy."

Dock hit Morgan in the kidneys with his first pitch.

By this time, both benches were agog. It was Mayday on May Day. The Pirates realized that Dock was doing what he said he would do. The Reds were watching him do it. "I looked over on the bench, they were all with their eyes wide and their mouths wide open, like, 'I don't believe it!'

"The next batter was Driessen. I threw a ball to him. High inside. The next one, I hit him in the back."

Bases loaded, no outs. Tony Perez, Cincinnati first baseman, came to bat. He did not dig in. "There was no way I could hit him. He was *running*. The first one I threw behind him, over his head, up against the screen, but it came back off the glass, and they didn't advance. I threw behind him because he was backing up, but then he stepped in front of the ball. The next three pitches, he was *running*. . . . I walked him." A run came in. "The next hitter was Johnny Bench. I tried to deck him twice. I threw at his jaw, and he moved. I threw at the back of his head, and he moved."

With two balls and no strikes on Johnny Bench—eleven pitches gone: three hit batsmen, one walk, one run, and now two balls—Murtaugh approached the mound. "He came out as if to say, 'What's wrong? Can't find the plate?' " Dock was suspicious that his manager really knew what he was doing. "No," said Dock, "I must have Blass-itis." (It was genuine wildness—not throwing at batters—that had destroyed Steve Blass the year before.)

"He looked at me *hard*," Dock remembers. "He said, 'I'm going to bring another guy in.' So I just walked off the mound."

5. *Rome Kicks Carthage Ass*

In his May Day experiment, his point was not to hit batters; his point was to kick Cincinnati ass. Pittsburgh was *down,* in last place, lethargic and limp and lifeless. Cincinnati was fighting it out with Los Angeles, confident it would prevail at the end. And for Pittsburgh, Cincinnati was The Enemy.

In 1970, Cincinnati beat Pittsburgh in the Championship Series for the National League pennant. In 1971, with Cincinnati out of it, Pittsburgh took the pennant in a play-off with the Giants, then beat Baltimore in a seven-game Series. In 1972, three months before Roberto Clemente's death, Cincinnati beat Pittsburgh in the Championship Series, three games to two.

"Then," says Dock, "they go on TV and say the Pirates ain't nothing. . . ." Bruce Kison adds, "We got beat fairly in the score, but the *way* the Cincinnati ball club—the players sitting on the bench— were hollering and yelling at us like Little Leaguers. It left a bad taste in my mouth. I remember that. When I do go against Cincinnati, there's a little advantage."

In the winter of 1973-74, and at spring training, Dock began to feel that the Pirates had lost aggressiveness.

"Spring training had just begun, and I say, 'You are *scared* of Cincinnati.' That's what I told my teammates. 'You are *always* scared of Cincinnati.' I've watched us lose games against Cincinnati and it's *ridiculous.* I've pitched some good games at Cincinnati, but the majority I've lost, because I feel like we weren't aggressive. Every time we play Cincinnati, the hitters are on their *ass.*"

"Is that what the players are afraid of?" I asked.

"*Physically* afraid," said Dock. In 1970, '71, and '72, he says, the rest of the league was afraid of the Pirates. "They say, 'Here come the big bad Pirates. They're going to kick our ass!' Like they give up. That's what *our* team was starting to do. When Cincinnati showed up in spring training, I saw all the ballplayers doing the same thing. They were running over, talking, laughing and hee-haw this and that.

"Cincinnati will bullshit with us and kick our ass and laugh at us. They're the only team that talk about us like a dog. *Whenever* we play that team, everybody *socializes* with them." In the past the roles had been reversed. "When *they* ran over to *us,* we knew they were afraid of us. When I saw *our* team doing it, right then I say, 'We gonna get *down.* We gonna *do* the *do.* I'm going to *hit* these motherfuckers.'"

When Dock had announced his intentions, he did not receive total support.

"Several of my teammates told me that they would not be there. When the shit went down, they would not be on the mound. Bob Robertson told me that. It really hurt me. I *believe* he was serious."

"Why?"

"Because this was benefiting him. He wasn't hitting but one oh two. Pitches coming up around his neck."

From time to time a batter who has been hit, or thrown at, will advance on the pitcher, the dugouts will empty, and there will be a baseball fight. Mostly, baseball fights are innocuous. But Dick

McAuliffe once dislocated Tommy John's shoulder, and Campy Campaneris threw his bat at Lerrin LaGrow. But Dock thinks and plans. "I talked to other pitchers who have dealt with them on this level, one being Bob Gibson. He hits them *at random!* In fact, Pete Rose and Tommy Helms tried to whip Gibson, and Gibson got in *both* of them's stuff, in the dugout. He just went in and *got* them.

"I took everything into consideration, when I did what I did. Because I had to figure out who would fight us. Manpower per manpower, it had to be them. That's the *only* team that I could see would really try to *deal* with us. I was thinking of the physical ability of the two teams, and that was the only one that was comparable to us. The only one I could think of that was physically *next* was Philadelphia, and they wouldn't want to fight us. No way would they want to fight us. If I hit twenty of them in a row, they ain't going to fight."

As Pittsburgh endured a dreary April, Dock's resolve intensified. "The team was down. I had to do something for the team. Everybody was complaining about this and that. We weren't winning, and every time I hear someone talk, he's talking about whose ass he's going to kick. On our own team, I mean." The defense was abominable—not just errors, but hits that could have been called errors, like the fly ball that drops in front of an outfielder, or the ground ball that an infielder seems unable to bend over for. Pitching and relief pitching were spotty, hitting streaky, with some of the team's best hitters looking sluggish and halfhearted. "So I said, 'I'm tired of hearing you talk of how *bad* everybody is. We're going to get the shit *on.*"

One of the troubles with Pirate hitting was *fear;* batters were standing away from the plate; opposition pitchers were dusting them, moving them back, and then suckering them with balls on the outside corners. "My hitters weren't aggressive at the plate," Dock says. And a hitter would complain, "My pitcher wasn't protecting me," since retaliation is the best defense.

The game before Dock started against Cincinnati, a Houston relief pitcher hit Wilver Stargell on the head. If Dock needed fuel for his fire, this was sufficient. "They hit Willie in the head!" Willie Stargell and Dock were two of the tightest players on the club. "Houston had hit him on the head last year, and whether it was intentional or not, they hit him in the head again this year. And the next time I was to pitch was Cincinnati, and I had said *before* that I was going to get Cincinnati anyway, so everything more or less fell into line. I *could* have picked out the team that hit him on the head, but I took my anger out on the team that I felt *our* team was afraid of.

"Because now you had the team from the Western Division which was the champs, and the team from the Eastern Division which *should*'ve been the champs—both of them physically supposed to be strong, and on the field strengthwise as far as hitting goes. In the clubhouse I say, 'Well, we going to whip some ass.' It was a message I was trying to convey, to other teams throughout the league, to *leave my hitters alone.*" It was also a message Dock intended for the Pittsburgh Pirates.

6. *On Aggression*

In the country of baseball, the citizens talk about aggression. Athletes talk about aggressiveness the way businessmen talk about profit margins. Many middle-class Americans—workers and clerks, teachers and small businessmen—have problems dealing with their own aggression. Aggression is human and necessary, built into us by the craft and power of survival, but in our lives it can be destructive. We need to disguise it (as love or sexual drive, as gregariousness or good works) in order to live with it. Or we turn it inward on ourselves.

By definition, the athlete is someone who has few problems with his own aggression. Of course he must inherit and develop a skillful and powerful body, but the body is not enough. Everyone has known the superb athlete who never made it, because he clutched; who would excel in practice or in warm-up, but in the heat of battle drop the ball. Recently a professional football team recruited a punter, from civilian life, who could hang the ball as high as the Goodyear blimp. But at a crucial moment of his first professional game, he fumbled a perfect pass from center, and his team lost. He turned in his uniform after the game.

The professional athlete—say he is twenty-seven—has been meeting challenges for twenty years. When he was seven and playing in the Little League finals, when he was seventeen and pitching for his high school in the state tournament, the tension was ultimate. There is no way that the World Series, when he is twenty-seven, is going to be a greater challenge than his high moments at the age of seventeen and seven. Over the years, this athlete is self-selected as the man who is most able to summon and use his aggression.

Although a team is a collection of people with developed aggressiveness, something can happen collectively to depress this quality. A team, as a whole, can become depressed. Dock's insight—about Pirate players acting chummy with the Reds—diagnosed a team neurosis, an epidemic of fear and weakness. Making the diagnosis, the physician applies it to himself. In the lobby of the Pittsburgh Hilton, Dock Ellis bumps into Tony Perez, Cincinnati first baseman. Perez looks affable, says, "Hey, man, what's happening?" but Dock, pursuant to his designs, mutters something noncommittal and adopts his haughtiest expression.

Such a neurosis, the result of whatever trauma—maybe Clemente's death, maybe the stumbling loss to the Mets in 1973—can be cured, some think, by shock treatment.

It didn't work. Or, if it did, it took ten weeks for the electric current to shake up the synapses. Ten weeks largely spent losing ball games. When aggression fails, depression deepens.

"The only thing I did was prove that I was going to do what I said. I don't even think the guys on the team realize why I did it. That really hurt me. They couldn't understand why I did. That really hurt me, that they didn't understand. Even the guys that I did it for, they respect the fact that I did what I said I was going to do—but that's *all*. Like Stargell told me, he said that some of the brothers on the team might not like what I did. He said, 'It could hurt not only the brothers on this team, but the brothers throughout the league.' "

"So I said, 'Hey, Starge, I don't give a damn.' I know he'll tell me what he has on his mind. He was the only one that told me anything about it."

If you did it again, would you do it differently?

"I wouldn't do it again. My feelings was hurt."

Newspapers were full of stories about Dock's wildness, quoting Manny Sanguillen, "I never seen nobody so wild." Danny Murtaugh, told that it had been a deliberate act, summoned Dock and announced that he was fining him two hundred dollars. "Murtaugh pretended he didn't know anything about it," says Dock. "To this day, he's still looking for his two-hundred-dollar fine. Which is ridiculous." General Manager Joe Brown also called Dock in, and suggested that instead of mowing them down, Dock "beat them with the ball."

But, "that wasn't my mission," Dock says. "If that had been my mission, I wouldn't have thrown at anyone. I would have went out and pitched. My mission was to *hit* them. . . . I try now to relate back to the feeling I had when I was doing it. 'Ooh, buddy! Let me try to get him!' That's all I was into—how could I get him, how could I get him."

Around the ball club, nobody *talks* very much. The players chatter continuously—and no one more than Dock—but most of the chatter is light, a steady breeze of teasing, kidding, taking humorously the game and the combat which is deadly serious to them.

Before a game in which he will pitch, Ken Brett sees me early at the ball park, watching batting practice, infield, pepper, coaches hitting fungoes to the outfield. "What're you doing here so early?" he asks, cocky and fresh and friendly. Oh, I tell him, I love baseball; I'll watch anything, even calisthenics. Brett shrugs and smiles, "It's just a boys' game," he says. But when Murtaugh removes him for a pinch hitter, the Pirates losing by three runs early in the game, he stands in the dugout near his manager, staring at the wall behind Murtaugh's head, yelling, "Motherfucker! Motherfucker! Motherfucker! Motherfucker!"

Everybody, we can suppose, is really serious about his own career, and to varying degrees about his team and about winning and losing. But most of the time, it doesn't do to *act* too serious; acting serious is for baseball politicians, for organization men. So when Dock announced his intentions, nobody knew for sure if he was serious. When Bob Robertson said he wouldn't defend Dock, Dock couldn't be sure whether he meant it or not. When Willie Stargell told Dock that some of the brothers on the team hadn't appreciated the gesture, he didn't say who, or explain why—and Dock didn't ask him. Maybe asking would have seemed too much like caring. And anyway, after the event as before, nobody talked about it much.

Later in the season I asked Bruce Kison what he thought of Dock deliberately hitting the Cincinnati team.

Kison's face organized itself, and he said carefully, "Are you sure it was deliberate?" Kison speaks slowly, and seems to compose a sentence with all deliberate speed. When I assured him that the word had come from Dock, Kison's face relaxed. "I *loved* it!" he said. Then he remembered Dock's talk, beginning with spring training. "We didn't know if Dock was *sincere*. Most everybody was aware . . . but whether he was going to go *through* with it. . . . ? Even after it happened, we could hardly believe it. . . . It was his idea that he was going to shake the ball club up. We were just going through the motions."

I told Manny Sanguillen what Stargell told Dock: that some of the brothers on the team were displeased.

Manny is incredulous. The muscles move in his ropy, mobile, sensible face, his forehead arches like a fly to center field. "Some of the

Pittsburgh brothers? The Pittsburgh Pirates? The Pittsburgh *black brothers?*"

Gene Clines, sitting next to him, says, "I wouldn't doubt that at all."

Manny does not seem to hear Clines. His face becomes firm, even grim. He has decided he knows the reason anyone would disapprove, and it does not accord with his own set of values, which are firm and precise like his religion.

"Maybe the brother was scared," he says. "I'm not scared." Clearly, he speaks the truth. "Dock knock somebody down, other pitcher wait to knock you down too. Somebody get hurt. Me, I don't knock down too easy. I can move. I can move. When you throw the ball at me, sometime I catch it with my hand before it hit me." He gestures quickly, from the chair he is sitting in, and mimics a man snatching a baseball from a spot near his chin, like someone quick enough to catch houseflies in bare hands. He laughs. Then he is grim again. "I'm not scared," he says. "I know I'm going to die . . . and I know where I go when I die."

Two months after the incident, I chatted with Pete Rose about Dock.

"At first I just knew him playing baseball. I got to know him a little better at the All-Star Game in Detroit. His wife was there with my wife, and they were good people. We went out and ate, and he's a real good guy. Dock's just the type of guy—there's a lot of guys like him—he just wants to be left alone by reporters. When a reporter finds out that he wants to be left alone, then they really pester you.

"I like Dock as an individual, and he has a good arm. I can attest to that because he hit me the other day. He hit me right in the back and the damned thing hurt for about three days. I know he's still throwing good.

"A lot of small things happened to Dock. He's one of those fellows where controversy's always going to be around. Cassius Clay, he's the same way. In this life, you can't make people happy all the time. You go out of your way to sign a hundred autographs. Maybe one or two people you're not going to sign. They're going to go out and tell everybody you're an asshole."

"Had you heard rumors, before the game, that Dock was going to hit Cincinnati batters?"

"No. But when we left here we went to Houston, and the guys at Houston said that Dock said that he was going to hit the first five guys up." The Pirates had finished a series with Houston just before Cincinnati arrived May first. "I didn't quite understand that because

Dock's not like that. If somebody hits me, they *hit* me, you know. That might ruin me. He had some heat on it, at my head. When you know a guy's throwing at you, that's not kosher, as we say. I didn't quite understand why he was doing that.

"You see, I like Dock. I like a guy that's an honest guy and I like a guy that if he wants to tell a guy to get fucked he'll tell them to get fucked. I like an honest guy, a guy that ain't scared to hide nothing. If Dock don't like you, he'll come right out and tell you. You've got to respect a guy like that. I don't necessarily like it when he says he's gonna hit the first five batters. You never know what might have happened. If we'd have known that before the game, there might have been a brawl."

Pete pauses, Pete makes a move. "But I'm *glad* he hit me, because I don't usually get too many hits off him, and he just saved me an at bat. He got me a run scored."

"What did the players say, when they found out for sure that Dock had hit them on purpose?"

"Some of the guys say because he's pissed off at the management. I don't know if he's pissed off at the management or not. It was before the trading deadline.

"He's got a good arm, he's a good bunter. I noticed that the last couple of years, he's made himself a good hitter. Learned to switch-hit, make a little contact on the ball. He works hard. He does his bats, and he's on the field on time, and things like that. Usually by himself, but there's a lot of guys like that. Some rookie comes along and stands by himself and nobody says anything, but because he's Dock Ellis, if he stands by himself in the outfield they say he's militant, they say he don't like nobody. He's always said Hi to me, and asked how my little boy is."

Dock is crazy about Pete Rose's little boy. Pete takes his son to the ball park for Cincinnati home games. "We've got a cage underneath the stadium. He can *hit*. He's four, now. I like to bring some of the opposing players and show them what a little work can do. Many of the other guys got little kids and they don't hit like my little boy. They don't work at it like he does. It's amazing. You'd be *amazed* to see how a four-year-old kid can hit. He's *aggressive*. I introduce him to all the players and he watches them. He goes to the games and he watches them on TV. It's a big thing for him."

A year earlier, when young Rose was three, Pete asked Dock under the stands to pitch to the boy. "He's just like his father," Dock says with admiration. "He *stands* just like him." Dock asked him where he'd like the pitch. "Get your shit over the plate," the boy said. "Get that damned shit over."

When I told Dock later that Pete Rose complained that his back hurt for days, Dock crowed with delight. "You see, that's the type of dude he is." It didn't hurt him at all, Dock claimed—but Pete knew that word would get back to Dock, and he was trying to psych him. When Dock heard that Pete said that he was *glad* that he was hit, because he doesn't bat too well against Dock, Dock roared with laughter. "He's lying. He's trying to *psych* me. That's what makes him so great. I hated for him to roll that ball back to me! He's a professional ballplayer."

I ask Dock: "Did you get any reaction from other Reds' players?"
"No," he said. "Only Joe Morgan. He say he got a hundred and fifty dollars reward out, for any pitcher in the league that will hit me."
"Did you talk to Morgan about that?"
"I tell him, 'Hey, you're making a beautiful living playing baseball!' "

When aggression fails, depression deepens.
Dock didn't get a loss in the May Day game, because the Pirates tied it up—but then they went on to lose the game anyway. They lost most of the time, early in 1974. As they found themselves flying to Cincinnati, six weeks into the season, the Pirates had won only fourteen games, and they had lost twenty-six, for an average of .350, and they rode well into last place. Dock was losing pitcher in twenty percent of the Pirate losses.
Dock was scheduled to pitch the first game at Cincinnati, four weeks and three days after May Day. But Murtaugh called him into the office and told him that he would miss two starts. He was giving Dock a rest, Murtaugh said, because of his "bad luck."
"I said okay. It was *child psychology,* and I didn't want to hear about it." Dock's "bad luck"—statistically speaking—was a one and five record and an ERA approaching five. He had never missed a turn in May. Possibly the Pirate management, knowing that Dock had deliberately hit the Reds six weeks before, feared that he would repeat himself, or that the Reds would retaliate against him.
(He would not have thrown at them. On the telephone I asked him if he was tempted to mow the lineup down again. "No No No," said Dock, like a trill on a piano; then, with delicacy and precision, "I—have— *delivered—my—message.*")

Then Murtaugh suggested that Dock might sit in the bullpen for a spell. Murtaugh explained that they "just wanted to take me out of the rotation. To let the winning pitchers—the ones that were hot—just keep pitching. They wanted to bring Bruce Kison in there. I listened to him *talk*. Well, the man has been successful with me, and I have been successful with him. I know for a fact that my fastball wasn't as lively as it had been before, because they had hit many home runs off me, more on me this year already than they had all last year. I know for a fact my arm is not up to par. And so I just had to say, well, maybe the man is right."

But then the press picked up Murtaugh's words about the bullpen. "In Cincinnati, the sportswriters—and you can't pay too much attention to what they say—were bringing up the question of me taking Giusti's job, going short relief. And that would be cool. But I would definitely say they would have to pay me some *money* for it. To *relieve*, that would mean that I would have to cut out a lot of my extracurricular activities. It would break me down more or less as just being a *baseball* player. To be a short man, I'd have to be available every day."

So Dock talked to reporters, and again Dock Ellis made the wire services, showed up in headlines in Boston and Little Rock. It was the annual flap, 1974 edition: ELLIS REFUSES BULLPEN. What he said, what he meant, and what he is quoted as saying interweave like braid. He would never relieve. He would relieve if they paid him. He would never relieve unless his team needed him desperately. A week later, I asked him what he really said.

"I said I would never go to the bullpen, and I would never pitch to a hitter, not even one inning, not even one pitch. I was misinterpreted, as far as the sports announcers go. They were saying that I would *never* pitch in the bullpen."

"But that's what you just said," I pointed out.

"But to be a member of a *team*, and a participant on this team, in order for them to *win*, if I have to pitch to a batter, I *will* pitch to a batter. What I meant was I would never go to the *bullpen*, to be *in* the bullpen. But to pitch to a batter, or to win a game—Now if I was to go to the bullpen, then we'd have to talk about money. If I'm going to take an ace's job, then I want an ace's pay."

"What?"

"Giusti makes a hundred thousand dollars a year. I make seventy-two thousand five hundred."

After the newspaper flap, in order to save Danny Murtaugh's face, Dock threw some pitches in the bullpen in Cincinnati. He wasn't wearing a cup, which was his way of proving to himself that he had no intention of entering the game.

Who can say what lurks in all those hearts? Maybe he was removed from the rotation because Cincinnati management warned Pittsburgh management that matters could get out of hand. Maybe Danny Murtaugh, an expert at manipulation, was applying some shock treatment, attempting to psych Dock into greater effort and concentration.

Maybe Murtaugh really felt that Dock might develop into a relief pitcher, especially since Giusti was having problems. Or maybe he felt that if Dock underwent the humiliation of being long man—the reliever who enters the game early when the game is already lost—his hurt pride would restore his fastball. If Murtaugh really expected him to do relief, then Dock outpsyched the psycher, with his blasts to the press. (The Manual of Aggression includes a chapter on the use of public relations.) He pitched no relief in 1974.

7. *Sparky Steps on Spanky's Foot*

The general depression continued, in the first half of the season.

On July 10, the Pirates were still in last place. Dock started against Atlanta, gave up three runs immediately, and was relieved in the first inning. It was his eighth loss against three wins.

Cincinnati came to town, the first visit since May first, for a five-game series including two doubleheaders. The Enemy won four straight, giving Pittsburgh another five-game losing streak. Reuss, Rooker, Demery, and Brett all started and lost. Brett, whose pitching so far had been the brightest moment of the season, gave up a three-run homer to Tony Perez in the first inning of the first game of Sunday's doubleheader, July 14, and pitched immaculate ball thereafter, but lost three to two.

The Pirates were undergoing humiliation. They were down, they were low, and they felt mean. Cincinnati was riding high in pursuit of the Dodgers, a pursuit that most of the players, as far back as July, believed would succeed. But Cincinnati was also aware that on its last visit, it had been thrown at. The mob was restless. It was Bastille Day. In Bruce Kison, who started the second game, the mob had a leader.

Kison is a reliever and a sport starter, with an uneven record and great courage. He comes from the side, frequently, powerful against right-handed batters, and finds himself in trouble with left-handers. Spotty though his record may be—he ended the regular season, in 1974, with nine wins and eight losses—he rises to the challenge. Everyone remembers his performance as a twenty-year-old rookie in the 1971 World Series. At the end of the 1974 season, he rose from a series of setbacks to beat the Cardinals in St. Louis—the game that put Pittsburgh ahead—and next pitched a three-hitter to beat the Mets and sustain the Pirates in their push toward the Eastern Division title. In the third game of the Championship Series with Los Angeles, Kison gave up four hits and no runs to the team with the best record in baseball.

Pitching to right-handed batters, Kison's fastball breaks up and in. Pitching against the right-handed Cincinnati Reds—George Foster, Johnny Bench, Tony Perez, Dave Concepcion—his fastball kept riding toward chins. When Concepcion went down from a fastball in the second inning, the umpire behind the plate, Ed Sudol, walked to the mound and warned Kison not to throw at batters. Both benches emptied. There were words. Nothing happened.

When Sudol returned behind the place, Kison resumed the task of pitching to Concepcion. As he put it later, "I assumed that he would be looking for a pitch down the middle, after I had been warned; so I jammed him."

In the fourth when Kison batted, Cincinnati pitcher Jack Billingham hit him with the first pitch. When the ball knocked Kison's helmet off, everyone assumed that Billingham had hit him on the head. Actually, the ball hit Kison on the left arm and bounced to his shoulder, "one of the few places where I have any meat," and thence to the bill of his helmet. "It didn't cause any pain. I lay on the ground, and I was kind of dazed. I thought he called it a foul ball. 'You've got to be kidding.' By that time, everything had started. Sanguillen was out there, but I never even *knew* he was out there, he was so fast getting out there. I wasn't mad. I wasn't mad at all. Obviously, whether I was doing it on purpose or not, a lot of their hitters had gone down."

Manny was mad. Quick as a hummingbird, with his perpetual smile, Manny Sanguillen is the more affable and the most volatile of the Pirates. He is also, probably, the best boxer. "That smile," says Dock, "That smile is *dangerous.*"

Around the mound, and at various points in the infield, the rival players confronted each other. Sparky Anderson, manager of the Reds, and Spanky Kirkpatrick, Pittsburgh utility man, were standing next to each other. At first, Dock watched from the base line. "Sparky stepped on Spanky's foot. Then Spanky pushed him. That's what they say started it." Andy Kosco, Cincinnati reserve, threw the first punch, after seeing Spanky push Sparky. Unlike most fights in the country of baseball, this fight had some fighting in it. It lasted twenty minutes.

"All hell broke loose," says Dock, grinning. "Manny was hitting everyone. It was ridiculous, he's so quick. If one of our players got in the way, *he* got hit. He didn't hit them in the face or nothing, but he was *swinging*. He was body punching, just like a boxer. When I saw him, I wanted to do it too.

"That's when it started around third base. I was trying to get to Billingham, because it was him that hit Kison. The umpire was pushing me. Fists started flying, and you didn't know what was happening. I would see three Cincinnati ballplayers on a Pirate, which at that time was [Daryl] Patterson, and somebody had him by the hair. So I started to step on the dude's hand, but I was afraid to step on Patterson's head. Stargell just took his thumb back, and bent it. That took care of that.

"Before Borbon grabbed Patterson by the hair, Patterson had him in an armlock, and was going to pound his head in. Ain't no way he could have got away from Patterson. And the Cincinnati ballplayers was begging him to let him go. I could hear them, 'Please let him get up. Let him get up. Let him get up.' And I looked, I saw Daryl had him, so I saw there wasn't any need to be dealing with that. When I looked back over there, Borbon had him by the hair. When Patterson let him go, Borbon *bit* him. Bit him bad. Like an animal bite. He had to have a tetanus shot. Pulled part of his skin away, with his teeth."

The Pirates went on to score, after the dust had cleared, and after Sparky and Spanky, together with Andy Kosco, had been thrown out of the game. Kison pitched well, and left the game in the seventh inning only when a blister puffed out on his middle finger like a button mushroom. Giusti was perfect in relief, and the Pirates won, two to one. The Pirates agreed that they had won the fight as well as the ball game.

Aggression Returns. Son of Aggression. Aggression Rides Again.

Later that Sunday night, over drinks all over the city, the ballplayers rehashed the fight. The team that had been dour and sullen transformed itself.

In the dugout the next day, everyone was cheerful and ebullient. No one could forget it. Every detail was repeated with care and detailed attention. There are events we wish would never stop, which we repeat endlessly, like television—doing over and over again a stunning moment: the deflected forward pass which wins a championship, the first step on the moon. Even in the press club, where the reporters drink gin and eat sandwiches free, everyone was cheerful, everyone repeated what *he* saw, what *he* heard someone say.

And everyone apportioning credit or blame asserts that this skirmish, in the war between the clubs, began not when Kison decked Bench on a curveball in the first inning, but on May first when Dock knocked down three in a row. "It was *bound* to happen," Jack Billingham said, in the clubhouse after the game; "Dock hit three in a row. . . ."

In Cincinnati in August, the Pirates took two out of three, and there were no fights. From Bastille Day on the Pirates averaged a little better than two out of three. First, they won eight straight games, beginning with Dock's complete game victory over Houston the next day. Then, after losing one, they won nine of eleven. From last place they rose steadily, with little vacillation, until they passed St. Louis and Philadelphia to take first place on August 27. They were kicking ass.

Two: Black Graffiti

1. *The Neighborhood*

Because Dock Ellis grew up in Los Angeles, and because he is black, it is widely known that he grew up in Watts. He did not.

After a game with Houston in April of 1974, I saw Dock in Pittsburgh at a party to celebrate the publication of *Playing Around*. Dock had invited two friends from the Astros: Lee May who next season went over to Baltimore, and Don Wilson who died in Houston nine months later. Lee May was a great suave hulk, Don Wilson's roomie and a friend of Dock's since Dock came up. Don Wilson grew up a few blocks away in Los Angeles, and they had known each other—and scuffled more than once—from the ages of nine or ten. "Three no-hitters from one Neighborhood," said Dock as he introduced me to Wilson. "Not bad." Don Wilson threw no-hitters in 1967 and 1969, Dock in 1970.

Late in the party, Dock found me in the kitchen making a drink, and dragged me out to the living room to hear what Don Wilson had just said.

"We didn't grow up in *no ghetto*," Wilson repeated with some force. When baseball took him east and north from Los Angeles—he continued—and he saw how black people lived in the slums of Philadelphia and New York, he was appalled. Not even Watts approached Harlem.

"Hell," interrupts Dock, "we didn't grow up in no *ghetto*. We grew up in *Hollywood!*"

47

The Neighborhood—as everyone calls it—occupies two city blocks between 135th and 139th, to the southeast of Los Angeles, near the cities of Gardena and Compton. The Neighborhood is prosperous, immaculate, and middle class. Each lawn is as smooth as a pool table, with trimmed shrubs and borders of flowers. Garden hoses lie coiled beside the garage, and emerge at twilight along with the clippers and trimmers and mowers. The houses themselves are ranches, low and wide, with two-car garages, new cars, pictures on the walls, and cellophane over the lampshades. Floyd Hoffman, Sr., has built a tidy bar next to his living room, barstools and broad, dark wood bar, and anything you like.

When the Pirates flew to Los Angeles to play the Dodgers in June of 1974, Dock took me down to the Neighborhood.

Driving my rented car down 139th Street, he sees a large young man riding a bicycle. Dock waves and yells, "Hey, Big Man!" He turns to me: "That's a *big* motherfucker; I knew him when he was a little bitty boy."

Through all the streets he waves, shouts, stops for brief conversations. Everyone wants to talk, and he wants to talk with everyone. He visits, collapses, relaxes, laughs, thinks of a neighbor, and runs off to pay another call. He is the long-lost uncle from Australia, the sailor home from the sea.

He parks at his mother's house. Where the garage used to be, his mother and stepfather have made an extra sitting room. Most of these houses still retain the big garages, with knee-high door handles. When Dock was a boy, he got in trouble throwing baseballs at door handles, practicing his control.

Dock Philip Ellis, Sr., and his wife Naomi, moved to Los Angeles in 1944. Both were born and grew up in Louisiana, Naomi from Nakatuchi, and Dock, Sr., from Waterproof. Dock, Sr., had served in the army, and was invalided out in 1944 with asthma. At first, the couple lived on Fifty-third and McKinley: "ghetto," says Dock, "East Side ghetto." Dock Philip Ellis, Jr., was born March 11, 1945. In 1950, with two girls born after the son, the family of five moved to the present house in the Neighborhood. A GI loan helped them buy it.

Dock, Sr., worked in the post office, worked on the docks believe it or not, and saved enough money to become independent. On a street corner in Compton—Rosecrans and Central, within walking distance of the Neighborhood—he opened a shoe-repair shop. Later he leased a dry cleaners in the same building. Dock and Naomi, helped later by Junior, ran the two businesses.

Everything was for the children.

Dock grew up in the suburbs, the son of hardworking parents, knowing always that he would go to school and college, that when he was sixteen he would have a car, that he would dress well and be clean, and most of all that he was *worthwhile*. When he discovered, at the age of ten or eleven, that portions of the white world doubted his worth, his response was not humiliation nor hurt but outrage. Nothing would ever displace the sense of worth that his parents, in the black suburban fifties, had built in him.

When he was four, at Fifty-third and McKinley, Dock threw a baseball across the street. His only other memory from the old house is looking up girls' dresses.

A year later, he remembers throwing a ball with his father in the front yard of the new house.

It is a hot day in summer, his father home from the shoe-repair shop, and the sun is still high. They are wearing new baseball gloves. The baby sisters stay inside the house with their mother, who is home from running the cleaners, making supper. Dock, Sr., will not play catch with his son often. His breath comes hard. When his son is in his second year of junior college, just before signing a baseball contract, only thirteen years in the future, his accumulated ills will finally kill him. No one will ever know the exact nature of his disease, because Dock will not allow an autopsy. "No one was going to take a knife to my father."

In the Neighborhood, athletic competition was everything. Football, roller skates, foot races, basketball, jumping, bicycles, baseball, gymnastics, rabbit chasing, and pigeon catching. Only ice hockey never got going.

Outdoors all year long, the children ran and jumped, threw balls, and eluded each other. Nine months of the year, school was an interruption suffered as a required waste of time, like sleep. In summer, they played from dawn until after sunset, pausing only to replenish their energy for more play.

The acres around the Neighborhood are built up now. New houses, freeways, factories, and warehouses spread out over the scrubby land. Now the Neighborhood is enclosed, a suburban island in an industrial sea; it used to be bedrooms isolated in a playground of horses and rabbits. "We would get up Saturday morning, and go out all day, hunting rabbits," says an old friend, reminiscing. "Bows and arrows!" Dock leaps in. "Walk in tall, beat them on the head with sticks! And dig *this*. We would *eat* those rabbits. We'd kill them and we'd *eat* them!"

Much of Southern California track and field came out of the Neighborhood, and did its first wind sprints chasing rabbits.

We visit Dock's mother, leave to visit Big Big Daddy—otherwise known as Floyd Hoffman, Sr., father of Dock's best friend Big Daddy— and call on Dock's old playground supervisor, talk with old and young neighbors on the street, and come back to Dock's mother's. When I meet new people, Dock often leaves me alone with them for a while—so they can talk about him behind his back, and so he can call on someone else. Then he pops back and sweeps me off to another neighbor. Usually, he pauses long enough to interject the last word.

Naomi Ellis Craven is a compact and handsome woman in her fifties, rather proper meeting a stranger, fiercely protective of her children. She sits on the sofa, tugging her dress down over her knees.

"Dock was always an active child," she says. "He can't stay put. His father was like that too. And I am too. So I guess he's got a lot of things *double*. He was riding a bike when he was three years old. When he was *four* years old I used to give him spankings for throwing balls against the wall. Every time he would find a ball, he was throwing it against the wall! They would be on the streets, between the houses, playing *all* the time. One of my neighbors, next door, he used to tell her, 'This arm is going to make me a millionaire.' "

Elementary school was Avalon Gardens, and for Dock school was the playground. Tag football, baseball, basketball. Summer just meant he spent *all day* on the playground. Even when he had gone off to junior high, Dock returned to the Avalon Gardens playground for sports. The task in the playground was to be *best*: jump higher, throw faster, run faster, kick ass. But as the children grew, in the Neighborhood, some of the sport took on another tone. It diverted itself from sport to pranks, from pranks to petty crime; but it was hard to draw the line.

2. *Pigeon Farming with Big Daddy*

Dock and Big Daddy collected pigeons, for Big Daddy's pigeon coop. Big Daddy took his name from his size; he was always tallest, six feet four inches by the time he was twelve. He was also the best pitcher in the neighborhood. ("Big Daddy"—the old friends reminisce, shaking their heads—"he could *really* bring it!") He was also the most cunning, the shrewdest of scamps, con men, or petty criminals. He and Dock did not *collect* pigeons, they *stole* pigeons even if the pigeons appeared to belong to the air. Stealing pigeons, Dock and Floyd—both "Junior" to their parents, "Nut" and "Big Daddy" on the streets—climbed a water tower in the field behind Floyd's house, where the pigeons roosted at night.

Big Daddy is a fireman now. He and his wife Marsha come to Dock's suite at the Los Angeles Hilton, after a game, and we talk with them for hours. Dock introduces us, leaves us alone, comes back, and goes out again.

Marsha is pretty, sharp, and cynical about people's motives. Floyd is cynical also, but amused to remember the lies, the thefts, and the cons of sweet youth. His eyes shine when he talks about stealing pigeons or Gallo wine. But for the present he is—as his parents were before him—responsible and mature and conservative. When we had chatted for a few minutes, I asked him about the pigeons.

"I had a pigeon coop, and my father would give me about fifty cents a day, per day during the summer. Good pigeons cost one-fifty. So if I bought a pigeon, that meant three days I had to sacrifice my potato chips and sodas. But we found out that there were pigeons up there, in the tower. They were very easy to catch. They were sitting there, just waiting for you to grab. In gunny sacks, you know."

The real goal was not to acquire pigeons, but to elude the watchman, who carried a gun. One night, when they were ten years old, both boys had climbed up the tower when the watchman appeared and fired. Floyd says he jumped down from the tower, and when he hit the ground, Dock was there ahead of him. "I found him behind a hill. He was trying to laugh, and shaking at the same time. I looked down and his pants was wet. 'Hey, man. What happened to you?' 'Nothing.' He had pissed all over himself."

Big Daddy:

"I moved there in fifty-two. It was just before Christmas and I got these skates for Christmas. I skated on down to Dock's house. He put his skates on. We was racing up the street trying to skate. He never could beat me—it would just *piss* him off—he was never able to catch me on skates . . . he was *running* on skates.

"I had an old bicycle. I would go down to the corner and turn around and come back real fast, on the sidewalk, and Nut, he would grab hold of the back, and ride. This time he grabbed and I stopped, and he went over.

"Dock flew forward, one knee cracking into the cement sidewalk." (Dock sticks his head in the door: "We had *sidewalks* in Hollywood!" Big Daddy goes on talking.) "That's when he broke his leg. Ever since then, he's had that water on the knee problem. We stood him up, and pushed him home backward on the skates. He had a cast on from his toe all the way up to here. That didn't stop him from playing though. We'd let him have left field open where he could get him a base hit. He'd stand up there on that one leg, cock it some kind of way to balance hisself, he'd haul off and hit the ball, get down and grab his crutches, and crutch on down to first base."

Big Daddy:

"We used to play a game in the Neighborhood. Me, Dock, and just the complete Neighborhood, about twenty guys. We all got together, and we took a fire hydrant, two guys to each hydrant, and the game was to turn on the hydrant—the hydrant is going to sound a bell alarm, a water flow alarm—the fire department and the sheriffs were going to come, and you couldn't run until they were a block and a half away. That was the game, to get away. Me and Dock, we were the only ones who had sense. What we would do, when the cops would come, was knock on somebody's door, and tell the people that these guys were trying to beat us up. Could we use the phone, to call our father? Okay? So we'd pretend to use the phone, and we'd say thank you. Then we'd walk on out. If the cops stopped us, and they would, we'd say, 'Why, we just came out of this house.' And they'd knock on the door and ask the lady, did these kids come out of this house? And she'd say yes.

"I think we were the only two in the Neighborhood that never got caught."

At an early age—junior high, maybe earlier—Dock and Big Daddy founded their first club. Behind Big Daddy's house, construction work was beginning. There were holes and piles of dirt, and huge cardboard spools, bigger than sewer pipe, which had held roofing material. The boys rolled a spool into a hole, piled dirt over it, and made themselves a cave where they hid out on hot summer days.

Big Daddy:
"There was a fruit stand on San Pedro and Rosecrans, Japanese owner, and they had beer and wine and fruit. We used to go in the summer—hot, eighty-five, ninety degrees—and we'd have great big heavy coats on, fathers' coats, and we'd go to the store, browse around. We'd take sunflower seeds, stick them down our pants, five or six bottles of wine. There was four of us—Teddy, me, Samearl, Dock. We'd stick five or six bottles of wine down in our sides, button our coat up, go up to the front of the stand, and buy a piece of bubble gum. So we stocked this tube full of nothing but wine—like port, white port—and then we'd steal us some lime Kool-Aid, or some grape Kool-Aid, and mix it, pour in the wine, and shake it up, get rid of that nasty Gallo taste.

"Every day we'd wake up in the morning, we'd go over to Nut's house or one of the others, we'd get together and we'd go on down to our cave, and we'd sit down there and just get drunker than hell. And then we'd go back to the store. . . . I would be up front, Dock would be next to me. We always, me and him, had to be together. . . . He was the only one I could have faith in. I'd take a great big juicy watermelon and throw it to him and he'd throw it to Samearl and Samearl would throw it to Teddy, all the way across the street. We had an assembly line!

"We'd have five or six watermelons. We'd take them to our little cave, and bust them up, and just get the heart and throw the rest of it away. We ain't got time for seeds. It's *free*."

Dock's father had academic ambitions for Dock, part of his general ambition for his children: play baseball, but go to school too. For all the athletics, for all the pranks and the petty crime, home was important and secure. Dock still moved in awe of his father. Despite pigeon killing, wine stealing, and pony riding, he and Big Daddy were relatively conservative among the boys of the Neighborhood. "That was our fathers. I really appreciate the way I was brought up, now. Ninety-nine percent of the guys we grew up with, in the same Neighborhood, have been in jail or still are. Bribery, murders, cutting throats, or whatever. Like I say, our fathers scared the hell out of us. We knew what kind of trouble we were *in*, if we were caught at it."

3. *Mr. Thompson, and Mr. Thompson's Son*

For those without fathers, or for those who needed more father than they had, the Neighborhood supplied auxiliaries. These fathers coached, and preached athletics—because they loved sports, because they might have made it themselves without the color line, and because they wanted "to keep the boys out of the streets." Where now—half a generation later—fathers and teachers advocate medical or law school, in Dock's youth they advocated sports.

Dock needed more father than his own father. By the time Dock was thirteen, his father had become an invalid, in and out of the hospital, no longer the force that he had been before.

Of the four auxiliary fathers who helped Dock, his baseball coach Mr. Brewer was the foremost, but Dock did not meet him until the age of fifteen. Earlier, there was Mr. Nicholson, a white father who stood by him during troubles in a white section of town. Within the Neighborhood itself, there was Mr. Thompson and there was an old prizefighter named Mr. Williams, who played dominoes with the boys. All of the fathers are called mister.

Mr. Thompson taught at Riis High School, where "they sent everyone who couldn't stay in regular high schools—problem boys." In his own neighborhood, Mr. Thompson worked to keep boys from becoming problems. In his own backyard, he made a basketball court: one basket, with pavement to dribble on, big enough for six or eight boys to play. He also set up rings for gymnastics, a broad-jump pit, and space for the hop skip and jump.

Dock started his basketball career in Mr. Thompson's backyard, when he was eleven or twelve, and the big boys showed him tricks. "Tasker and James Horn, they showed me how to pass off. Tasker in particular showed me how to dribble and shoot with my left hand. That little court back there, you couldn't drive. All you could do was a jump shot." He learned how to fake to his right, come back to his left, and make the shot. And on defense, "Tasker is the one who taught me to watch people's eyes. He used to tell me: 'Don't watch the ball or the body, watch the eyes.' "

Dock takes me to Mr. Thompson's house, but Mr. Thompson is away, working at his camp for problem boys. Mr. Thompson's son Keith is there, a little younger than Dock, with a friend named Leon. From Leon, Dock gets the sort of welcome usually accorded returning heroes, something like, *Can you spare us five minutes of your time?*

Because of such greetings, people who become even moderately famous often protect themselves from their old friends, they become "snobs," they don't have time for their old friends anymore, they are "different." The weight of envy pulls down every conversation, makes all utterance a test. The famous find themselves comfortable only in the company of others like themselves, where they are free at least from the bitter accusation that they are "successful."

But not Dock. He brushes away the accusation like a housefly. Paying no attention to it, he is immune to it; bad feeling disappears, because he refuses to acknowledge it. *He* knows he is the same. Soon, everyone else knows it too, and amazement enters the room and speaks itself. Leon says to me, "Dock, he never changes!"

Keith Thompson wants me to understand something, about sports and the Neighborhood. Growing up, all the children attended Avalon Gardens together. Through the sixth grade, their lives reflected each other; their lives cohered. Avalon Gardens was black. The world was wholly black, and so the children were not aware of blackness. Once an uncle asked Keith how many of his teachers were white, and how many black; he hadn't the slightest idea.

But when the black kids from the Neighborhood became a minority at the white and Japanese junior high school, the world disintegrated. The blending of the races exposed differences of culture. The black kids were faster, stronger, and better athletes; the Japanese and the Caucasians could read better, figure better, and did their homework. "While *we* were playing ball, or having races, and our parents were trying to make that dollar," Keith tells me, "*their* parents were getting them books, or talking about things, or taking them to the symphony or something." The teachers and administrators reinforced the division which began at home; they sent the blacks to industrial arts or to agriculture, while the whites and Japanese took academic subjects.

The Japanese were the best scholars. "The Buddhaheads were the straight A's," says Dock, overhearing and interrupting. "I used to howl every time there was a left handed Buddhahead sitting next to me. Couldn't cheat."

A fourth ethnic group was the Mexicans. Mexicans and blacks got on, and blacks got on with Japanese—though "mostly they weren't around when the fights got started." But between whites and blacks, the tension was general. "I was in the house of Mexicans," someone told me. "I was in the house of Japanese. I was never in the house of white people, and they weren't in mine." The tension began the first day of school, but the blacks were prepared, and doughty; the older black students, who had gone to Gardena before them, "taught us how to hang together. If you fought one of us, you had to fight all of us."

4. *Thornburg Park*

Little League was part of the general Neighborhood passion for sports. Dock played his first organized baseball with the Seven-Uppers at El Segundo playground. Playing center field, he was so strong—and so wild—that he threw the ball over the catcher's head, trying to beat a runner to the plate. When he made the same error his second year in Little League—playing over at Gonzalez Park—his coach suggested that he take up pitching.

For many years he played other positions as well as pitching, especially third base and catcher. Even with Mr. Brewer, he played infield for a while when he couldn't pitch.

The most important ball park—for the shape of Dock's life, if not for the shape of his athletic career—was Edward L. Thornburg Park, in the white city of Gardena. When he was nine years old, Dock was recruited from the fields of the Neighborhood by David Nicholson, another nine-year-old, and David's father, otherwise known as "Mr. Nicholson." David was a good athlete, and Mr. Nicholson coached him in Peewee football and basketball and baseball. Father and son recruited Dock as the only black player on Mr. Nicholson's white team. Dock and David perforce became friends.

Mr. Nicholson's teams took over Gardena. His tag football backfield included the white quarterback Don Horn, later a professional, a black halfback (Dock), and a Japanese halfback (Neil Minami, Dock's friend). His basketball and baseball teams, also interracial, also triumphed.

(The friendships made at nine remain. In June of 1974, Dock took David Nicholson's young sons through the Pirates' locker room. He had his old friend stay outside, as he explained it, so that the kids would have something on their old man. And Dock called at Sam Minami's sporting goods store—Neil's father—and chatted with Neil's young wife.)

For three years, Mr. Nicholson picked up Dock in the Neighborhood just after five o'clock, on his way home from work. Out of school between two and three, Dock would play in the Neighborhood until five, then ride over to Thornburg and play until eight o'clock. In winter, he would play basketball under the lights at Thornburg. Spring would come and the Apaches would change to the Cubs, basketball to baseball. At the end of the summer, baseball would shift to tag football, and Cubs become Apaches again.

One morning Dock and I drive to Thornburg Park. We walk from the parking lot along some link fence, past the squat shack of the supervisor, onto the playing fields. We pass the basketball hoops, and walk toward the diamond laid out in a far corner.

"It started over here. I was nine years old. That's when they didn't want any blacks at all over in this city. This is the ball park, this is the park where one night we were playing a basketball game, and they had a lot of rough guys out here, and they didn't want me over here. So they were talking about how they were going to kick my ass. So Mr. Nicholson—he knew some of the neighborhood hoods around here, so he told them he would pay them to kick *their* ass. I had no more trouble over here, at this ball park.

"And this is the football field. And Don Horn was the quarterback here. He used to send me up in that end zone up in there, and just say, 'Jump up!' I used to catch passes all around here. At nine, ten, eleven, twelve. Flag football.

"Right here is where I used to pitch and catch. I used to catch for the Peewee Cubs. This is where I used to hit home runs, when I was a little fellow. That's when I could hit.

"David Nicholson, he took a lot of shit, because I used to stay over at his house sometimes. We used to hang together.

"Right over here they used to have a barn; they had hillbilly music. They didn't *like* that shit, you know. They'd be coming in here and I'd be out here playing football, and baseball, and they really didn't like it. At that time, I didn't understand."

When it became impossible to misunderstand, his reaction was outrage and violence. "Right here, one time, they were watching us play basketball, and they got to name-calling, and a guy—he's not living now; he got killed down here at a streetlight; Peter Rucker—me and him was about the best little basketball players around this area." Pete Rucker was white, and sometimes visited Dock in the Neighborhood. "We just did a *job* on some people, right over there in that corner—right by that tree right there, that same tree. We had one in between that tree. He had him one way, kicking him, and I had him another way.

"Those are the memories I have of this park.

"I also remember the day they put the boundary up. The boundary to let you know where you could live to play over here. And I saw that I was eligible to play here. And the next day they *changed* the boundary. They followed David Nicholson's father over to where we lived, and they cut the boundary off. From the time I saw them cut that boundary up, I never did come to this ball park this way. I always came that way." Dock no longer walked past the office, but detoured around the park to enter the far end, away from the little supervisor's shack with its bulletin board. "I never wanted to pass by *here*, to pass by this office, because I knew who did it. The person who did it was the guy in this office.

"This place here. This is where it started. The hate."

Talking about her son, Dock's mother told me she had little trouble with him. "The only thing I used to tell him, I used to tell him a lot of times to grit his teeth at a lot of things that's being spoken or said to him. But he said, 'I can't do it, Mother, I can't do those things.' "

5. *Bad Dudes*

All sorts of things replaced teeth-gritting: hard work, crime, black pride, black separation, stealing cars, athletics, beating people up.

When Big Daddy and Dock attended Perry Junior High, they became gangsters, shakedown artists, protection racketeers. "The time we was going there," Big Daddy told me—grinning, lolling in Dock's suite with a drink in his hand, speaking slowly and emphatically—"it was two loads of blacks, and the rest was white and Japanese. We ruled the school. We had everybody paying us insurance. We played it like we were from Watts. I was telling the white kids, if you don't give me fifty cents insurance, Dock is going to kick the hell out of you, and so they would pay me. Then Dock, he would say to the same guy that *I* was going to jump on him if he didn't pay Dock fifty cents insurance. So we had this going. . . ."

When Dock talks about the insurance racket, he begins to explain it in terms of economics, and ends by acknowledging racial anger. (This double motive recurs when his friends talk about stealing cars and other crime.) "We are getting about twenty-five or thirty cents a day to eat on," says Dock, "so we used to just take other people's money."

"What kind of people?"

"It was always white against blacks."

"Now do you think it was wrong?"

"No."

"Why?"

"Because at the time it was the thing to do. It was the *thing* to *do,* at that level. We were *forced* to go to that school, like forced busing. They *forced* us to go to this particular school."

Big Daddy, Dock, and two black friends were waiting by the bus stop at Perry when a group of white high-school boys approached undoing their belts. It was quite a fight. Some white construction workers joined the high-school boys. A black janitor threw brooms out a window to the blacks. Police came to break it up, and Dock and Big Daddy were expelled from Perry, and spent their final year of junior high at Gompers, which was black.

At Gompers, or in the vicinity of Gompers, Dock and Big Daddy had fights with blacks. To poor blacks from Gompers or—heaven knows—Watts, Dock and Big Daddy and the boys of the Neighborhood were a bunch of soft rich kids.

Big Daddy:

"We was coming from Gompers. Dock, he had an elective—woodcraft, I believe—and he had made him a big, tall, beautiful bongo drum. We was walking, and we got to the bus stop. He started beating on his drum a little bit. We were waiting for the bus. There was another gang across the street, at the other bus stop, called the D'Artagnans—black, a *rough* gang. They saw Dock's drum, so they started coming across the street. At the same time, our bus was coming. The bus came, and stopped, and opened the door, I got in, and Dock was *trying* to get in, when the D'Artagnans said, 'Hey, man, let me have that drum, or I'll whip your ass.' Dock said, 'No.' So they went to swing on him, and he—he has always been swift on his feet—he started running. From Imperial to our house was—it must have been about four miles. He was running toward home, straight down Avalon. The bus took off, and I was sitting in the seat, and he was just *running*. He had his drum up under his arms, and he was just *running*. The bus stopped every two or three blocks. He would just go on past. The bus driver wouldn't let us get off. (If we got off, he knew what we were going to *do*.) Then we didn't see him anymore. Then we seen the D'Artagnans stop, so I said I guess he's all right. We got down to a hundred and thirty-fifth and there was Dock—he outran the bus and everything!"

The D'Artagnans, the Low Riders, the Farmers—these were black gangs that the blacks of the Neighborhood feared. When they were little, and their parents left Dock and Big Daddy for an afternoon at a park in Watts, the Watts kids took their snack money from them. Watts stood to the Neighborhood as the Neighborhood stood to the whites at Perry.

For every white friend at Perry there were twenty "scaries," as Dock called them, who believed that Dock had only to blow a whistle and Watts would flood every aisle. For the scaries as for the sportswriters, black meant Watts. And for Dock and Big Daddy, the most protected of the protected middle-class Neighborhood, there was a lot to prove. How do you develop a reputation as Bad Dude, if your daddy won't let you smoke? The insurance racketeers, on their way to Perry one day, were caught smoking by Dock, Sr., who reported to Floyd, Sr., and the gangsters were punished.

They were the only boys in the Neighborhood who had to be in at night. If they sneaked out to join their friends, and got caught, their fathers came down hard. They were also the only boys whose fathers gave them cars when they were sixteen. Other friends in the Neighborhood proved their manhood by stealing cars, but Dock and Big Daddy didn't have an excuse to.

They had cars at sixteen, and earlier it was toys, bicycles, roller skates, or clothes. However they managed, their parents were determined to provide. Dock lays it to shrewd practices, rather than to wealth.

"When we were small, I always remember my father and my mother going to the rummage sale. Then at Christmastime we had a whole bunch of toys. The toys didn't cost over ten dollars, but we had a bunch of them. They were somebody else's toys—but we still had them. Things like that. And even like clothes, I remember my mother used to go to this place, Cheap Charlie's. I used to get about ten pairs of pants, for about ten dollars. That's how I became the best dressed at school. I could change pants every day!"

But it was *hard*, being well dressed and rich and owning your own car, because you had to be a Bad Dude too. In a reunion of old Neighborhood friends, there is happy reminiscence of crime. Distance makes the crime profounder. (Big Daddy remembers boasting about stealing cars and taking them to Mexico—a complete lie, something he picked up from the newspapers.) Although some of the men gathered in Dock's suite have been in and out of the slammer, others have never done time—and feel inferior; they are virgins. Like white, crew-cut salesmen, sitting in the airport bar, boasting about broads and chicks, the men of the Neighborhood talk about stripping down cars.

George Jennison reminisces about Gardena High, and crime. Playing football, he works out with the first team all week, and in the game plays only in the last quarter. Transferring from a black high school with high grades, he finds that he is placed in auto shop. "I didn't want that. Then you got in a hassle with the vice-principal.

"And money was hard to get, so we had to do something, so we stole automobiles."

Dock and Big Daddy and a few others from the Neighborhood took to invading Compton which was tougher than the Neighborhood. One night—three of them wearing newly fashionable trench coats—they crashed a Compton party and nearly got killed.

George Jennison:

"Everything was cool for a while, and then Dock fooled around with somebody's old lady. She was pregnant; she was sitting on the patio." (Dock interrupts: "I kissed her.") "The next thing I knew, the next thing I knew, my head went into the TV."

Dock: "I tried to get out the sliding glass door. Somebody knocked me into the sliding glass door. I was on the ground, and they was kicking me. This was on a hundred and fifty-seventh, what they call the Twilight Zone; we also called it the Land of a Thousand Women. They were beating me to *death*. I knew one guy from Compton, a guy named Gibson, so he picked me up and threw me over the fence, when I was almost killed. They were cutting at me with knives. The only thing that saved me was that I had on a trench coat and a suit coat underneath it. After I got up, the trench coat was in shreds. They beat the *shit* out of me.

"I just ran and jumped in Big Daddy's car. He had a fifty-three Mercury at the time. Jumped in his car. Didn't even touch the window. Just dove straight in it. They were driving off, and didn't know where I was at. And I was laying down, *out*. When I woke up, we were in the gas station where Big Daddy used to work. He was putting tape on himself. Somebody stuck him with an ice pick. He was putting tape across his stomach."

They returned to Horace Mack's (Magpie's) mother's house and Dock staggered into the bathroom, and took off his pants, and threw them out the window. "That's what happened. They beat the *shit* out of me."

6. *Gardena High*

High school separated Big Daddy and Dock. By fraudulent use of an aunt's address, Big Daddy went to the black school, Fremont. Dock attended Fremont for two weeks, until the authorities discovered where he lived. He had wanted to play basketball and baseball there; at Gompers, he had played on the nucleus of the All-City Fremont basketball team. Probably he could have managed to attend Fremont if his father had not wanted him to go to Gardena. The white school was academically better.

But not for black males. Black males were counseled to take crafts: ceramics, photography, shop.

In his first year at Gardena High, Dock surely had a Bad Attitude. Frustrated in his wish to go to a black school, called "Watusi" and "nigger" in the corridors—names he had first heard at Thornburg in the same city—he cared nothing for classes; he cared only for fighting. He returned to shakedowns and other minor crime, like pilfering lockers. School was constant confrontation with the vice-principal, chief disciplinarian, who told Dock he would never be *anything*. Dock constantly challenged authority, never accepted anything put upon him. He tilted his head back, half closed his eyes, and *questioned:* his manner drove authority wild. The vice-principal tore up scholarship applications (UCLA was interested in Dock for basketball), saying you could not get a scholarship with a 1.9. Dock tells me the story, and adds, "That ain't no ERA, either."

Basketball was his outstanding sport. In his first year at Gardena he played on the B team, and the B coach hated him. Then Mickey Panovich, the varsity basketball coach, grabbed him away, and he was team MVP for two years, and led the team to the city tournament. At six feet three and a half inches, he was tall for a high-school guard.

Playmaking was his thing. *Shoot,* his friends kept telling him, but he preferred to pass off, and he made as many as thirty-two assists in a single game. As his old coach remembers it, Dock was unselfish: he helped out other players in practice; he was virtually an assistant coach; then in the game he set up other players' scoring.

"Any troubles he had in school," Panovich says, "probably came from people who expected him to *snap to,* and do what they said immediately. He reacted kind of slow, or looked at them." Panovich mimics Dock being haughty. "He had a way of looking with his head back, not exactly down his nose. It looks as if he's saying, 'Are you going to *make* me do this?' He looked *sassy.*"

Dock and Panovich were fond of each other. Here was one white at Gardena High who was ready for Dock Ellis—as whites in Gardena, in subsequent years, have learned to be ready for other blacks who did not *snap to.* Panovich had known another black athlete when he attended UCLA. "I would compare Dock in a way with Jackie Robinson. Not as good an all-around athlete of course. I went to school with him. When he was a senior, I was a freshman, playing basketball at UCLA, and we used to scrimmage the varsity once in a while. We always tried to get Jackie to guard, because he did so well. He made us look silly. Jackie got into a lot of problems because he didn't *snap to* immediately, you know, when people asked him to do something. He had pride. He had some kind of pride. He would get into trouble once in a while when people expected him to snap to. When people were *reasonable* with him, they would get along fine with him.

"Like Dock."

When he matriculated at Gardena High, Dock fully intended to play baseball. But in the spring of his first year—with the name-calling and the reputed attitude of the baseball coach—"All I wanted to do was fight. I didn't want to play no baseball."

Later, "Once I got smarter than the name-calling, I said, 'Well, I don't want to play for *them.*'" He played baseball, but he played elsewhere. During his second year at high school he began to play on Mr. Brewer's team. Hearing of Dock's success, the Gardena coach tried to recruit him. "I told them no." He could have sat out Mr. Brewer's team during high-school season, if he had wanted to play for Gardena. Mr. Brewer's other players starred for their black high school: Willie Crawford and Bobby Tolan for Fremont; Don Wilson and Roy White and Wayne Simpson for Centennial; Ronnie Woods for Compton. Dock conscientiously objected to Gardena High baseball.

Then, in his senior year, "They caught me in the bathroom drinking wine and getting high. They told me, 'You play on the baseball team, and we won't kick you out of school.' " Things would have been awkward at home, with his father ill. "So, I played on the baseball team. I played only two games, and I made all-league. No, I take it back. I played four games. I pitched two, and played third base the other two."

7. Baseball City

A permanent smog and sulfurous gray dome, like the top of a vast stadium dedicated to emphysema, curves over the concrete lanes, intersecting and crawling everywhere and nowhere, on which the carcinogenic machines hurry and scurry. But Los Angeles is also a vast plain of low houses, fields, warehouses, and baseball diamonds. Southern California has become the great hothouse of baseball players. While poor neighborhoods in cities of the Midwest and the East have space only for basketball courts, making basketball the city game, the flat acres of Los Angeles grow diamonds like weeds.

It is the biggest city of the country of baseball. Everywhere you look, driving from the Neighborhood to Compton or Gardena, baseball fields settle in corners of land, among houses and churches and oil wells and liquor stores and factories. Tiny diamonds for the small children, school fields, municipal fields with grandstands—everywhere the precise notations of base paths, pitchers' mounds, and backstops. Although most boys mimic the seasons of professional sport, trisecting the year, in Los Angeles the seasons are artificial. If you want to play baseball all year, you can do it. Somebody is always playing baseball, and the sound of the bat hitting the ball, or the ball smacking into the catcher's mitt, is never wholly absent, under the gray dome.

8. Harbor J. C.

After graduating from Gardena High, Dock attended Harbor Junior College for a year and a half.

First, two teams tried to negotiate with Dock's father, to sign Dock to a professional baseball contract. (It was the year before baseball initiated the draft.) Dock's father turned them down, saying that the offers weren't big enough. Maybe Dock's father was reinforcing college, when he found the offers wanting. Dock's father wanted and expected him to go to college, and Dock did what his father wanted and expected him to do.

"At this stage," says Al Rambo, who attended Harbor with Dock, "blacks were supposed to *go* to college, but nobody taught you anything about *studying* in college. Nobody was ready for it. The crowd I was in, some went to Harbor J. C., some went into service. My type thing was Harbor J. C."

Dock's type thing was to *go*, but not to *study*, Al implies. Dock's sisters both went to Harbor—it was all right for girls—and both graduated. But Dock's heart wasn't in it, and as usual he offended people, in particular all coaches. Because athletics was the reason for going to Harbor—to improve his grade point, to matriculate at UCLA and play basketball—it wasn't sensible to offend coaches. But Al shrugs his shoulders. "Even today, I see where Dock speaks his mind, and a lot of people are upset. It was the way he was brought up. This is the way that *he* is; this is not the way that somebody told him to do. He can't be any other way and still be himself.

"I can remember an incident. To shock his father, he carried a copy of *Muhammed Speaks*. That day, that was *really* something. The movement hadn't really grabbed a hold at this time. For Dock to be thinking along these lines was *radical*. This was right at the time of Harbor J. C. Dock was the kind of person, even then, who was going to stick with whatever was in his mind."

Dock wasted no time in alienating the white coaches on his arrival. Maybe he didn't really want to go to college *at all:*

"The first car I got was a fifty nine Impala, and I kept it until nineteen sixty-four. And the remarkable thing, one of the coaches, he was jealous of me having a car. Because he didn't have a fifty-nine, he had something like a fifty-three or something like that. He failed me in a basketball class, and the test we took, I didn't miss a shot or anything.

"But I *was* the kind of dude, I would say, 'These honkies don't know how to shoot a basketball'—and he didn't like that."

He went out for baseball. One day Dock arrived at the park to discover that he was to pitch against Orange State. He was unprepared, got bombed, and quit the team to return to Mr. Brewer. "I was used to playing with professional athletes. That was the Little League, the way they did it; I wasn't going to deal with it."

9. *Low-Riding with Roy Jones and The Bug*

The first year at Harbor J. C. was relaxed and wild. Dock traveled especially in one small clique, known as the Sons, or Big Daddy and the Sons. Big Daddy, Dock, Al Rambo, Ray Jones, Willie Crawford, and Vaughn Chapel ran and partied together. And there were women they ran with too, like Rudy-poo, eating at the hamburger joints, riding crazily all over town in their low-rides, playing cards. When Dock saw *American Graffiti*, he thought of the last year of high school and the low-riding months at Harbor. He wanted to make a film *Black Graffiti*.

The second year at Harbor was a bad time. Discouraged in his academic subjects, unable to enjoy sports at Harbor, Dock one day tried to enlist in the service. His mother persuaded him to change his mind, for his dying father's sake. But when his father died, Dock quit school and signed a baseball contract. Just before going to spring training, he and Ray Jones stole a car, were caught, jailed, released, tried, fined, and put on probation.

Al Rambo—The Bug—coaches and teaches physical education in a Los Angeles high school. In the summer, he and Ray Jones and Earl Brown coach a baseball team, the E-C All-Stars. E-C stands for Ellis-Crawford, since Dock and Willie—at the behest of the coaches—sponsored the team by requesting money for uniforms from Mayor Tom Bradley of Los Angeles. Many players on the team are gang leaders, and baseball keeps them off the streets and out of jail. When Dock comes to town in the winter, Al and Ray introduce him to young ballplayers, and from time to time Dock takes one of them around Los Angeles with him. Sometimes he takes a kid to the airport, where a fancy restaurant suspended from tall concrete legs turns full circle once an hour. Dock tells the boy, 'You can do anything you want. You can eat in that restaurant *every day*, if you *want*. You *do* something."

We arrive at eleven-thirty, after the night game. Ray Jones is already there, and The Bug arrives a little later, in baseball uniform. The E-C All-Stars just lost a game, six to three. With him he brings a sleepy-eyed black kid, about sixteen, who will play basketball at The Bug's high school next winter. "What's happening, my man?" says Dock to the boy. The boy grins, shy, meeting Dock Ellis. Dock is relaxed, paternal, gentle respectful, and firm all at once. Then he teases The Bug about illegally recruiting his basketball team.

The Bug tells me about the E-C All-Stars. "It's specifically for people having trouble in school, who can't get along with their instructors, can't *relate*. They're going through the same type of thing we were. Some of the guys on the team played basketball together last year. Dock came home for the winter; he followed the team quite a bit. The idea we had, forming this club, was really the same idea as Mr. Brewer was doing ten years ago."

I ask Ray Jones about stealing the car. Ray is relaxed, high, continually laughing, very handsome and wicked, with the slight paunch of an ex-football player.

"We was up to Centennial High School. We was about seventeen I guess. Dock had this fifty-nine Impala. He done dropped it, and put the mags on it, mag wheels. We in there shooting basketballs, and we come out, and the car is sitting up there on crates! Somebody took all the wheels! So we got some tires, some kind of way. Took it on home.

"The next day—he done thought about that all night; he's pissed off now—he says, 'We going out here, and we going to steal a car!'"

"We drove out to Harbor, and he gets out of the car and takes his keys with him, and went over there and started up a fifty-five Chevrolet. So I look over there, and it's blasting, and he's sitting in it. So I thought, 'You don't have no choice, now, but to move it.' So he moved it, and I followed him in his car. All the way from Harbor Junior College to his neighborhood, over on a hundred and thirty-fifth and San Pedro. We go over there to rip the wheels off, and a dude looks at us, and tells us, 'Hey, man, those are fifteen inch!' And we had fourteen inch on the Impala! And they don't fit no way. So we done stole something we can't even use!"

Dock pushes the door open just then, hears the last phrases, and interrupts: "The police saw *him*. And then they come back to get him. He gave them some I.D. When they found out that the stolen car was in that area where he was, quite naturally they just figured he did it."

Ray: "I had nothing. I played it so innocent that day. I must have acted good."

Dock: "Yet he still had my wallet under the seat. Because I always kept my wallet under the front seat. That proved to them that he didn't steal my car. Next thing I knew his mother called me and said, 'They got Ray in jail, and looking for you.' That's when I went down there."

Dock went to the police station on his way to a ball game, because they already had Ray. "And they said, 'Come on in, Mr. Ellis.' And they said, 'Ray Jones signed a confession that you stole a car.' I said, 'I didn't steal no car.' I knew what I was doing. I told them to go get Ray and let me hear him say it. So they went and got Ray, and he say, he bend over and say, 'They got your fingerprints!' He forgot I had gloves on. I said, 'Wait a minute, Ray. I didn't steal no car.' It could have been my word against his, but he had signed the confession, so . . ."

Ray: "He had his baseball uniform on, coming in there."

Dock: "I had my baseball uniform top on. And a pair of pants over the rest of it. I used to just go to the ball park and to to the bathroom and put on the baseball pants, and come out."

Dock and Ray spent a day and a half in jail. At the trial, Mr. Brewer appeared as a character witness. Both men were fined, put on probation, and Dock was free to play for the Batavia (New York) Pirates. Dock was supposed to report to the police of every town he visited to play in. It was impossible. After the first year, the court relaxed his probation.

Ray Jones:

"We just all started running together. We was friends, and that was cool. And then we just happened to meet a man like Mr. Brewer. Mr. Brewer used to discipline us, in his own little way. He would always look at Nut like that, and look away from him." Ray mimics a glance of dignity and disdain.

"That semester he went to college, that did it, that turned him around. That made him realize that he'd better go play him some baseball."

"Because he knew he was wasting his time?"

"Right. Because he got *done*. Because some people out there *hated* him. His trip was entirely different from my trip. Just the opposite. I could get everything done, he couldn't get nothing done." Ray acknowledges his salesmanship; he smiles winningly. "That's just how they *felt* about him. They didn't even know him. They just saw him one time, and they say, 'I'm going to hate this nigger.' That's what they say, 'I'm going to *hate* this nigger.' When they *seen* him. And they *hated* him. He's always in the spotlight . . ." Ray collapses laughing, praising, laughing.

"That's Nut," Ray goes on. "He could go to China, and he would live just like them people. If he went to Japan and played ball, he would probably spend less than any American over there today, because he would get down with the people. (*They* saving money, some kind of way. They getting too big over there, *not* to be saving some money.) He could go over there and fit in. He could go to Thailand, and he could fit in. No matter, anywhere in this world, he could fit in. Especially with his master's, now."

Three: The Season, and Mr. Brewer

1. *One and Five*

The Pirates started their trip West, at the end of May 1974, by losing two out of three to Cincinnati. In Los Angeles the Dodgers took them three straight. On their first day in San Francisco, the Pirates lost their fifth straight.

They were in last place. They were playing all kinds of bad baseball, but their defensive play was worst of all. Dave Parker pulled a muscle badly and gave right field over to Richie Zisk. Zisk started hitting the ball, and finished the year with a .313 batting average. There was no way to get him out of there, but for the first half of the season, his fielding was appalling. A left-fielder all the way through the minor leagues—no wheels, no gun—he found Willie Stargell firm in left field at Three Rivers Stadium. In right field, he stood transfixed while balls dropped in front of him for singles or scooted past him for triples, errors that could not be called errors. If you pull up short on a ball that you could have caught—that Truman Capote could have caught—and pick it up on the second bounce and heave it into second base, the pitcher has given up a single. If you get a late start on a ground ball twelve feet to the left of you, and the ball rolls past your glove, and you lumber after it like an ostrich, and lob it to second base while the batter slides into third, the pitcher is recorded as having given up a triple. The pitchers did not like to talk about Richie Zisk, in the first half of 1974—except when his batting won them a game. In the second half, his fielding picked up as the team picked up, and everybody was friends.

At third base, the Pirates play a good bat named Richie Hebner, who would make a first-rate designated hitter. He hits right-handed pitching with considerable consistency. But as a third baseman, he is handicapped by his inability to bend over. Again and again—early in the season, especially—an easy ground ball would snap out toward third base, a few feet from Hebner, and Hebner would run to field the ball—and then he would seem to forget to bend over, and the ball would trickle out into left field. In the number of chances handled, he was eighth among ten National League third basemen. He didn't handle so many chances because of his strange inability to bend from the waist.

At second base, Rennie Stennett fielded brilliantly, with great range for a second baseman, but with unsettling frequency threw the ball to the wrong base, or to the right base which his shortstop had neglected to cover, or nowhere at all.

"You can buy a good glove at the five-and-ten," says Dock. "That's what they always say. I say, 'Well, let's go buy some of those five-and-ten gloves!' "

The pitchers grew malcontent. Malcontent, they threw home-run balls.

One of the games in Los Angeles, the Pirates played almost well. They came from behind in the top of the ninth to tie the game at three-three. Jim Rooker was pitching precisely, the defense making the necessary plays. Then in the bottom of the ninth the first batter hit a home run off Rooker and the game was over.

In the clubhouse, Dock took shelter. "Hebner was *throwing* things. Chairs. Stuff. He's baseball crazy. Rooker was throwing things. People are going crazy. Man, I'm getting *out-of-here!* Somebody's going to get *killed.*"

But the Pirate ballplayers did not assault each other. In the time of defeat, each man draws more and more into himself. Some stew and fret and go home and beat their wives. Others remain calm. Deliberately calm.

Though the ballplayers don't criticize each other, tension shows itself in a hundred ways. People pop off to the press. Zisk tells a reporter that Murtaugh is a liar. Later, Zisk apologizes to Murtaugh in front of the team. Word spreads among the players that Murtaugh threatened Zisk with never playing baseball again if he didn't apologize. Then they remember: a week before, Al Oliver had apologized to the team, for

something he had told a reporter. Maybe they threatened Scoop? You
don't usually threaten a $100,000 centerfielder who hits .308. No,
probably—Dock says—"They just got into his head."

Murtaugh calls a team meeting, because "Someone on the team is
snitching to the press. Someone is telling the press *exactly* what we're
saying in the clubhouse, what *exactly* is happening to different
individuals on the team. And then the press comes back to Murtaugh
and asks him. He said, 'If I ever find out who it is, he will never play on
this team again. He will never play baseball again.'

"That is a *threat*. You can't do that. You can fuck around and get killed,
threatening a ballplayer. If they ever put a threat on me, I'll do
something bad to them."

The last of the three losses in L. A. was a laugher, six to nothing:
errors—official and unofficial—and futility at the plate and bad pitching.
John Morlan came in for a long relief, and before throwing a pitch
balked in a run. (He balked a throw to first. Possibly his fingers
were arranged to throw a curveball, and he suddenly remembered in
midthrow.) It was typical of the first half of '74. Afterward, no one threw
chairs or screamed in the clubhouse, as they had done the night before
when they lost in the ninth. Heavy depression spread over the room.
Then the team filed into the bus to take them to the plane. Since the
hapless game had taken a little over two hours, they could look forward
to a long wait at the airport.

But the bus driver took an hour and a half to accomplish the
thirty-minute drive. "They run a *game* on us," Dock told me in San
Francisco. "Going from the ball park to the airport, the bus driver went
way out of his way. I could have gotten from the ball park to the airport
and back to the ball park *two times*. A lot of guys were screaming. 'Hey,
where we going?' I started running the directions down.

"I kept saying, 'Bussie, do you know where you going? Bussie, I'll give
you *fifty dollars* if you'll turn around and go back to Sepulveda!

"I figure they did it to keep the ballplayers out of the airport bar."

2. *Visiting Mr. Brewer*

The day before the Pirates left Los Angeles, Dock took me to meet his
old coach, Chet Brewer. Mr. Brewer—Dock had been telling me all

along—was the most important man in his life, after his father. When his father died—Dock in late adolescence—Mr. Brewer more than anyone else supplied the discipline and the model that Dock needed.

He had played brilliant baseball in the Negro leagues for more than twenty-five years, but few people know about it. *The Baseball Encyclopedia*, Macmillan's huge volume, lists every man who ever played in the National League, in the American League, and even in the National Association (1871–75), and brags on its jacket that the book contains over one million three hundred thousand facts—but it carries no mention of the Kansas City Monarchs or the Pittsburgh Crawfords. Josh Gibson's name is absent from the players' register, and Satchel Paige makes the pitchers' register as a chap who staggered into the major leagues as a forty-two-year-old rookie, and no footnote accounts for his earlier experience. Barnes's *The Official Encyclopedia of Baseball* prints one page of information about "Negro Players."

A book about Negro baseball, *Only the Ball was White*, tells us a little more, but is short on detail. *Voices from the Great Black Baseball Leagues* prints interviews with old players. We know that black and white played together in the early years of professional baseball, and we know that Cap Anson refused to field a team against a black pitcher in 1884, and we know that many segregated teams of black and Latin players flourished from the twenties to the fifties, when black and white finally came together again. We know the names of some of the famous teams, and even the names of some of the players. The baseball Hall of Fame, in a late gesture, elected Josh Gibson, Judy Johnson, Cool Papa Bell, and Buck Leonard. But it omitted many other black players who starred in postseason games against white major leaguers, and whose consistency in Negro baseball year after year argues that they would have been a great major leaguers if bigotry had not excluded them.

A black sportswriter named Doc Young argues that the hall should forget about electing more old black players, because the exercise is hypocritical, including only players whom the media has made famous because of their colorfulness. "Among other old time Negro League stars who qualify," he said in *The Sporting News* in 1975, "are: Bullet Joe Rogan, Bingo De Moss . . . [and] Chet Brewer (a truly outstanding pitcher for whom Satchel Paige should be a campaign manager). . . ."

When Dock played for Mr. Brewer, he played at a level equivalent to Class A. Here are some of the people who played for Chet Brewer from the Neighborhood and nearby: Reggie Smith, Bob Watson, Dave

Nelson, Willie Crawford, Bobby Tolan, Don Wilson, Roy White, Dick Simpson, Enos Cabell, Buddy Bradford, Ronnie Woods, Leon McFadden, Wayne Simpson, Rudy May, and George Hendricks.

Dock told me about Mr. Brewer as we drove to Mr. Brewer's house:

"Oh, it was ridiculous, the talent he had! And he was a scout for the Pirates. Not a scout but a bird dog. He had all the talent in L.A. On one team. And they plucked them from him. Tolan went to Pittsburgh originally, Roy White went to the Yankees, Reggie Smith at that time went to Minnesota. And he didn't get credit for handling them, or assigning them.

"At that time, all he had to do was tell us, 'Don't sign unless I tell you to sign,' and we would never have signed. He could have made a million dollars.

"He had the nucleus of the big leagues, almost, right in the Neighborhood. Scouts was just coming around us, and saying, 'We want to sign you!' I think Mr. Brewer, he was just *overwhelmed* to see us *sign*. To get a chance to play ball. Rather than to try to get his part out of it, which he deserved.

"Every time I progressed, the scout got money." The scout was Jerry Gardner, who was, in Dock's mother's phrase, "a Caucasian fellow." "When I got to the big leagues, for ninety days, I got five thousand dollars. The scout got it too.

"Oh, Mr. Brewer put in a lot of time with us! Even with Reggie Smith. Reggie said Pesky taught him how to play shortstop. Hey, man! I used to say, 'Why is Mr. Brewer hitting all them ground balls to Reggie? Them balls jump out and knock your tooth out.' I said, 'Reggie's a fool to be out there letting Mr. Brewer hit hard ground balls and bust him in the mouth and everything.' And, Mr. Brewer is the one that had him switch-hitting."

We descend from the freeway, and nose our way through suburban streets. I ask, "What did he teach you about pitching?"

"He's always trying to teach me how to throw a curveball. He says *today* I don't know how to throw a curveball."

Later, I asked Big Daddy to tell me about playing for Mr. Brewer.

"Mr. Brewer had a fifty-six Buick, a Century. He used to come home from work, from the aircraft plant. He'd come home from work and his wife would fix his dinner, fix his plate, and he would get in the car and I was the one who would drive to the park, while he was eating. Every night!

"As we were driving down to the park, or home from the park, he would start telling us about Satchel Paige, all the ballplayers. Sometimes he would bring out the pictures and all the books he had on the black baseball leagues. Kansas City Monarchs. We read about him and Satchel Paige—all the dudes. It was really interesting to me. That was something I had never done. I had never liked to read anything. He would open up those books to us, and it was just fascinating.

"He knew all phases of the game. He would help everybody, but he helped me and Dock more than he helped anybody. Nut, he has always had the curveball and the drop, which I had never had. I had the fastball, and a mediocre change-up curve. He started on me and Dock. The main thing was the jumping fastball. He wasn't worried about the curve.

"He was throwing batting practice to us. And we had an old guy named Tommy—that's all I knew him by, was Tommy—he was about sixty-five then and he had played with Brewer. Tommy would throw us batting practice—he had a four-finger mitt, no strings—and he couldn't throw hard, but he had more shit on that ball! Couldn't nobody hit him! He would actually relieve for us. Managers could play in the Muny League, and he was player-coach. When we'd get in trouble, we'd just bring old man Tommy in."

Dock parks the car in front of a gray house on a gray street. Inside, the living room is untidy—Mr. Brewer's wife had died suddenly four years before, the morning after Los Angeles held a testimonial dinner for him—and cluttered, mainly with trophies from the country of baseball.

Because Dock wants me to talk alone with Mr. Brewer, to get to know him a little, Dock invents an errand that takes him away.

Chet Brewer is tall and slim, light brown, handsome, his great dignity combines with a foxy look. He is in his sixties now. Today, he moves continually among the four rooms of his house, fetching objects to show me: books of clippings, plaques, cups, photographs. From a Mexican newspaper comes the translation of a news item— CHET BREWER WORTHY OF THE HIGHEST HONORS—which begins, "A giant entered the hotel where the immortals of Mexican baseball are staying . . . " Although much of what he brings attests to his fame and to his accomplishment, Mr. Brewer displays himself without appearing vain; he is *beyond* vanity.

Chet Brewer played Mexican baseball in the winter, and in the Negro leagues in the United States in the summer. He pitched for the Birmingham Black Barons, the Pittsburgh Crawfords, the Baltimore

Elite Giants, the Chattanooga Black Lookouts, and the New Orleans Black Pelicans. Mostly, he pitched for the Kansas City Monarchs along with Satchel Paige. While he and I talk, an old Negro League ballplayer named Bill Evans telephones, and after he and Mr. Brewer have chatted, Mr. Brewer tells him that he is being interviewed, and hands me the telephone. I meet Bill Evans on the telephone, who tells me that when the Negro League old-timers voted on their best all-time pitchers, Chet Brewer was one of seven chosen. And when he was young, Bill Evans says, Chet Brewer pitched against the Black Sox—the White Sox players who threw the 1919 World Series, were banned from baseball, and barnstormed for years—and "they said he was one of the best pitchers they *ever* saw."

When Bill Evans and I hang up, I ask Mr. Brewer to tell me about his baseball life, right from the start.

"Oh, well. I've been in baseball a number of years."

(I lean back on the sofa, listening. Mr. Brewer tilts back in a chair, his cane across his lap, one leg straight out. His voice is slow, and persistent, understated, ironic until he talks about coaching the young; ironic about his own accomplishments, maybe because the world no longer acknowledges them.)

"I played in the colored leagues. They didn't let us play, then, before Jackie Robinson.

"We had to learn the hard way. We didn't have specialized coaches the way they have now. We learned from the older players."

"How long did you play?"

"In the colored leagues? Oh, I'd say about twenty years. I played about forty *seasons,* because we used to go play winter ball—in Puerto Rico, in Cuba, Panama, South America. One winter we went all the way to the Philippine Islands. Stopped over in the Hawaiian Islands. Nineteen fifty-three was my last year.

"I played ball in Mexico, and I had the opportunity to go to a college down there. I had two years of college. In Tampico, I studied Spanish. It proved to be quite useful, because the last three years the Pirates have sent me to the Mexican League in the spring, as instructor and scout.

"At the time I was going to school and learning Spanish there, it was so that I could communicate with the girls. Not thinking that in my older days it would be useful, professionally speaking."

Late in his baseball career, Mr. Brewer used to patch together a team and play major leaguers, barnstorming on the West Coast at the end of the regular season.

"I was one of the sponsors of the team. We brought colored stars out here and we played major leaguers. Like Bob Feller would bring his Major League All Stars out here, and we would play them all up and down the coast. And I had Satchel Paige with me, and Luke Easter played for me, Larry Doby, and those kind of fellows."

"Did you pitch for that team?"

"Yes, I pitched when I felt like it. If they needed me. Because I had fellows like Booker McDaniels who pitched for the Kansas City Monarchs along with Paige. I had Connie Johnson out here. He was another pitcher for the Kansas City Monarchs, who played briefly with the Chicago White Sox. Oh, I had a real team. We had to be, to play the major leaguers. One year Bob Feller brought a team out here—he had Hogan from the Indians and Hemsley from the Cubs, catchers, and at first base he had Mickey Vernon, who had just won the American League batting championship, second base they had Johnny Beradino, he played with Cleveland—he's now on TV in General Hospital—and they had Ben Chapman from the Athletics playing short, and they had Ken Keltner from the Indians playing third; in left field they had King Kong Keller from the Yankees, center field they had Stan the Man Musial, and in right field they had Big Jeff Heath, from the St. Louis Browns. And the pitching staff was Bob Feller, Johnny Sain, Bob Lemon, and Mike Garcia. Those are the kind of players that we were playing against. And we were successful. We won as many games, or more, as we lost. Nineteen forty-five and nineteen forty-six."

"How did you learn to pitch, when you were starting?"

"I learned from experience. My elbow swelled up so much I could hardly get my hand in my pocket. Pitching every two, three days. We had three or four pitchers, but we were playing every day, and doubleheaders, and triple-headers on holidays. I remember a Fourth of July, when I was playing out in Philadelphia. We played a ten-thirty game in the morning, played a doubleheader that afternoon, and got in the bus and rode over to New York, and played in New York State *that night*. That's four games in one day. Our uniform never got dry. We got a dollar and a half a day, meal money."

"What were your salaries?"

"They paid five hundred or six hundred dollars a month, top players. I remember when I started playing in the colored leagues, I was getting a hundred and seventy-five dollars a month. Back in nineteen twenty-five. Right out of high school.

"Nineteen twenty-five. Nineteen fifty three. That makes *twenty-eight* years playing baseball."

"I said I played forty seasons. That takes in riding on the buses, eating out of paper sacks. We would go places, and because our face was black, they wouldn't feed us. Some of the places, they'd tell you to go around back and get something to eat, and eat over the garbage cans.

"Some white people today don't understand the young colored man. He's not holding still for what we had to go through. Because it wasn't right, it just wasn't *morally* right. We were dressed clean, intelligent people. When I came into baseball, most of us were high-school graduates at least. Just a few of the old-timers hadn't been to school. The others kept *them* straight. We had a real fine baseball team. Some of them were going to college, and just using baseball as a means to a college education. This is the type of team that I was on with the Kansas City Monarchs.

"A fellow called me up and asked me if I would back a book called *Bingo Long's Travelling All Stars*. You ever hear of that?" I had. A white author had written a novel about the Negro leagues. "As far as I'm concerned, it's trash. I told this man, I said, 'No, I can't push a book like that, because this type of ballplayer that you are picturing in that book, it wasn't that way with us.' I heard they were going to make a movie out of it. Oh, boy, some of that stuff, I don't see how they're going to make a movie out of it. Some of the language that they use. They can't never make a movie out of that. It's degrading, as far as I am concerned."

When Mr. Brewer stopped playing professionally, he started to coach the young. "I've been working on the playground about eighteen years." Four years ago, the city of Los Angeles gave Mr. Brewer a testimonial dinner, and awarded him a plaque which credited him with five thousand hours of voluntary unpaid work on the playgrounds.

"I always have time to work with kids. I like to work with dropouts. Some kids have dropped out of school, and they don't have any direction. I try to stay close to them, and see if I can help them with their problems. I've been quite successful. The kids seem to have confidence in me, and respect me, and this is all I ask. I don't ask for any money or anything. I just want to try to make good citizens.

"I've had a lot of experience from traveling. This is why it's easy for me to communicate with people, because I've met so many different types, and I'm just hung up on youth. In my neighborhood here, all the little kids call me, 'Hi, Papa.' That makes me feel real good. They gave me an address book! I had this one here"—Mr. Brewer shows a battered address book, full of the names of young players—"and you need to be an Einstein to cipher it out. So these little kids came here one day and brought me this new address book. And I'm proud. This little girl—she's eight, her brother's ten—she says, 'Papa, you know why we like you? Because we think you're a nice man.' So this is how I got my pay, things like Dock dropping by here today. So many of these fellows that are in the big leagues, they don't even call me up. Like Reggie Smith, he's one."

"Do you remember Dock from the beginning?"

"Yes, I remember. I was living out in his Neighborhood. They had a little junior league team, thirteen- and fourteen-year-olds. I was new in the Neighborhood, and they told me, 'Whatever you do, don't get Dock on the team, because he's a troublemaker.' And that was a big mistake, because I could have used him. I scuffled with these kids. Some of them, they didn't know which end of the bat to hold, But I made the season with them, and we almost won the championship. Had I had Dock, we would have won it. The next year I said, 'Well, since I'm into this thing, I'm going to play the boys that I want to play. You parents don't give me any help anyway. I'm going to run the thing the way I see fit, and have play who I want to play. Like Dock.'

"We had a real fine relationship. They said a lot of things about him, but deep down, Dock is a real fine person. A real fine person, if you know him. They said he wants to fight. Yes, he did like to fight. That's normal for a red-blooded boy. They'll fight. But he wasn't using tire irons, and all that stuff. I never had any trouble with him. I told him, you want to fight, get out there and use all that energy *pitching*. He played third base for me too. He did a good job. We made the championship."

"What did you work on with Dock, especially?"

"The main thing I worked on was his temperament. So he wouldn't be so hot-tempered. Tried to make him concentrate on just being a nice citizen. Be *right*. You don't always have to want to pick a fight. This was the main thing, and I talked to him a lot, and we got pretty close. I told him when his father was sick, and he had a little girl that he was courting, I said, 'By the time you two get married, Dock will be in the big leagues.' He was a *natural* athlete."

"You didn't have to show him how to throw the ball?"

"Oh, yeah, I showed him a few things about that. But he was a natural, he could throw a curveball already. This is the hardest thing to teach young pitchers. How to throw a curveball. Dock *still* needs some help in the area of short-arming the ball, and making his elbow sore. He told me that he had that whipped, but apparently he hasn't. I want to talk with him when he comes back about that. Because I'm going to demonstrate something to you."

Mr. Brewer pulls himself up, stiff, and walks over to me. He stands me up, and takes my right arm and manipulates it, showing me how a pitcher can throw the curve with his arm entirely outstretched, just snapping the wrist, or he can throw it short-armed, crooked at the elbow, snapping it partly from the elbow—and in the process hurt his elbow.

"If you break your elbow like this, before you throw the breaking stuff, where do you feel it? Right in the elbow!" Mr. Brewer demonstrates with my reluctant arm. "See now if you *extend* your arm, and just break the wrist, there's no pressure on the elbow. You've got it *all* back here in your shoulder." Demonstration concluded, Mr. Brewer sits down and looks satisfied.

"Did Dock have any deficiencies as an athlete?"

"Well, he wasn't much of a hitter. You got to have a God-given ability. You can't take a pick and hammer and make a watch. No way! But that's about the only thing. It amazed me how he improved in his running. He's a real nice runner, now. They use him for pinch running, sometimes. He was slow when he was young."

Waiting for Dock to return, Mr. Brewer starts to fret about what he read in the paper, about Dock saying he wouldn't pitch one ball as a relief pitcher. I tell him that Dock considers that he has been misquoted. Mr. Brewer shakes his head; he knows about misquotation. "I talked to Don Osborne, the pitching coach, at a banquet one night. He said he'd be sitting there in the clubhouse, and those newspapermen would ask Dock something, and Dock would answer them, and the next day it was so *distorted*. It wasn't the same thing that Dock said, but it was *good news*. They built him up as a bad boy; this is what the media does and it is not good. They want to sell papers." Then Mr. Brewer remembers the time a security guard at the Cincinnati ballpark maced Dock, when Dock tried to enter the stadium without identification. Mr. Brewer shakes his head. He has spent years as a security guard himself; he knows you don't have to mace anybody; he knows why the guard maced Dock.

I'm not sure what to ask. I want Dock to come back, so that I can hear the two of them talk baseball. It's obvious that Mr. Brewer has a number of questions for Dock—about what's wrong with Dock's pitching this year, about what he said or didn't say to the press on the subject of the bullpen. I think of a question.

"You know," I say, "Dock is proud of *using* the press sometimes, like when he named himself starting pitcher in the All-Star Game. What do you think of that?"

Mr. Brewer shakes his head. Clearly it is not his way. It reminds him of something.

When the Pirates won the World Series, Dock felt that management should give Mr. Brewer a World Series ring, because of his contributions. The Pirate organization was slow in awarding it to him.

"When they didn't give me a ring, Dock just hit the roof. He wanted to put it in the paper and make a big something out of it. I said, 'Dock, the man I work for out here says he's going to get me a ring. It might take a little time, but he's going to get me one.' And this man is Jerry Gardner"—Pirate scout for whom Mr. Brewer bird-dogs—"and he hasn't lied to me yet, all the time I've been working with him. 'I got confidence that this man is going to see that I get a ring. Your way—I don't like that way, and I'm not going to do it.'

"And I got my ring. Took a little time. Dock was impatient. Oh, man, he raised Cain about it. I said, 'Well, I don't go about things the way you do. But I'll get results.' "

Mr. Brewer thinks of an analogy. "I was working out there at North American, as an inspector, and they made a white fellow an A-inspector in front of me. And boy, the colored union guys said, 'Hey, let's take this through the union.' And I said, 'No, I don't want to do that. They've given me promotions. They gave me the job in inspection in the first place. I was the first colored fellow in inspection. And everything he said he'd do, he has done.' "

I think of Dock's mother talking about how she and his father had gritted their teeth.

3. *Brewer and Son*

Dock returns from his errand. Immediately, Mr. Brewer telephones a friend, making sure that Dock can hear him. He tells his friend that Dock and Willie Crawford have bought uniforms for another Los Angeles sandlot team, *not* Mr. Brewer's, although Dock had promised to *give* him five hundred dollars for uniforms. Immediately, Dock jumps to his own defense. "No, I didn't!" he says, his voice high and insistent. "No, I didn't!" He is the child falsely accused by a father. "I didn't buy anything!"

Mr. Brewer's voice continues, calm and gentle, talking to his friend. "Yeah, well, I need the uniforms *now*, not in August when he comes back." The conversation concluded, Mr. Brewer hangs up and sits down. Dock pleads innocence, denying and denying.

But Mr. Brewer stands firm. "How come Earl Brown" [associated with Al Rambo and Ray Jones in coaching the E-C All-Stars] "got those uniforms?"

"I don't know. I don't know."

"Well, he said you and Willie Crawford . . ."

This subject continues under discussion for five minutes. A few seconds of silence after a denial are broken by a new flurry of accusations. The pauses begin to lengthen. Suddenly Dock leaps to change the subject, recalling a topic which he thinks may distract Mr. Brewer; he brings up World Series rings.

Dock and Mr. Brewer compare their rings. Mr. Brewer competes: "You just got 'Ellis' written on yours, haven't you?"

"That's all I need on there."

"Yeah, well, I've got 'Chet Brewer,' the whole name, on mine. Pittsburgh gave it to me."

Dock: "Yeah, after the World Series was over three years."

Mr. Brewer: "It makes no difference. I got it."

Now Mr. Brewer wants to change the subject. He says to Dock, "You know, I've got some cold beer in the fridge."

Dock, absolutely straight-faced, apparently offended: "You know I'm a baseball player, Mr. Brewer."

Everybody has a beer.

Mr. Brewer has been saving other remonstrances for Dock. First, he mentions the newspaper stories which said that Dock refused to go to the bullpen. Mr. Brewer says he understands that Dock was misquoted.

Dock: "I said they're not going to put me in the *bull*-pen. I said I would not pitch to one hitter, not even pitch . . ."

Mr. Brewer (outraged): "That's what the papers *said* you said."

Dock: "But they were saying it like I wouldn't do it to win a game. I meant the *bull*-pen."

Mr. Brewer: "Well, what do you mean? How are you going to be a relief pitcher if you're not in the bullpen?"

Dock: "You know, like going in if the score is eight to nine and we are winning, and get a guy out, then we win, right? But that's not going to be my *job*."

Mr. Brewer: "Why not?"

Dock: "Because I'm not going to the *bull*-pen."

Mr. Brewer: "Why?"

Dock: "They'll have to give me some money, if I'm going to take the ace's job. The ace gets one hundred thousand dollars."

Mr. Brewer: "Well you've got to do the job first, before you get one hundred thousand dollars."

Dock: "They've got to give me the money."

Mr. Brewer: "I don't see your reasoning. They are paying you now, and you are not doing the job. They are not going to keep paying you if you don't get better than a five-run earned run average." This is the ammunition Mr. Brewer has been storing up; he is furious about Dock's record.

Dock: "Their best bet to do is to trade me then."

Mr. Brewer: "They will send you to the minors. They sent Steve Blass down there."

Dock: "They can't do that to me."

Mr. Brewer: "Why?"

Dock: "I don't have any more options, Mr. Brewer. And I believe they're afraid to mess with me like that."

Mr. Brewer: "How did they send Steve Blass?"

Dock: "Blass couldn't find the plate. I *know* where the plate is."

Mr. Brewer: "Yeah, well, you're not getting nobody out."

Dock: "I'm one and five . . . but I'm not going to the *bull*-pen, Mr. Brewer."

Mr. Brewer: "Well then you're going to the minors."

Dock (voice rising): "I'm not going to the minors! I'm not the type of person to go *to* the minors! I have played in the minors! So when it come time for me to go to the minors, I'm not playing!"

Mr. Brewer: "Well, it's time for you not to play if you can't get nobody out."

Dock: "I can get people out."

Mr. Brewer: "Well you're not getting them out."

Dock: "That's the Pirates—"

Mr. Brewer: "That's what I want to talk to you about—"

Dock (he begins to be angry): "You can't *deal* with me in baseball right now, Mr. Brewer. There's nothing you can tell me about baseball that I don't know. Right now. Especially the Pirate organization, you see, because it's all changed."

Mr. Brewer (conciliatory): "You're on the inside of everything. I don't know . . ." Pause. He returns to the attack. "But I can *see* what you're doing out there pitching. . . ."

Dock: "Ain't nothing wrong with me."

Mr. Brewer: "Got to be something wrong with you."

Dock: " 'Cause I lose, doesn't mean nothing's wrong with me."

Mr. Brewer: "We're talking about *how* you lose."

Dock: "You lost. You've lost, and nothing was wrong with you. Right? You've gotten popped, right?"

Mr. Brewer: "Yeah, I have."

Dock: "Last year I lost five in a row."

Mr. Brewer: "I never remember being one and five."

Dock: "Last year I lost *five games in a row.*"

Mr. Brewer: "Were you one and five?"

Dock: "I won the first three."

Mr. Brewer: "You won the first three."

Dock: "And then I lost five."

Mr. Brewer: "How? Why?"

Dock: "I'm still doing the thing I always do: pitch."

Mr. Brewer: "Wait a minute. Now listen to me, Dock, doggone it. When you get on a losing streak, there's a reason for it. There's a reason for everything that happens."

Dock: "I got a ninety-five-hundred-dollar raise last year, and I had a twelve and fourteen record. You want to know how I got a ninety-five-hundred-dollar raise? Because I didn't talk about what's going on *now* last year. I waited until they got ready to negotiate. *Then* I said, 'What about the twenty-one unearned runs I gave up?' I don't say nothing about the guys booting the ball behind me. Nothing until it's time to negotiate."

Mr. Brewer (with sarcasm): "So that's why you're one and five now?"

Dock: "That's right. I didn't say, 'We're losing because we have Little

League infielders: they catch the ball and don't know what to do with it.'
I don't say that *now*. But when it comes time to get that money, I'm
going to tell them."

Mr. Brewer: "They're going to tell *you*, if you don't do what the man
says. If he says for you to be a relief pitcher, you're going to be a relief
pitcher."

Dock: "They've got to pay me."

Mr. Brewer: "I can see if you are the short man and you're out there
saving games or winning games . . ."

Dock: "If I'm going to be the short man, I'm going to be the short man.
But I'm not going to be no *bull*-pen *pitcher*. I'm not going to come in in
no fourth or fifth inning and pitch."

Mr. Brewer: "If you was working for me, you . . ."

Dock: "Mr. Brewer, you talking just like the Pirates!"

Mr. Brewer: "I'm making sense! You going to deliver, before I pay
you."

Dock: "They know how to stop it."

Mr. Brewer: "They will, eventually."

Dock: "Well, eventually it will come."

Mr. Brewer: "Soon."

Dock: "But I'll still be *me*.

Pause.

Mr. Brewer: "Yeah, you been *you* all your life. That doesn't make you
right. All the time."

Dock (conciliatory): "I never right all the time. Or else I wouldn't be
one and five."

Mr. Brewer (with rising volume): "So tell me why you're one and five.
Is it because you've got Little Leaguers can't catch the ball?"

Dock: "They just can't think, don't know what they doing. Plus they
confused. The guys on this team, they not used to losing. They don't
know how to handle it. That's why they all screaming."

Mr. Brewer: "This is true. I believe that."

Dock: "And therefore they make a lot of mental mistakes. All trying to
carry the load on themselves."

Pause. Mr. Brewer pauses to *believe* Dock, then decides it cannot be
exactly as he says. He returns to the attack once again.

Mr. Brewer: "I've been watching that thing, and you've got an earned
run average of almost five."

Dock: "Well, it was seven before that."

Mr. Brewer: "Yeah, I know. Well, it's almost five now."

Dock: "I ain't *got* to be one and five."

Mr. Brewer: "With an earned run average that says so?"

Dock: "I could easily be four and one."

Mr. Brewer: "With an earned run average of almost five?"

Dock: "My earned run average don't have to be like that! Last year, when they messed up behind me, I come back and got that man out, before they scored their run. If they boot the ball this year, okay they boot the ball. I get a man out. Another man drives in a couple of runs."

Mr. Brewer: "That's two unearned runs."

Pause. Again, Dock changes the subject, "Well, we not here to talk about my one-and-five year, we here to talk about *you*."

Mr. Brewer: "Me? I'm no news. I'm just a plain old poor scout. Starving to death. Skulking around trying to keep a team together and we can't get no uniforms and you and Willie Crawford go buying . . ."

Dock: "I told you I didn't buy no uniforms! I ain't bought nothing!!" (But during the argument, Dock has remembered what he *did* do.) "I set up the proposal to go to the mayor."

Mr. Brewer: "To the mayor?"

Dock: "Everyone he had on the team was in a gang, or a gang leader. They all got potential to be major league ballplayers. Bradley *got* to give up the money. If he see someone working with *gangsters*. Keeping them out of the streets. Playing baseball. He can check their high-school record, he can see they All-City basketball players, or All-City baseball players. He *got* to give them the money.

"I didn't give them none. I bet you Willie Crawford didn't either."

Dock mentions Big Daddy. "Couldn't he *fire?*"

Mr. Brewer shakes his head, in admiration and regret. "Oh, he *could.*"

"Now," Dock says, "he couldn't lob the ball across this room."

While I listen, my eyes wandering over plaques and trophies, the old pitcher and his protégé talk about arms, and about short-arming the curveball. Mr. Brewer remembers how he taught Sam Jones to throw a curveball. Then they talk about staying in shape, about not getting fat in the off-season. Then Mr. Brewer turns to me: "The fattest thing about Dock is his *head*," and the two men collapse in laughter.

We stand and say our good-byes, and drive away waving to the tall figure in the doorway. Driving, Dock chuckles about the old man's nagging remonstrances, and tells more stories. We reminisce about the hour just past. Dock would never miss a chance to visit Mr. Brewer.

I ask, "Why doesn't everybody feel that way? He told me that Reggie Smith never came to see him."

Dock nods. "He doesn't like that. It hurts him. A lot of people *change*. I understand it, because I'm around it. Money can do a lot of things to people.

"Tolan goes back, but he don't have no time. He'll speak, say, 'Hi,' and he's *gone*. When Tolan's with me, he seems strange. Say we'll be around someone that he's known and I've known and he hasn't seen him for even longer than I have, and he says, 'Hi,' and then he wants to go. 'Let's go. Let's go.' "

4. *The Pitching Day*

Humiliated by the Dodgers in Los Angeles, the Pirates flew to San Francisco, where the Giants were doing about as badly. In the opening game of the series, Larry Demery made his first start in the majors.

Twenty years old, a graduate of Locke High School not far from the Neighborhood, he is a fastballing right-hander like Dock nine years ago. He looks younger than he is; his eyes always popping slightly, he looks scared. In 1972, in his first spring training, eighteen years old, Demery started an exhibition game against the Detroit Tigers, and threw a memorable first pitch. He threw the first ball over the backstop.

But now, in a Pirate uniform after burning up Triple A, he isn't scared of anything. The day before the start, Dock asks a bunch of us to a taco lunch at his sister Elizabeth's house. I ask Larry if he isn't frightened, and he pretends not to understand the question. "What about?" he says.

Cool alone is not enough. You need support. That night the Pirates scraped together only two runs off John D'Acquisto, and Demery left the game for a pinch hitter, and ended up losing pitcher, although he pitched well. After that game, on June 7, the Pirates' record was eighteen and thirty-two. They were in last place in their division, nine games out of first.

Dock did not see the game Friday night, because he was starting Saturday afternoon. He drove out to Candlestick on the team bus Friday afternoon at five, dressed, ran a little, and took infield. He loosened up by fielding at second base, bending down from his high waist to scoop up the grounders hit by third-base coach Bob Skinner. Then Dock walked back to the clubhouse, showered, and took a cab back to San Francisco, where he had a suite on the twentieth floor of the elegant and pretentious Hilton Towers. He waited for a young woman to come by, who had earlier planned to visit, and when she did not appear, stayed up by himself and watched television, drinking a little Pouilly Fuissé—his favorite wine; Willie Stargell introduced him to it—and smoking a few Kools. He stayed up late so that he would sleep in the morning until it was time to catch the team bus.

Up at ten, quick shower, no breakfast, and onto the bus at 10:30. At the ball park, coffee and orange juice.

On a day when he pitches, Dock normally takes batting practice. Because it is Camera Day at Candlestick Park, there is no BP. Dock remains in the clubhouse, while the trainer Tony Bartirome rubs him down, and plays with the iron ball—so heavy it makes a real baseball, when you handle it afterward, feel as if it were inflated with helium.

On the field, when the llamas and cameras are put away, the teams practice shagging flies and fielding grounders. Left-hander Jim Rooker stands to the left of the plate, hitting fungoes to outfielders in right field. To the right of the plate, Dave Giusti hits flies to outfielders in left field. Bob Skinner slaps grounders to third base, short stop, second base, and first base, and then rolls a bunt for the catcher, with the rhythm of ten thousand coaches and ten thousand summer afternoons.

At 12:35—the game to start at one—starting pitcher Dock Ellis walks onto the field for the first time, entering from the visitors' clubhouse deep in right field. He joshes with the fans as he walks along the box seats. At the dugout, he removes his jacket, and strikes a pose for a newspaper photographer—stretched forward, ball aimed at the camera, as if he were about to release a fastball. He stops to chat for a moment, perfectly relaxed, and we arrange for dinner after the game. Then he turns back, ball and glove in hand, and saunters toward the bullpen where he will warm up. Fans yell at him. Backup catcher Mike Ryan and pitching coach Don Osborne mosey after him.

Heat rises from the plastic grass, making little waves on the air. Now it is 12:45. Groundsmen sprinkle water on the patches of dirt at the bases, and vacuum-clean real dirt from the plastic grass.

Dock starts to throw easily, half-speed, three-quarter arm. Twenty-

year-old habits pull themselves together. Willie Stargell strides down to
the bullpen with a bat, and provides a figure for his old roommate to
measure himself against—a mean-looking huge, left-handed figure. By
12:50, Dock is throwing harder, though not at full speed. He throws
curveballs for four minutes. At 12:54, he begins to throw hard. Willie
stands in, flicking his bat on occasion as Dock winds up. One fastball
begins to drop as it approaches the plate; another rises and moves away
from Stargell. Don Osborne watches without expression, arms folded on
his chest, as the pitches pound into Ryan's glove. At 12:58, team captain
Willie Stargell leaves the bullpen; he must present the lineup in the
ritual home-plate meeting between umpires and team representatives.
Dock throws twice more—curveballs—and walks to the dugout putting
on his jacket. This time he does not chatter at the crowd.

"The Star-Spangled Banner." As the first notes boom out, Dave
Giusti and Tony Bartirome find themselves caught in the infield,
hurrying toward the dugout. Both revolve to face the flag and freeze at
their random places. The rest of the Pirates stand with hats over hearts,
hearts aimed at the flagpole, but only Don Leppert appears actually to
sing. The song done, Giusti and Bartirome thaw out, and slouch into the
dugout, where everyone sprawls to watch the game. Dock towels away
his sweat.

Top of the first. The Pirates make two quick outs, then Hebner
singles. Willie Stargell, cleanup as usual, grounds out on a close play at
first. Willie is struggling. By the end of the day, he will have gone oh for
twenty-three.

Now Dock walks slowly to the mound and takes his warm-up pitches,
signaling with his glove hand—the familiar wrist chop—when he is
ready to throw a curve, making an over-the-shoulder gesture when he
tells Manny that this will be his last warm-up, and that Manny should
throw to second base. Now Bobby Bonds steps in, old friend of Dock's,
with whom Dock paid a USO visit to Vietnam in 1971. A curveball is a
swinging strike. On a second curveball, Bonds tries to bunt and misses
the ball. Frank Pulli shouts, "Strike." A third curveball, he swings, a
tipped foul which Manny holds onto. One out. K.

Second man up is Chris Speier, who gets two fastballs, and then a
curve which becomes an easy fly to the outfield. Two out, Garry Maddox
up. With the count two and two, Maddox lifts a pop fly to shortstop.
Mario Mendoza circles under it like a dog flattening a bed in a hayfield.
The wind is crazy. In the outfield, the flags stand straight out, from right
toward left. In the infield, the wind is equally strong—but it blows from
third toward first. Mario Mendoza is a rookie, playing his first game at

Candlestick Park, and the pop fly drops untouched. Maddox, running like a dash man all the way, stands on second base. Dock has just given up a double. A patented Pirate-defense double.

Then Ed Goodson hits a ground ball to Mario, who handles it easily, and Dock returns to the dugout, toweling his face and laughing.

"Baseball is *fun*," he tells his teammates.

In the top of the second, Zisk triples, Sanguillen doubles, and Mendoza singles. Two runs in.

In the bottom of the second, Gene Clines loses a ball in the wind for a two-base error. Next man singles, and Zisk throws the runner out at the plate.

In the third inning, both sides go out in order. Dock has pitched three innings of shutout ball.

(That evening at dinner, he told me how it feels, when baseball is fun again. The rhythm is natural, the body feeling itself move as it has learned to move over twenty years. As the game moves on, he feels more and more in control. His release point is right. The fastball is not moving much—there are days it strides, there are days it budges—but it moves where he wants it. He learned something, he tells me at dinner, loosening up in Los Angeles. Trying to throw the sinking fastball, he had begun to turn it over, like a screwball. "Sangy was telling me, standing there watching me. That's not throwing it naturally." Throwing it naturally in San Francisco—not *trying* so hard—it dropped more abruptly. And his curve was better. "Today I was throwing curveballs from *everywhere!* You can do that when you drop quick. Instead of striding way out. You stride way out, then you've got to come through with the ball. But if you have a *short* stride, you can snap quicker. I was doing it on every pitch."

(Mr. Brewer had hassled him about his curveball.)

And while he throws, and while he sits in the dugout to watch his own team bat, afternoon unwinds in the country of baseball. Wind swirls sand into the faces of the players, heat rises from the plastic, in the stands the cries of vendors alternate with the shouts of the Camera Day crowd, the kids and the fans. Bright blue sky, cool sun, guards and groundsmen lounging at the edge of the field, vendors everywhere, so that at every tense pause in the action of the game, the air is filled with the word, "Beer!"

The Pirates go down in the top of the fourth.

In the bottom of the inning, Dock walks the first batter. Ed Goodson hits a foul which is almost an opposite-field double. Manny runs out from behind the plate to confer with Dock, and Rennie Stennett joins them. It looks as if they are alarmed.

("What were they saying?" I ask at dinner.)

("They told me I should move Stargell over, because, they said, 'The left-handers are not pulling you.' So I said, 'No, I'm going to pitch this guy *in.*' Instead of moving Stargell, I told Rennie to move Zisk over toward the right-field line.")

Goodson flies out to Zisk.

Dock tries to pick Maddox off first, and throws in the dirt. Ed Kirkpatrick cannot dig out the throw and Maddox takes second, going on to third when Steve Ontiveros grounds out. Two out, man on third. The fans start rhythmic applause.

(At dinner I ask, "Can you hear it?")

("No, you don't hear it. You're too involved in the game.")

Dock fires two dropping fastballs at Gary Thomasson, who fouls them off, and then doubles, scoring Maddox. Bruce Miller grounds out. The score is two to one.

Dock leads off, in the top of the fifth. He looks awkward and frightened at the plate, leaning over from his high legs as he chops at the ball. He resembles those toy birds that tip periodically down to drink from a glass of water, stiff and abrupt.

He has been afraid at the plate since he was hit on the elbow at thirteen, and he is a switch-hitter out of fear. "Oh," he laments, "I used to hit just like Clemente"—meaning until he was thirteen. "I could go to right field. I could do anything with the bat. When the pitcher threw the ball, I threw my elbow up like that, and he hit my elbow, and ever since then, I'm afraid of the ball from a right-hander."

(But he is quick. He hit .238 in 1974, mostly chopping and running.)

Now, at the top of the fifth inning, Dock moves around in the box, batting left-handed against a right-hander. Jabbing, he hits a little tapper back to Tom Bradley, which Bradley has trouble picking up. Dock keeps running. When Bradley finally gets hold of the ball, he throws it into right field. Dock slides into third base for a Little League triple.

Dock slides into third base despite Bob Skinner's signal to stand up. "I went for the third baseman's fake. I thought he was reaching for the ball. He wanted me to slide. To hurt myself. I was *watching* the coach, but I *went for* the fake. They all told me on the bench I could have walked to third.

("Actually, I felt like laying down anyway.")

Clines singles to drive Dock in. Three to one.

Bottom of the inning, Dock starts by giving up a single to the catcher. The pitcher bunts him to second, and Bobby Bonds comes up to hit again. Dock has been getting him out on curves. Bonds hits a curveball foul. He takes another curve for a ball. Then Dock looks in at Bonds and sees something.

("I know how he holds his bat, and I see him looking for a curveball with the *bat*. I throw him a fastball and he pops it up.")

The runner takes third. Chris Speier up. Two fastballs out of the strike zone, the second one brushing him back. Then two foul balls, the second a line drive just foul. Then a called third strike, the fastball that sails up and in, to right-handed batters. Speier, enraged, gets Frank Pulli to throw him out of the game. Tito Fuentes takes over second base.

(It is a pitch that Dock likes to remember, after the game. "When it's down low, and rises a bit but stays inside the strike zone, it's a hell of a pitch, the pitch I struck Speier out with. The ball came *back*. But it was *down*. He was looking for something *away*.")

In the sixth inning, Dock drives in a run with a Baltimore chop single. Four to one.

Bottom of the sixth, Dock sets them down in order, and his confidence parades itself. When the third batter slaps a ground ball in the general direction of Rennie Stennett, Dock leaves the mound and is halfway to the dugout by the time the out is made.

The Pirates quickly down in the top of the seventh, Dock walks out to the mound again. The first batter bounces a ball over Dock's head, an infield single. No out, man on first. The crowd seems listless, and does not clap, but in the bullpen Giusti and Hernandez get up and start throwing. Murtaugh must worry that Dock will tire in the last innings.

Pop fly to Clines, one out. Then two outs. Dock seems to be concentrating, telling himself to *fire*, challenging batters with fastballs. Now the Giants send up Chris Arnold to pinch-hit for their pitcher. Dock motions, and Manny Sanguillen lopes to the mound. Chris Arnold seems only vaguely familiar.

Without a book on Arnold, Dock mixes a change-up, a fastball, curve, fastballs. Two and two, Arnold hits a single. Men on first and third, Bobby Bonds up, and Giusti throws harder in the bullpen.

Dock gets Bobby Bonds to pop up a curveball.

At bat in the eighth, Dock misses the ball on hit and run, and Mario Mendoza is thrown out at second. Mario brings Dock his glove and ball at the end of the inning, and they exchange a few words.

"I told him I thought I tipped it. He told me he got a bad jump."

The Giants go out one-two-three in the eighth.

In the top of the ninth, Kirkpatrick hits a home run. When Dock takes the mound in the ninth inning, he has a five to one lead.

He walks the first man, on fastballs. It was the fastball that rises and moves in, which was riding in high.

"Were you tired?" I asked him after the game. We were drinking vodka and orange juice in his suite, before going to dinner.

"I was a *little* tired. I couldn't get the ball down. My *arm* was tired. I was releasing the ball here, instead of here." He mimes releasing the ball at ear level, instead of releasing it at shoulder level. "That's what happens when you get tired. It will go *up*, if you don't get on top of it."

"What do you tell yourself?"

"Throw strikes. Reach back and bring it. Fire."

The bullpen starts working again, this time Kison the right-hander instead of Giusti.

Dock strikes out the next two batters, Thomasson and Miller. Then Kingman pinch-hits a single. Then Dock walks Matthews pinch hitting. Bases loaded, two outs, and a five to one lead. Bobby Bonds comes to the plate. Dock has handled him all day with ease. However, this season Dock has thrown a few home-run balls. A home run, and the game would be tied. At this point in this season, Murtaugh trusts nobody. He sends Don Osborne out to the mound, and Dock takes the long walk to right field and the clubhouse. The circle that started two and a half hours earlier, when he left the clubhouse to warm up, touches down where it began.

Bruce Kison takes over on the mound. He wild-pitches a run in, five to two, before getting Bonds to ground out and end the game.

Winning Pitcher, Dock Ellis. Record as of June eighth, two wins and five losses.

After the game, drinking his vodka and orange juice back at the Hilton, he looks elegant and sassy, but he is modest about his

Fourteen years old, at Gompers Junior High.

Dock Philip Ellis, Sr.

Dock's parents at Thanksgiving, 1961.

The young ballplayer, with his own caption.

The Batavia Pirate, Dock's first
pro uniform.

Paula and Dock, 25 September 1965.

With Charlie Howard in Kinston, North Carolina.

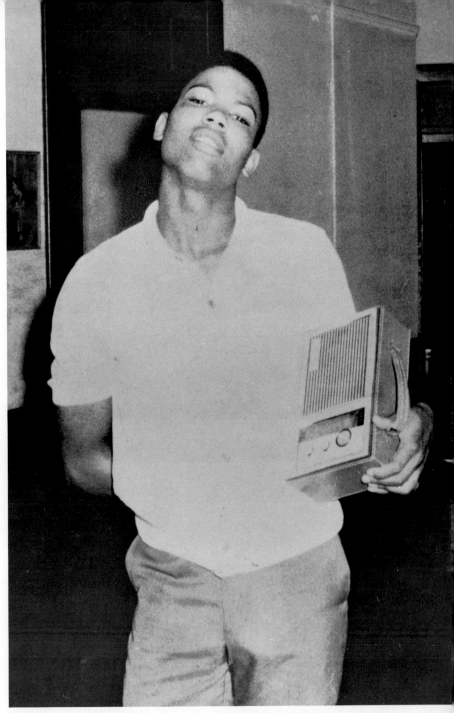

At Kinston, North Carolina.

Visiting New York with the Pirates. Lorenzo Lanier, Willie Stargell, Dock, and Bob Veale.

Pitching in Dodger Stadium.

Jane Kenyon

In the dugout after the no-hitter.

Jane Kenyon

Talking with the kids, Dodger Stadium.

In the dugout.

Jane Kenyon

achievement. "I didn't have exceptional stuff, but I was keeping the ball down, keeping the ball low."

"You didn't throw many changes, did you?"

"I only threw three changes, and they were wild. I threw one I *thought* was a strike, but he called it a ball. All I threw was curves and fastballs."

"How did you like being hooked in the ninth, with two out?"

"When they say you're gone, I'm *gone*. I just give them the ball and keep going. I never say nothing about it, because the manager has made up his mind and he's going to take you out. A lot of guys argue. Why argue? Because the man is saying, 'You *gone.*'

"Although I couldn't see why he would take me out against Bobby Bonds."

After dinner at a French restaurant near the hotel, Dock returns to his suite, where the telephone rings every few minutes. Other players telephone to ask him to parties, or to run the San Francisco streets, but he is entertaining friends. A girl he knew in St. Louis—friend of Connie's, from Dock's protofamily in St. Louis—drops by with her husband and her husband's brother. She and her husband, a photographer who spent a year in the army in Vietnam, have recently adopted African names. Dock memorizes the names carefully, writes them down. Then everyone sets out seriously to drink wine. Dock tells stories about Tito Fuentes and voodoo. Dock tells stories about touring Vietnam with Bobby Bonds. The phone rings. More people drop by. It is good to win. It is also good to be yourself.

Back in Los Angeles, by this time, Chet Brewer and Mr. Thompson and Big Daddy and The Bug and Magpie—all the fathers and all the brothers—know that Dock won another baseball game. Ray Jones felt all along that Dock was being psyched into winning, by the master psychologist Danny Murtaugh. Speaking of Dock sitting out two starts, Ray Jones ruminated to me: "The man had to do *something*, Murtaugh had to do *something*. Maybe Murtaugh had his reasons? Maybe Murtaugh wanted to wake the nigger up? Nut *like* that man, Murtaugh. On the bench, maybe Nut is *thinking* again, 'Must be doing something *wrong.*'

"And these people, they *know* he going to see Chet. They know that. They know he's doing something wrong, but they can't see it. *Chet* sees it. He just wind up one time, and *Chet* tell him!"

Four: The Gas Man Keeping It Low

1. *Batavia, New York*

When Dock turned nineteen, on March 11, 1964, he found himself in Florida beginning life as a professional ballplayer. Rookie camp was at Daytona Beach, and for Dock it might as well have been Gardena High. He fought seven fights with white rookies over "racial things. Name-calling." If the major league Pirates, now, breathe Utopian tranquillity among races and nations—as I believe they do—the players won that tranquillity after painful years in the minors. You learn more than baseball in the minor leagues.

Dock was assigned to the Batavia Pirates, and opened the season against Geneva, New York. A fan started rolling the epithets toward him—the tall thin black, never before out of California.

"That's the time I went into the stands with a leaded bat. The first time I pitched. We were playing the Geneva Senators, and a guy was calling me Stepin Fetchit. At that particular time, I was *wild*. I couldn't stand to hear this kind of shit. I'd go crazy. I had a black manager, named Gene Baker. I was up in the stands swinging a leaded bat. They had to come get me in a hurry.

"They say the same things in Pittsburgh, but you can't *hear* it like you can in the minor leagues."

"It was beautiful country," Dock tells me. We sit in one of the endless hotel rooms, drinking extra coffee after a room service breakfast. He is

101

telling me about ten years past. "Batavia, New York. We didn't travel by bus. We drove cars. I was in the back asleep."

"Class A?"

"I called it high school. They called it Pony League." P is for Pennsylvania, NY for New York. "I didn't even stay a year. My arm swole up. And they told me to go home.

"Plus I was *screaming* to go home anyway, because I was homesick."

His father had just died, his mother and his sisters were back home in the Neighborhood, and he was lonesome. "Oh, I wanted to get *out* of there, out of Batavia. There was nothing but two or three black families there. It was near a blind school too. *All* I was seeing was *blind* people and shit.

"Eventually they let me go. Gene Baker told me to go back to Pittsburgh and let them look at my arm. They put me on the disabled list. That's the way they got me through the draft. No one would draft a sore-armed pitcher. The Pirates told me to say that my arm hurt from here to here." Dock gestures with his left hand, drawing a line from his right shoulder down to his fingers. "Clyde McCullugh—he was managing the Auburn Mets—he told me, 'We're going to draft *you!*' I was *firing* the ball. But the Mets wouldn't have me. There was a scout for Chicago named Doc, and he used to say, 'I'm going to draft you. By the way, what's wrong?' Me not knowing any better, I said, 'It hurts from here to here.' "

I ask Dock, "What *was* the matter with your arm?"

"Nothing. I'd never pitched that much, and I was throwing a lot of curveballs, and it was cold weather. That's the first time I saw snow, shit."

So after a Batavia career of six weeks, Dock returned to L.A.—to the family and to the friends. He lived at home, to his own relief and his mother's. "It was real hard for him the first years," she says, "because he had never been away from home. He used to call me up any time of the day or night."

She had looked after Dock's girlfriend Paula, and had organized the rest of the Ellis universe with competent spunk. "They sent a letter for him to report to selective service one time. I went to the selective board—this was his first year in the minor leagues—and I told them his father was a number two veteran and deceased. They said they can't take him, he's the surviving son."

Mulling over these anecdotes, I ask Dock, "Did your mother bring you up a lot?"

"Well," he says, "my sisters call me Mama's Boy."

In later years, Dock has not been quite so lonesome for home, though he telephones and makes frequent visits. Those first years, he was missing not only his mother but his black Neighborhood. He also missed women; he was around *men* all the time. Of course there were girls, in all the towns, but Dock needed not just young girls but maternal women. Now as he travels from city to city he has auxiliary families everywhere—Connie in St. Louis, Big Mama in Chicago—where he can crash anytime for talk and tacos.

When he returned to California, he discovered that his mother was seeing a man. Both he and his sisters were appalled.

"After I got remarried it was all right," Mrs. Craven told me, "but when I started going out—it was only my husband I went out with—they . . . they felt I should just sit here and look at the four walls.

"I said, 'Listen, Dock. I'm still a young woman! I can't, I got to have somebody. You a grown man, you understand life.'

"Finally . . . he knew I was a mother to him. He could come home at any time and find me at home. If I was gone, he knew where I was. But it was hard, for a while, for him to get himself adjusted."

Bill Craven was a friend of Dock, Sr.'s, and ran his business from the building that housed the shoe-repair shop and the dry-cleaning establishment. Bill has been a prosperous bookie, and just recently retired from his profession.

Dock is aware, of course, that the commissioner might not enjoy this family connection. Every spring at Pirate City, when management reacquainted the players with baseball's rules about gambling, Dock reinformed Pirate management that his stepfather was a bookie. "Because *he* told *me, I* have to tell *them.* They talk about how you get in trouble, because of people you're running with. Someone is watching you—after the McLain thing."

I wonder out loud if Bowie Kuhn knows about it.

"I don't know. He probably does. I don't know if they think I'm joking, but every time they have a meeting about it, I *say* it."

Dock gets along handsomely with his stepfather. One day he was telling me something about Bill, when he suddenly stuck out his right hand, resplendent with rings. He pointed to a wide gold band with a diamond. "This is my stepfather's ring. I got it, before he could marry my mother."

"He gave it to you?"

"He had to. He had to give it to me, to marry my momma. I wouldn't have let him in that house."

2. The Kinston Pirates

By the time Naomi and Bill got married, Dock had finished his second year of professional baseball in the United States, and was playing winter ball in the Dominican Republic.

Spring training started badly. Dock wanted to go to Kinston, North Carolina, that year, which is also Class A, but *fast* Class A. "You can come from there to the big leagues." But the Pirates at first had other plans. "They wanted to leave me at Batavia, and I told them to go to hell. I said, 'Send me home then. I'm not going back to Batavia.' "

"Because you were homesick there?"

"No. Because I wasn't going *back*, in baseball." Batavia would have been back; Kinston was forward. Then Elmo Plastkett argued on Dock's behalf. Plastkett was a black catcher, on his way down from the major leagues, who would spend the year at Kinston. In 1965, the Pirates followed the old practice of stocking their minor league teams with a mixture of veteran players, to help teach the young. "He *fought* for me to go to Kinston," and Dock went. "This was their way of getting someone to teach me how to pitch."

"What kind of things did he teach you?"

"How to move the ball around, how to set up hitters. I used to move the ball down from the side, which the Pirates stopped me from doing. They started fining me, every time I dropped from the side. First it was five dollars, for about three times. Then they said ten. We got up to fifteen. I couldn't deal with it, because I was making only eight hundred and fifty."

While he was in Kinston, black Los Angeles burned. The Neighborhood is not Watts, but it is black, and Watts is no great distance away, as the tank rolls. Dock telephoned his mother, who reported that rioters were shooting at airplanes from factory roofs, next to the Neighborhood, and tanks were rolling down the streets. At one point, Dock's mother was surrounded by rioters, ready to jump her, mistaking her light skin for white. As she got into the car she heard someone say, "No! That's Nut's mother!" Back in Kinston, Dock tried to take leave. "They wouldn't let me go. If I had had the money, I would have been *gone.*"

In small-town North Carolina, racial relations continued as usual. "I was pitching one time at Wilson, North Carolina, and they was calling me nigger. I struck out the last batter—I never will forget the guy's name, Charlie Manuel; I think he still plays for Minnesota; he was a white dude—and when I struck him out I just turned around and did *this.*" Dock stands and wheels slowly, a complete circle, wearing his haughtiest expression, and holds forth his right hand, middle finger fully extended.

Dock lost his first three games at Kinston. "Then I won eleven or twelve or fourteen straight, almost. Then I went to Pittsburgh for two weeks."

In his second year, at the age of twenty, Dock came up to the majors. He was not activated, but he wore a Pirate uniform, pitched batting practice, and sat in the dugout during games. The Pirates brought him up to pitch an exhibition game at Cleveland. But why did they keep him around for two weeks? "At one time I had thoughts that they were going to keep me in the big leagues. I said, 'What in hell are you keeping me here for, for *two weeks?*' Then I started thinking: them sons of bitches probably don't *want* me to win twenty games down there." If he won twenty in Kinston, how could they keep him down?

He is still unsure that his suspicions are accurate. "I don't know. I was supposed to get familiar with the team. I had a hunch that Harry Walker"—managing the Pirates, in 1965—"was trying to work me in. I have a hunch he might have worked me in, if anybody had got hurt. I was flat bringing it then. I didn't know where it was going, but I could bring it! And I had a hell of a curve. Better than the one I have now."

He looks happy, remembering how well he pitched at the age of twenty.

"If you were faster then, and your curve was better, how come you're here now?"

"Smarter. You get up here, you don't *want* to throw the big, breaking curve. We call that a high-school curve. You want to throw the quick-breaking curve, to right-handers.

"But down in the minor leagues, I didn't have no trouble with left-handers—with that big curve, and my ball cutting across."

"How did you do in the exhibition game?"

"We won the game. I was pitching a no-hitter for six innings. Young. Scared. Rocky Colavito pointed a bat at me. I had Leon Wagner, Joe Azcue, Vic Davalillo. There was a crowd. Thirty-three thousand six hundred and sixty-six. A record for an exhibition game, I believe. Vic still talks about that game." Davalillo was utility man for the Pirates early in 1974. "He was the fastest man I have ever seen. He hit the ball, and I looked around he's sliding into third.

"It was five innings no-hit, not six. They took me out in the sixth or seventh. They wanted Wilbur Wood to get some work."

Dock's mother flew from Los Angeles to Cleveland to see him pitch the game, and Paula flew with her. "He was shaking like a leaf on a tree," his mother says. "His father used to be nervous too. He pitched a real good game that day. After the game, we were walking back to the hotel, and this fellow—I think his name was Galbreath—and his son, and Joe Brown, were in a car, and we were walking, and they stopped us and said, 'You're Mrs. Ellis, Dock's mother, aren't you?' He told me that Dock was a real good pitcher. They felt he should have a little bit more experience before he came to the major leagues."

So Dock went back to Kinston, let up, and lost some games. He was bored with Kinston, after the glories of Pittsburgh and Cleveland. He won only one game, the rest of the season at Kinston, and lost five.

So they promoted him for one game, at the end of the season.

"They sent me to Columbus. Triple A. I pitched the last game of the season for Columbus."

At least, he started to pitch the last game of the season for Columbus. He walked the first three men who came to bat. Larry Shepherd was managing Columbus then, who later managed briefly for the Pirates, and now acts as pitching coach for Cincinnati.

"I walked the bases loaded. I never will forget, because Larry Shepherd came to the mound, and he said, 'You horseshit motherfucker, you can't pitch. Who told you you could pitch?'

"He can get on you bad. He can make you feel mighty low. So I told him, 'You get off the fucking mound, and watch me throw!'

"So I struck out the next three guys. And he told me, 'Go take a shower.'"

I am puzzled by these ups and downs. "Why did he do that?"

Dock is puzzled too. "I don't know. Shepherd . . . that Shepherd, *he* might do *anything*."

3. *Marriage and Baseball*

Ballplayers marry the prettiest girl in high school, cheerleader and homecoming queen, whose untouchable beauty they watched secretly in the corridors with the green lockers—while all the glib boys teased and flirted with them, and the athlete, shyer and quieter, only watched and dreamed. Then when the athlete, golden and famous, scored the touchdown and led the team to the quarter finals of the state basketball tournament and hit .400 playing center field, this gorgeous untouchable creature found him, discovered not only that he existed but that he was *cute,* and went to the Legion rodeo with him, and encouraged his tentative essays into sensuality.

Then after a year or so in Class A, nineteen years old, center field marries centerfold, and they come to live in the country of baseball.

In this country, marriage is often traditional in the roles assigned the sexes, and heavily indebted to the double standard. That it is not impossible, that any marriage endures, can be attributed to the wives and husbands, in the country of baseball, who prefer traditional sexual roles and the double standard.

Bitter mouths disfigure the handsome faces of cheerleaders turning thirty, in the country of baseball. It is not easy to be wife of an athlete. It is not easy to be twenty-five, and watch eighteen-year-old girls chase visiting ballplayers, two days before your husband goes on a road trip. It is not easy, for the prettiest girl in the class, to grow wrinkles and hips—among all the prettiest girls from all the classes, younger every year.

Paula Hartsfield was beautiful; she was no armpiece. They had known each other since 1960, when Dock was fifteen and Paula twelve. When Paula was homecoming queen, at Washington High, Dock was her escort. Daughter of a lawyer, Paula was an accomplished athlete, a swimmer, and a good student. They were married when they were seventeen and twenty, in 1965, and their daughter Shangalesa was born in 1969. In 1972 they separated. If you wish to be other than decorative and hypocritical, it is not easy to stay married during the years of baseball. Today Dock is divorced, but feels that he could sustain a marriage; maybe it would be better, he thinks, to marry just before leaving baseball.

4. *The Asheville Pirates*

In 1965, when he went back to the minor leagues after pitching at Cleveland, Dock had hoped for promotion to Asheville, North Carolina, in Double A. "The league was too slow for me down there. I had a tendency to *relax*."

In 1966 the pattern repeated itself. "When I got to Asheville, I overpowered the league. I was nine and oh, with a one point something ERA. I wound up ten and nine. I relaxed again, because I felt like I should have been taken to Triple A.

"They *did* bring me to the Pirates that year, sixty-six, but I didn't pitch. I was here for sixty some days, and Harry Walker didn't even know my damned name. He talked to me in the office one day when we were coming to L.A., the coastal trip, and I was asking him if I could stay at home. He started talking about Jackie Robinson and Bill White—some old bullshit about the black and white situation." It was the year after Watts, a sensitive year. "I started to tell him I didn't want to hear that bullshit, I just wanted to know if I can stay at home. He said to me, 'You come from that riot place?' I said not exactly, but I'm over that way, and he went into his thing. Stargell was outside looking for me, screaming my name, and the clubhouse guy was looking for me, and they was yelling, 'Dock! Dock!' When I got ready to leave, he didn't even know my name. He said, 'Bye . . . uh . . . uh . . .'

"I said, 'Dock. Good-bye.'"

"Wasn't it discouraging to be up in the major leagues for sixty days and never play?"

"Not a *pitch*."

"Did your arm get stale?"

"I was always throwing the ball in the bullpen every time we were on TV. I *had* to throw on TV, to let the people back home see me. If I wasn't going to pitch, at least they could put the camera on me and say—Dock does his Curt Gowdy voice—'That's the rookie Dock Ellis warming up or getting loose or something.'"

"They let you throw anytime you wanted to, down in the bullpen?"

"Oh, yeah. I was *noted* for that. *Every* national TV game, I was *up*."

Back in Asheville, the team was socially coherent. "Every weekend

we'd party together. We always partied over the guy's house named
Charlie Leonard. He was an old ballplayer, on his way down, there to
help the young ballplayers. He could hit, he could still hit."
   "Black or white?"
   "He was white. He could express his feeling on the black and white
thing, and it was cool for both sides. One night we had a party and they
called the police on us. This house was next to a cemetery. Now who the
fuck can we disturb?"

   Pitching for Asheville in Greensboro, North Carolina, Dock threw a
change-up to young Bobby Murcer. "He was the first dude ever to hit a
change-up off me for a home run. And I lost the game one to nothing.
Then somebody called me nigger."
   Dock went into the stands with a baseball bat again. "I missed his head
by the skin of a hot dog. They had to *subdue* me."

   In Asheville Dock's friendship with Bob Robertson began, which
flourished in the minor leagues. Some ballplayers entered a White
Castle in Montgomery, Alabama, where the Tigers had a farm.
Somebody in the White Castle sneered the word "nigger." Dock says
admiringly, "Robertson locked the door. He was ready to *kick ass.*"
   Dock was touched. "Robbie, what you do that for?" Dock asked him
later. "What the fuck you do that for? Were you going to get killed, over
some nigger?"
   "And he said, 'What?' "
   Robertson was not known for his eloquence, but for better things.
"He's *loyal*," Dock says. "It didn't make any difference to him, black or
white, although he was from Maryland. As time went on, we got close.
The thing happened again. We was ready to *go down*, back to back,
together."
   At this time, Dock was into his "heavy black thing," and so the
friendship with Robertson was anomalous. In earlier years at
Thornburg, his white friend Pete Rucker had been "ready to *go down*,
back to back, together" when Dock was the victim of racial assault. But
at Gardena High and at Harbor, it was only the blacks who made a virtue
of loyalty, using their solidarity to compensate for small numbers.
Robertson was a white man with a difference, one of the émigrés to
blackness. "We really talked the same language," Dock says. "He really
cut into a black dude. Robbie spoke that black language, he liked black
music. They separated us."

"How did they separate you?" I ask.

"We wanted to room together, next year at Columbus. The Pirates wouldn't let us. There hadn't been any black-white roommates before. That way, we would have gotten *very* close. We would have been right there together."

"What happened to the friendship, when you got to the majors?" Dock shakes his head. "To this day, I can't tell you what happened. I still feel that management hurt Robertson. I think it was the challenge they put on him, that battle between him and Al Oliver for first base. That was a black and white thing. We had always called him the Great White Hope. What the fuck, he didn't mind that."

5. Voodoo

After the Kinston and Asheville seasons, Dock played winter ball in the Dominican Republic—loading up on extra courses in summer school, as it were, while he accelerated toward his degree.

In the Dominican Republic he roomed with Manny Sanguillen from Panama. The two men became friends, and gave each other language lessons. When Dock made a mistake in Spanish, or Manny in English, the teacher was allowed to hit the pupil as hard as he could. "I didn't talk too much Spanish," says Dock. Manny had been a boxing champion in Panama.

Eventually, they whomped each other into a usable vocabulary of idioms. When Dock returned to the Neighborhood after a winter of baseball, and Boxer's Berlitz, he visited his old Spanish teacher at Gardena High. "I explained to her in Spanish that I was now pitching for the Pirates. She didn't know what I was talking about! I was talking slang that I had learned from Sanguillen."

Manny Mota, Rico Carty, Tito Fuentes, Manny Sanguillen. Dock spent his time with rookies and major leaguers both, in the Dominican Republic. He sat up all night with Rico Carty, listening to talk about the major leagues.

Dock also heard talk about zombies, over the border in Haiti. He wanted to see some. "I got a guy from over there—one of Manny Mota's friends—to get a jeep. Manny Mota had told me about it: 'Don't go up there!' I said, 'I'm gone!'

"Sangy had his jeep, but I didn't want Sangy to take me because Sangy turned that jeep over one time. I tried to get Tito to go with me"—but Tito wanted no part of zombies.

"I *had* to go. Zombies. It *could* have been zombies. We were in a jeep. We got to a certain area. I saw these people walking—four of them, zombies, and a woman too—but they were walking *funny*. I say, 'This shit's got to be like Knott's Berry Farm, animated like for a show.' I was talking shit like, 'Well, the circus is over,' and they didn't *move*. I wasn't too hip on coming to a stop.

"I ain't saying it *was* zombies.

"When I got back to the Dominican, I told people. Tito Fuentes, he believes in me. He knew I went and saw the shit."

I ask, "Does Tito believe in the magic?"

"One time I saw him with leaves on his shoulder. That was voodoo. He had a bad shoulder, and he had leaves and stuff on it. He had the light flashing on the cross, and the cross made a shadow on the wall."

"Does anybody else do voodoo, that you know of?"

"There are plenty of them. Rico Carty. One day in Atlanta I tore a dollar bill in half and gave the clubhouse guy half of it and told him to give it to Rico Carty. I meant something like, 'If you get another hit off me, you get the other half.'

"And Rico said he was going to *kill* me, because I put the voodoo on him. I didn't know. And dig this: I loaded the bases up, and hit Rico on the hand, broke his finger, and he swore *that* was a voodoo!

"Prior to that, I drew a voodoo doll on a ball, and threw it to him in the outfield."

In the country of baseball, the Latin outfielder picks up a ball in practice, pulls back to throw, and sees a voodoo hex drawn on the ball! "And he threw that motherfucking ball over to us, and he was trying to *kill* somebody. I'm telling you the truth!"

6. *Keeping It Low*

To many observers, it seems that the Pittsburgh organization concentrates on hitting and lets the rest of the game take care of itself—fielding, base running, finesse, and pitching.

Dock had little instruction in the minor leagues, and most of his teaching came from older players, rather than from Pirate coaches. One of the exceptions occurred at Kinston, when the Pirates stopped him coming from the side. When he pitched overhand regularly, no one coached him. Coaches videotaped batters, to perfect their swings; no one videotaped the pitchers.

So he studied on his own. At Batavia, when he was nineteen, he wrote notes for himself:

> I have 4 pitches that I can get across the plate at all times.
> #1. FAST BALL
>   1.A. Low and Away
>   1.B. Low and on the extreme inside corner
>   1.C. High and tight (High meaning near the batter's letters).
> #2. CURVE BALL
>   2.A. Low and Away
>   *******************
>   *Never Get It Up*
>   *******************
>   a. Drop my arm. Start curve back inside corner in the middle of the plate and with a lot of wrist it will be on the outside corner for sure.
>   2.B. Inside corner start it behind the batter and with a lot of wrist it will be a strike for sure.
> #3. SINKER BALL
>   3.A. Inside corner start it on the outside corner or down the middle of the plate and throw it about ¾ speed. For left handers start it at hip.
>   3.B. Outside corner to a left hander start it on the inside corner or the middle of the plate.
> #4. CHANGE UP
>   4.A. At All Times Low

The asterisks around *Never Get It Up* conjure a scene for me: back at the hotel, after an evening when the curveball floated high to the batter, then high over the left-field wall, the young pitcher makes an urgent addition to his notes on pitching.

At this time in his life, Dock was still throwing mostly heat: he was "a gas man." But it was the curveball, and the pseudoslider, which brought him to the big leagues and kept him there. As long as he keeps it low.

"Why do you suppose they don't coach pitchers more?" I ask Dock.

"I don't understand. If they are going to invest a lot of money in someone, it stands to reason that they should help him. Try, at least. They *will* invite the young guys down to spring training with the major leaguers, but the major leaguers don't give a damn; major leaguers are just out there getting in shape, and they're *gone*. I try to help some of them. I try. When Kison first came to the Pirates he heard strange things about me, but once I got to know Kison, I let him see my Book."

"Is that a metaphor, or do you have a book?"

"No, I have a *book*, on hitters, from when I first got to the league. I was writing in it every day, when I got up here."

"Do you still add to it?"

"Right now all the guys are the same. Some young guys that come up at the end of the year, I might throw their name in the book where I won't forget it."

"What about when a guy changes his style or his stance?"

"I don't have to put that in the book, because I'm looking at it."

"Do you let other people besides Kison see The Book?"

"Scouts want it. I'm not going to let them get it. No other pitchers, no."

"Why don't you show it to other pitchers, like Larry Demery?"

"A lot of people don't like you telling them what to do."

"Why Kison?"

"I liked him the first time I met him. He was gutty. He had a lot of heart. I admired him for that. For that reason I let him see my Book. He asked questions too. It *surprised* him, that I let him see The Book."

"Do other baseball clubs do more for their pitching staff?"

"The *Dodgers!* They have pitching coaches at every level. They take it *seriously!* And at Houston I've heard Roger Craig talking to pitchers while they warm up on the sides. He's telling them about different pitches, how to hold the ball, how to throw it, release it. They *do* teach, over there. And definitely with the Mets. That's their trump suit. And Johnny Sain! Johnny Sain, I stop him every time I see him. I get him to tell me something new about that baseball! Like I stopped him in spring training this year. He was walking through the clubhouse."

"After so many years of pitching, can you really learn from Johnny Sain now? Can you change your ways?"

"Not really. Well, I would say if I was with him one spring I could. Johnny teaches the rotation of the ball *with backspin*. It makes the ball jump. That's the Johnny Sain way of pitching: *pull down*."

So Dock went looking for advice wherever he could get it. "Stargell used to give me advice, on how to pitch to left-handers. And right-handers also. Even now, he'll tell me, 'Well, you ought to pitch this guy this way.' I try it. I've been successful with it. He *knows*."

"You talk to Stargell about pitching to other batters, and yet Stargell's a batter. Is there any sort of camaraderie among hitters even though they're on different teams? Or pitchers with pitchers?"

"Yeah, when it comes to rapping with the opposing team. I talk to the other pitchers. I don't talk to too many of the hitters."

"Why not?"

"I don't like them. Stargell say that is wrong, but I don't like them. Only a few of them will I associate with. Hitters, they're always trying to run a psyche game on you, twenty-four hours a day."

"Aren't you running a psyche game on them?"

"Only certain batters. I used to. I used to be really into it. I'm not into that, now, because I don't talk to many of them. I still interject a little, here and there. Like Bobby Bonds. When they were here last time, I set him up to throw him a couple of fastballs. I say, 'You've got to hit the curveball. I'll keep throwing it until you hit it.' So I struck him out on fastballs."

A starting pitcher works like a rich man, a few hours once or twice a week. A batter plays the game seven days a week, and by September starts praying for rain. The starting pitcher is the envy of all eyes. Dock didn't want to go to the bullpen, in 1974 and 1975, because he didn't want to drop from the executive suite to the assembly line.

Early in my conversations with Dock, I asked him, "How many pitches do you have?"

"I throw a fastball, a sliding fastball, a curve, a change-up, and a palm ball. I'd say five."

"Is that sliding fastball what they call a slider?"

"No. The hitters call it a slider. A lot of hitters will tell you I throw a slider, but I don't."

Pete Rose told me about Dock's good slider. Manny Sanguillen told me giggling: "Everybody think Dock have a slider. He no have a slider. He have falling fastball. It natural. He no have slider." He doesn't throw a slider because he already has a curveball. "When you throw a curve and a slider, one of them is not going to be good," he says. "You can't have a good slider and a good curve. There's only two or three guys who can. Take Carlton. Steve Carlton's got a good curveball and a good slider. Not too many of them."

"What's the difference, throwing a curve and throwing a slider?"

"You throw a slider like you throw a football. You spiral it, letting it peel off your fingers. Throwing a curve, you snap your wrist as you let the ball go.

"You know when you throw a football, you see a little point on the back of the football, spinning? When you throw a slider, you see a little round circle on the ball, spinning. That means you're throwing it right. It's spinning, and it's going to *kick* at the end. That's how the hitters can spot it too."

"Tell me about the palm ball."

"The palm ball. Your palm rests on the meaty part of the ball, and you grip the ball with your thumb and your little finger, with your middle three fingers making no contact." When you become skillful, you can let the middle three fingers rest on the ball, and you are more deceptive. "You just come right *over*," with it, with the motion appropriate to the fastball.

"How about the other fastball?"—the one that comes in on a right-handed batter.

"The fastball that bores in, to the right-handed batter, you hold two fingers across the wide part of the seams. The fastball that sinks, you put two fingers at an angle across the narrow seam." Sometimes he throws it with his fingers jammed together between the seams. He carries calluses on his fingers all season, from his sinking fastball.

"And to throw the curveball, I put two fingers on either side of one of the seams, at the narrow part of the seam. That's what makes it break *quick*." Sometimes he throws a slow curve for a change-up—one finger on top and the other finger guiding it. "One year, I threw it a lot. I threw it on the outside corner of the plate to left-handers. I don't play around with it anymore."

"Why not?"

"Because I don't have a chance to. I usually play around with it when I have a three-run lead." No more three-run leads.

"Do you ever throw a knuckle ball?"

"No. My fingers are too small. I have small, chubby hands."

"Do you work on new pitches?"

"I don't feel I have to. Unless I'm pushed in the corner. If I don't start anymore, I'm going to have to go in the bullpen, and come up with different pitches. That would be while I was warming up." So if he leaves the rotation, he can work on new pitches to get back in the rotation.

"Do you call your own game? Do you shake off your catchers?"

Dock says he has confidence in his catchers. Maybe he has shaken off twenty pitches in his baseball career. Plenty of times he has appeared to shake off a pitch, but by prearrangement with his catcher he is actually running a game on the batter. He throws the pitch his catcher asks for, and if his location is right, he throws it where the catcher asks for it.

7. *Columbus, 1967*

After three summers in the minors—summers which included two trips to Pittsburgh, but no major league pitching—Dock started the 1967 season with the Pirate Triple A team in Columbus, Ohio. And he started the season rebellious and angry. His manager at Columbus had been his manager at Asheville—Harding Peterson, now head of scouting for Pittsburgh—and "I figured he had fucked me over in Asheville, and he was going to do it again." The major league Pirates were already heavily black, and he felt that management didn't want the team to become *more* black, because a black team would alienate white fans. Instead, he felt, the Pirates kept him in the minor leagues when he could pitch major league ball—down in the South and the Border States, where fans yelled nigger at him.

"And I was into a heavy black thing then." He remained friends with Bob Robertson, though the Pirates refused to allow them to room together, but otherwise Dock insisted on racial separateness. "I didn't want anybody around my locker. I didn't want anybody messing with my clothes. I wouldn't let the little boy do my laundry. The clubhouse guy want to do my clothes? Shine my shoes? I say, 'I'll do it. Don't fuck with my shit.'"

Dock pitched the second game of the year for Columbus. (Johnny Bench hit his first Triple A home run off him.) But the season was rotten, and he never went up. In fact he went down.

"I know why they sent me to Double A. Because my hair was so long. I said, 'If this is true, then I'm going to fuck with the Pirates the rest of my career.' They sent me to Macon, Georgia; they like to *hung* me, there! So I shaved my head. Absolutely shaved it. Do you know, the next day they asked me back to Triple A? I told them to kiss my ass."

"So you didn't go."

"Oh, yeah. I went. They told me they'd fine me a thousand dollars a day if I wasn't there. I said, 'I'll be there in the morning!'"

"I went back to Columbus, but it was the same thing. I was always at the manager's throat, because I felt he screwed me over, him and the organization."

At the end of the year, before the Triple A play-offs, a majority of Dock's teammates signed a petition that he be dropped from the team, and share no play-off money. The petitioners did not approach Bob Robertson; they did not approach Manny Sanguillen nor any of the black players.

"What happened?"

"I was pitching and got hit with a line drive. I still have the hole in my leg. No one told me to put ice on it. A week went by before I was supposed to pitch next, and it was still swollen. It was puffy, soggy. I told the manager, 'I cannot pitch, on my leg.' He said, 'You go to the doctor.' I went to the doctor and the doctor cut the fucking jelly out. It was *jelly-like,* that's how long it had set in there. Now I've got ice on my leg every day, and it's getting close to the end of the season. They wanted me to pitch the last day of the season. I say, 'I'll go out and warm up and try to pitch.' But when I warmed up, I was giving to my leg.

"I said, 'I'm not going to throw my arm out here with a bad leg.' But we was going to the *play-offs,* next. I said, 'Now maybe if I have another three or four days of rest, maybe I can help the team in the play-offs.' "

But on the last day of the regular season, "I told them I wouldn't pitch. A lot of guys was watching me warm up, and I was bringing it, but I was falling to my leg. So they said, 'You chickenshit, you just don't want to pitch the last day of the season.' "

Dock was not a popular figure, among the Columbus Jets. "They had a lot of older guys that had been sent down from major league teams. They didn't particularly care for me, because of the shit I was doing"—the racial separateness, the "heavy black thing."

"When I got back to Columbus, the team goes off to the play-offs, and they leave me in a hotel. The season is over, they get beat. So now they going to divide up the money and I find they signed a petition that I'm not going to get my share."

Manny Sanguillen: "Nobody tell me nothing about it. Nobody tell me anything about it. Nobody come close to me." He mentioned someone from that Columbus team who played with the Pirates for a while, and was traded away. "That is why I think he is not with this ball club. He come from Texas, you expect anything. The way he acts, try to sneak behind your back. People like that have a bad heart inside."

8. *Kissing Johnny Pesky*

After the fiasco of 1967, Dock set his mind against returning to Triple A. He worked out at spring training with the major leaguers at Fort Myers, Florida. Manny Sanguillen was working for a job also, and it looked as if both of them would make the team. Topps photographed them both for baseball cards.

If you are trying to make a big league team, you watch for the attentions of the Topps photographers. They photograph maybe thirty players on each team. Because the roster will eventually reduce to twenty-five, their interest is not an infallible sign, but they are more reliable than most other indicators—like four-leaf clovers in the outfield, or the general manager's facial expression. "They *find out*," says Dock.

Then they were cut, yet once again to report to the minor league complex in Daytona Beach.

"Me and Sangy *cried* all the way to Daytona Beach." Dock was driving a new Cadillac. "They sent us both down. Sangy cried, playing his guitar, and wouldn't look at me. When Sangy was driving, I was shooting a gun, shooting at empty hillsides out the window. But the police couldn't get us, we were flying."

"Did you always carry a gun then?"

"Yes. I was protecting myself. Not anymore."

I knew that Dock was threatened all over the minor leagues. For that matter he still is. "You were angry all the time, weren't you?"

"You saw where it started. The Gardena blowout. Thornburg Park."

"So what happened when you got there?"

"I met Pesky. He was the manager of the Triple A team at Columbus that year." A new manager, and largely a different team from the group that had petitioned Dock out. "I met Pesky. I told him, 'I'm not gonna do a goddamned thing down here.'

" 'Well,' he says, 'you take ten days off. Don't do nothing. Don't come to the ball park. When you come back, though, I want you to pitch one inning every day.'

"I say, 'I am twenty-three years old, how can I be a Triple A relief pitcher?'

"He says, 'Don't worry about a thing. I'm gonna get you to the big leagues. Just be my *dog*.'

"He told me to be his dog for thirty days and he would get me to the big leagues. That's just what he did. Johnny Pesky. I kiss him every time I see him.

"I pitched every day for maybe four or five days, then he'd give me an off day. Then I'd pitch for three days, then an off day."

"What was his idea?"

"He knew I had arm problems, but he said, 'You can do it.' When I started off in relief, my arm wasn't responding I had a hell of a dude to work with, Harvey Haddix. I had to learn what to do with the fastball. Go in there and bust that ball on those hitters. I didn't come in there to pick at no corners. I came in there to get them *out*."

"So a pitching coach helped you, after all?"

"He's the one who got me throwing that sharp curveball. But no one in the organization told him to. He did it on his own. His *job* in Columbus was just to *run* the pitches. That's the pitching coach's *job*, with the Pirates. To stand and watch them run."

"How long did you stay in Columbus?"

"We played nineteen games and I was in twelve of them. No, I was in fifteen of them. I had twelve *saves*—and a two and one record.

"Johnny Pesky called me in one day and he said, 'Bye.'

"I said, 'Good-bye.' That's when I went up to the big leagues."

Five: Coming Up and Staying Up

1. *The Book*

In 1968, Dock started ten games, and relieved in sixteen; he completed two of his starts, gave up thirty-eight bases on balls and struck out fifty-two batters. He won six games and lost five, and wound up with a first-rate 2.50 ERA.

It was a good rookie year, on a sixth-place ball club. In retrospect, Dock thinks that he was lucky. "I got away with a lot. I had an overpowering fastball"—and relied on it too much, instead of using the curve and the change-up he had been at pains to acquire. He was a gas man.

Larry Shepherd was manager now. Harry Walker had been fired, and Danny Murtaugh summoned back to finish out the year. When the Pirates finished sixth, Murtaugh reentered his voluntary retirement. Dock remembered Larry Shepherd from one game at Columbus: "You horseshit motherfucker. . . . Who told you you can pitch?" They got on well.

Alvin McBean was still pitching relief. Dock had already known him, and had known Willie Stargell and others from his visit in 1965 for the exhibition game, and from his sixty days with the club in 1966. He continued to admire McBean. "When he was at one corner of the locker room, and I was at the other, and we was both screaming, you *had* to listen to us. He was a good dude.

"He would wear a five-hundred-dollar suit, and a two-dollar pair of shoes. He had *bad feet*.

"A lot of guys said, when we were screaming, 'McBean is *gone.*' Management didn't want him to ruin me, and they said he had a bad arm. He didn't have a bad arm." And in 1969 McBean went to San Diego, and in 1970 he returned to the Virgin Islands he had come from.

When he came to the majors in 1968, he began keeping The Book. In a school notebook he carried with him, he wrote the names of all the hitters in the National League, and the pitches they could hit—type of pitch, and location—and the pitches they could not hit. For information he cornered everyone he respected. Willie Stargell gave him advice, and Roberto Clemente. Vernon Law was pitching coach, just retired and his mind still crowded with sixteen years of throwing to National League hitters. Dock followed Law around, notebook in hand, going through rosters. "I used to bug him to *death*."

In addition, Dock asked advice from pitchers on other teams, notably Bob Gibson and Juan Marichal. "They were *superior* pitchers, plus they were black: I felt I could relate to them. Asking wouldn't hurt, and if they were willing to *tell* me? I asked them, and they *told* me. They even said—like, Gibson told me, 'I pitched this guy this way, but you have a change-up and I don't, so you change speeds on him. He's looking for everything from me hard.' "

"When would you see them?"

"Here or there. On the field. In St. Louis and San Francisco. I would meet Marichal in the runway, and I'd say, 'Hey, man, tell me about so-and-so!' "

2. *Mothers on the Road*

Life in the big leagues, half of the time, is life on the road. Now Dock flew airplanes to cities instead of riding buses to towns. He flew home to Los Angeles, flew down to San Diego, flew up to Montreal, flew across to Chicago or St. Louis. Life became a series of hotels. For Dock, life also became a series of clothing stores, each outfit more outrageous, extravagant, and glittering than the last. His beneficence and his boredom scattered dazzling maxicoats and jump suits from coast to coast, in the closets of his friends.

Friends were many, old and new, through family or through other ballplayers. Parties were many also. He partied from coast to coast, night after night, stopping to sleep (usually but not always) on the night before he pitched.

Not even parties could keep life on the road from becoming lonesome. He missed in particular his home and family, and feminity, not as it is met in admiring young women at the ball park, or in acquisitive groupies in the hotel lobbies, but as discovered in kitchens among women wielding skillets. Gradually, over his first years in the big leagues, Dock collected families in all of his major league cities. "There's Connie and her family in St. Louis," Dock told me; "there's a family in Houston.

"When I go into a town, the people I know, I have *fun* with them. I don't have a boring moment. I meet a lot of people. A lot of people I meet are not young, either. They sort of adopt me, and take me in. 'This is my son.' When I first met Big Mama in Chicago, she was calling me Young Blood.

"These people, they accept me for being me. Being with them, it's being with people you like to be around, that you don't *have* to be around."

Like ballplayers, for instance. You have to be around ballplayers six or seven hours a day, every day, so why hang around with them in coffee shops and bars, or watching "Love of Life" in your hotel room while your roommate eats peanuts?

Connie Fenner met Dock soon after he came up to the major leagues. She invited him to eat with her family—daughter, three sons—and now he comes to call whenever the Pirates play in St. Louis, and usually at least once a year in the off-season.

Connie is in her late thirties, handsome, shy at first, then gradually warm and warmer. "He has patience with young people," Connie told me. "He tells them the right road. The children love him."

"What do you mean, the right road?"

"My sons, they want to become professional baseball players. He tells them, like, 'Get your education first. Go to school, keep your grades up—then you can have a choice.' He tells them it's not like it seems. If they want to go into it, he tells them he'll help them, but the basic thing he's trying to instill is 'Go to school.' "

But he spoils the children rotten. After he leaves town, Connie says, "I can't do anything with them. I have to put my foot down. When he's here, they get anything they want. Go to a store. Whatever it is.

"It's *hectic* when he gets to town," Connie laughs. "When he comes out to the house, all the children in the neighborhood are over to the house, talking and playing records, jiving around. It's just like a great big family. The people he meets, he brings them by. We had dinner for

Dave Cash, when he was with them. Al Oliver. But I can't say he brings them out all the time. When he's in St. Louis, he's like *away* from the ballplayers.

"Man, am I *tired* when he leaves! I don't know how he can do it. Get to bed at five o'clock, up and ready to go at quarter to nine. I can't do it."

Connie laughs, remembering one time. She hesitates to tell the story, then tells it anyway. "About three years ago, Dock came to St. Louis. He called from Washington. I don't know what he was doing in Washington." (He was testifying before a committee of the Senate about sickle-cell anemia.) "We picked him up at the airport, took him home, and he spent the night. He had quite a bit to drink that night. They watched the television off.

"Then he was on his way to the ball park. My daughter was taking him to the ball park and he needed some pants. He went into the store to buy some pants, and in the middle of the aisle he dropped his pants, and put the new ones on. Just in the middle of the aisle. But that's not the kicker. He didn't have any underpants on. Just dropped his pants and put on some more." Connie wags her head. "I'm surprised they didn't call the police, but he got away *clean*."

In Pittsburgh in the summer of 1974, Dock suddenly showed up every place—at the ball park, at parties, at restaurants and clothing stores and sporting goods outfitters—with a fourteen-year-old boy named Eric. For a week, they were inseparable, wearing identical white silk pith helmets. Dock introduced him, everywhere he went, as "Eric, my brother." Eric sat in the dugout before the game every day. Dock took him into the clubhouse with all the Pirates, and Eric did not ask for a single autograph—a world's coolness record for fourteen-year-old baseball freaks. Even a few old friends of Dock's began to wonder: *Could* he, somehow, have a younger brother named Eric? Maybe a *half* brother?

Finally, Eric disappeared. I asked Dock. "Oh," he said, "that's Eric, Connie's son. I call him my brother."

Visiting Los Angeles, Dock stays with his real mother in his real Neighborhood, tries to see as many old friends as he can, and eats tacos. Milk and tacos. His mother loves to feed him, and his response gladdens her bosom. "One of his *weaknesses* is drinking milk. He could drink half a gallon at each meal. When I didn't have hot bread for dinner, when he was a boy, he would take the loaf of plain white bread, and take all the center slices out. His sisters would get so angry with him! 'Momma, Dock is taking all the center bread out!' He was a big teaser. Still is. His father was a teaser too."

Now when he comes to his momma's house he may drink two or three quarts of milk at a sitting. His mother and sometimes his sisters fabricate enormous tacos—with ground beef, onion, tomato, cheese, avocado slices, and hot sauce. Very hot sauce. Dock will eat twelve of his mother's tacos sometimes. Fifteen.

And sometimes Dock brings friends for dinner. Dock's mother remembered:

"One year I had a *big* dinner, for the guys on Dock's team. We had a houseful, I think about ten players. Pagan, Willie Stargell, Gene Clines, Al Oliver, Spanish fellows, Caucasian fellows, Sanguillen. I don't remember. Dock had given me a menu. I had barbecued ribs, I had barbecued filet mignon steaks, hot links, chicken. And Dock asked me to cook this pot of greens. Mustard greens. I fixed a great big pot. Boy, those greens—I didn't think they would *go* for them like that. But they cleared them out before they did anything else. And I had potato salad, avocados, tomato and lettuce salad.

"When I know what I'm going to do, it doesn't take me long to get it done. My husband made me this big barrel that you can barbecue in. It's closed up. You get your coals prepared, and it's just like cooking inside on the stove, and you don't have to stand and watch over them. While I was cooking all them other foods, I just went out once in a while and checked."

"Oh, my goodness, everything *went*. We had this table full of liquor, beer. In the backyard, in the front yard. We had blankets out there. Everybody was coming over and wanted autographs. They spent five or six hours here, maybe.

"They had a wonderful time. When they left, Willie Stargell said, 'Momma, fix me a plate of cake. I got to have some of that cake to eat at bedtime.' "

3. Ladies on the Road

But social life on the road is not only a matter of mothers and surrogate mothers.

In the lobby of the San Francisco Hilton, as we head out for dinner after a game, we see a Pittsburgh Pirate sitting alone in a large, pretentious chair. This ballplayer is white, mustachioed, elegantly dressed, and he sits upright, cool, handsome, and dignified. "What's happening?" says Dock.

"Oh," says the ballplayer, sophisticated and detached, "I'm waiting for someone to pick me up for dinner." He pauses minutely, and just as Dock is about to speak, he continues, "I don't know who she is yet, but she'll be along." Then he squints down the dark hallway at a young woman registering. The squint is theatrical and exact. "No," he sighs. "Not her. I'm too beautiful."

The beautiful ballplayer is a married man, like most ballplayers, and like most ballplayers, chases women. Perhaps fidelity will never become the national pastime, and perhaps ballplayers when they chase women merely fulfill fantasies dreamed by legions of brothers and uncles back on the farm. Perhaps athletes, more openly aggressive than most males, are more open in aggressive sexuality.

In their first major league season, most young ballplayers cannot believe what is happening to them. It happened a bit in the minors, but the big leagues are big league, in groupies as in hotels and airplanes. After a season or two, the ballplayer begins to tell the desk clerk not to let any calls come through—except maybe from Sheila or Daphne or Dawn. When he comes to Philadelphia or Montreal, he consults his geographical address book—not The Book, but another useful tool in the majors—and his memories.

"You don't seek them out anymore?" I ask Dock.

"If they come by, they come by. But if they don't, they don't. I used to pound the pavement. Just out having fun. That's part of getting to the big leagues."

Marriages do not always thrive, in the country of baseball. "Before I got married, I used to tell Paula, 'I'm going to be a *baseball* player.' I used to try to explain to her that when you are playing baseball, you are *on the road.* And I'm going to come into contact with *a lot of women.* At that time I was a partying type person. No way you could keep me from a party.

"The first couple of years I was in baseball, I didn't get around that much, because I was in the minor leagues. But when we got to the big leagues—I had already told her about the other wives, because I had heard it and seen it. When I first got to major league camp, I used to hear the guys talking about it. I made sure she was prepared for this. The other wives, they're going to tell stories about seeing some other ballplayer with another lady. That's why I don't have a wife today, because she *listened* to all that mess.

"I could see it starting in sixty-nine. She wasn't busy anymore, like she used to be. She was spending a lot of time with the *biddies*."

Dock is not fond of ballplayers' wives—the former armpieces—with notable exceptions like Pam Cash and Delores Crawford. He tried to discourage Paula from keeping company with Pirate wives. "If I had another job," he told her, "you wouldn't be that concerned with knowing the other workers' wives. By 1970, he was saying, "I don't want them in my house. I don't want to be dealing with *remarks* from them."

"I used to hear little *remarks*," he told me. "But I'd laugh it off, or I'd say, 'I'm going to my women anyhow.' I tried to *prepare* her for that. She can see now how they got to her. She started to want to go to different affairs they were having. I wasn't going. Her going her way, and me going mine. I'd rather stay home, turn up the radio." All this time, Dock says, he was scrupulous to keep his philandering to the road.

"Well," I observed, "it must be hard to stay married if you're a ballplayer. All that separation."

"I would say so. If they do, they have to have a hell of a woman. Or one that's very naïve."

"How do the wives stand it?"

"A lot of guys, they put up a front with their families. 'I don't even go into a *bar*.' That's the biggest lie they ever told in their life! Or, 'I don't mess around.' *I* see them. How they going to hide from me?

"As far as women is concerned, you can always come in contact with the woman. If I enjoyed being with someone, I was going to be with them. That's it. I wasn't like *going through* women."

"Did you get assaulted in the lobbies by the groupies?"

"They didn't fool with me. I would curse them out. I met people through friends of mine. I wasn't out there trying to pick nobody up. I've seen a lot of ballplayers, they're just overwhelmed by women jumping over them. But even when I first came up, I wasn't really looking for no woman. I was out there having a good time."

As the years went by, Paula saw more and more of the other wives, but more importantly, less of Dock. The breakup came in 1972. Dock came in from a Pittsburgh party at six in the morning, and found Paula vacuuming the apartment. There was a fight. Dock went off on a road trip, and when he returned, Paula had moved out, taking Shangalesa. Shortly thereafter, she moved back to Los Angeles.

It was a marriage of opposites, Dock hyperactive and Paula increasingly passive. "Paula was always waiting on me to do something, instead of doing something herself, and I was always trying to program *her* to do something."

After Paula's departure, Dock in his Pittsburgh life alternated between domesticity and running the streets. He lived for six months with a young woman who, he later discovered, was still married to an acquaintance of his, a ballplayer no longer resident in the United States. "She kept telling me, 'After the season is over, I got something to tell you.' I happened to be going through some clippings about the World Series, and they had her in there as the Best Dressed Wife. I said, 'Oh!' then I said, 'No!' and I started remembering. It all came back. So I said, 'Where's Paco?' " (I have changed the name.) " 'Oh, he's back in Panama." Dock shakes his head. "I argued with Sangy, I said, 'Sangy, you're supposed to tell me something like this!' Sangy say, 'It's none of my business.' I say, 'Sangy, say the guy would come to my apartment, and I say, what's happening, Paco?' *Boom!* I wouldn't have known anything.

"I'm wondering where she got all those minks anyway."

Dock is clever with women, puts gracious and subtle moves on them, like an NBA guard moving to a basket. But when the breakup comes, it's likely to be quick and final. "Get your ass out of here." Speaking of one breakup, he says, "I cleaned house." And there is usually some missing property. Once I asked Dock if I could see The Book; it had disappeared. "When they go back to the minor leagues," he says, "when they get their release, they want to take a souvenir."

In 1973, Dock shared his apartment with Amaryllis, and he took her on the road with him, an infraction of a Pirate rule which management chose to ignore.

"They have a whole lot of rules. They don't pertain to *me*. They got rules 9A and 9B. He'll fine you two hundred and fifty dollars with a lady in your room, and two hundred if he catches your wife on the road with you. I say, 'Well, your wife is fifty dollars shorter than a lady. That's butting you short, buddy. Tell that to your wives!'

"Anybody they see me with is my cousin.

"And they fined Reuss, because Reuss's wife was with him. It's ridiculous for someone to be able to tell you that you can't take your wife on the road. Legally, they can*not* do it. Just call Marvin Miller."

I ask, "What happened about Amaryllis on the road?"

"Nothing. I was *deep* into the game, more than ever. But the wives resented that I had a lady with me. The wives tell the ballplayers, 'Well, Dock got a woman with him. Why can't I go with you?' What they don't know, their husbands don't want them around all the time.

"As for me, I was *heavy* into baseball. What you said, about the missing femininity? I thought about that, and you're right—like the friends I have in different cities. That woman image has to be there. Last year I must have spent ten thousand dollars for Amaryllis traveling with me, for the simple reason that I didn't want to go *out* then, looking for a lady. I didn't have time for that mess. I was heavy with *baseball.*"

4. *1969 and 1970*

In 1969, Dock became a regular starter, won eleven games and lost seventeen. He started thirty-three games, finished eight, and relieved in only two. With two hundred and nineteen innings pitched, he gave up two hundred and six hits, and his earned run average was 3.58. The ratio of bases on balls to strikeouts was fine—as it usually is for Dock—seventy-six bases on balls, and a hundred and seventy-three strikeouts.

"Did you get discouraged, losing so many?"

"How could I? I knew I was throwing good. I learned it the hard way. Pitching. There was no one telling me anything, so I had to go out there and learn it myself. I had to see what these guys were up to."

"Did you worry about being sent down?"

"No. My ERA wasn't that high. I had no fears of being sent down. I was a young pitcher, and they wanted me to have the experience. I didn't *want* anybody to tell me anything. This is when I found out I couldn't throw the fastball by everyone. I was slipping it by a *lot* of people. This is like Larry." Dock is talking to me in 1974, when Larry Demery has just come up. "He's going to have to learn that he can't do that. He's going to have to come up with that fast-breaking curveball. He *has* one, but he throws a slider, and you can't throw a slider and a curveball too." In tight situations, Larry, like most young pitchers, was throwing the fastball, instead of going to the curve and the change-up he had learned to throw.

"I was cocky, that year. One time they had a team meeting in Montreal, and they were talking about somebody going to the bullpen. This became a joke among the pitchers, because I stood up and said—how did I say it? Blass knows it by heart!—I said, 'Who's going to be the one to go to the bullpen? Not me!' And so they put Moose in the bullpen. He was fourteen and three, and they put him in the bullpen. There are some guys that they take advantage of."

In 1970, Dock was thirteen and ten. One of the thirteen was a no-hitter. His ERA dropped to 3.21. He started thirty games, relieved in none, and finished eight. He pitched two hundred and two innings, with eighty-seven bases on balls and one hundred and twenty-eight strikeouts. He was striking out fewer, and getting more outs.

"So things were better?"

"I was learning to vary my pitches more. Set up the hitters. Experience. Also, I was a very happy individual."

"That helps?"

"Oh, yeah. State of mind."

"Why did you have only twenty-three decisions?"

"I pitched two hundred and two innings, but I was out a lot with a sore arm. In nineteen sixty-nine I pitched more than two hundred innings, which I had never done before. In nineteen seventy-one I did too, but I haven't since. Over two hundred innings is good on this team, because of the five-man rotation. Plus, in the early seventies they were going to Giusti. I've been leaving games in the sixth inning—seven to one, eight to one—and he come in, got a save."

"Were they protecting your arm?"

"That I don't believe. I felt that they were building Giusti up, something to give him confidence as a reliever. He had just come to our team with a bad back. St. Louis has just gotten rid of him. They were giving him a new lease on life as a reliever.

"Giusti, *he* says, 'Dock, you can't do it! You don't have the stamina.'"

In May of 1970 the Pirates made their first western swing of the season, beginning with San Diego. They flew into San Diego on a Thursday, an off day. A twi-night doubleheader was scheduled for Friday, with Dock pitching the first game.

As soon as he had checked into the hotel, Dock rented a car and drove to Los Angeles, and went directly to the house of a young woman, old girlfriend of Al Rambo, whom Dock had not seen for some time. "The first thing, we turned Jimi Hendrix on, and we made some screwdrivers."

Dock and Al's girl talked through the night, drinking slowly, never quite drunk. "I don't think I ever went to sleep. About noon the next day I realized I was pitching!"

I can't believe what Dock is telling me. "You *forgot* you were *pitching?*"

Dock defends himself. "From the long drive, being tired, being a little high. I was under the impression that—I wasn't thinking right—we were playing in L.A.

"So then I realized I had to get out of there." He turned in his car, and he made reservations for a plane at five o'clock, under the impression—he still wasn't thinking right—that the game started at eight o'clock. "Then I remembered it was a doubleheader. And I was pitching the *first game.*

"So I got on the first thing smoking out of there.

"So I arrived there about five-thirty. The game's at five after six. They had just finished up batting. I ran right out to the bullpen and started warming up."

I observe, "You must have been pretty flaky."

"I knew what I was doing. I was in control. When I drank that coffee, that knocked that vodka out of there. Drank a *lot* of coffee."

It was probably not the first no-hitter pitched by someone who had spent the previous night drinking alcohol. *The Baseball Encyclopedia* remains unclear on this point.

Dock was fast, that day. Number one fastball was quick, and dropped off the table as it crossed the plate. Number two fastball rode up and in, disconcertingly chinwards. "I had 'em ducking and diving and hitting off the end of the bat. Pop flies. Ground balls. They hit two good balls off me." One of them was the almost hit, saved by a miraculous catch, which seems obligatory in a no-hitter. Ramon Webster pinch-hit in the seventh inning, and hit a line drive to the right of the elderly second baseman, Bill Mazeroski—hero of the 1960 World Series, still playing a steady game ten years later. Mazeroski dove to his right, and stretched his left hand across his body to make a backhanded catch in the webbing of his glove.

Webster was an unfamiliar hitter to Dock. "During the meeting they hadn't told me what kind of hitter he was," Dock complains, then changes his direction, "because I wasn't *there* for the meeting. I didn't know he was a fastball hitter. First thing I threw was a fastball. He jumped right on it. When I saw Maz *dive*, I knew he had it. Because he won't *leave his feet*, if he don't *know* he can get the ball.

"The other man was Clarence Gaston. No, it wasn't Clarence Gaston, because Clarence Gaston didn't play. It *was* Clarence Gaston, because Ollie Brown didn't play." Dock cannot decide. He waves the matter aside. "One of the two. He hit a line drive that was knuckling"— fluttering like a knuckle ball—"at Matty Alou. He came in and shoestringed it."

"What kind of a day was it?"

"It was misty, rainy that day. It was drizzling from the third or fourth inning on. There mustn't have been three or four hundred people there, five hundred at the most."

In the dugout Dock started talking about a no-hitter as early as the third inning. Thereafter, Dave Cash kept up a steady stream of teasing, whenever Dock rolled back from the mound. "You got a no-no, you got a no-no." Dock was grateful. "That kept me alert. A lot of guys, when they got a no-hitter going, they don't want you to talk about it. Dave knew I didn't care. What the hell."

"Do you remember the last pitch?"

"I struck out the last man. On a curveball. Sudol waved him out, and I just spun around. I screamed, A *motherfucking no-no!* ' "

"How'd you feel afterward?"

"I was zeroed out. I was *high*." There is a photograph taken as Dock sat in the dugout after the game. The game ball lies between his legs, his mouth is open, he stares blankly ahead. Zeroed out.

"Did you sleep for a couple of days?"

"No. Jumped straight up, drank some more vodka, getting high!"

The next day was Saturday, Game of the Week, and Curt Gowdy talked to Dock Ellis by telephone over national TV. Newspapers everywhere ran stories, and concentrated heavily on Dock as the man from Watts, Dock the convicted car thief, the man who came to baseball instead of going to jail.

It is possible that Dock was responsible for some of this romance. One story contained a sinister hint:

. . . He was up for grand theft and before that— "I'd rather not talk about that," he said, pointing the index finger at the hand which guided the arm that no-hitted the Padres last night. He did it in a manner which left the distinct impression that he's used a firearm before.

Dock has never fired a gun at anyone. He may possibly have sold a reporter a handful of wolf tickets.

Shangalesa Talwanga, eight months old, was spelled out from coast to coast. A wire story described Paula's reactions, hearing the game on the radio. It was said that Dock intended to enter the dry-cleaning business, upon his retirement from the country of baseball.

Nellie King, the tall and skinny ex-pitcher who broadcast for the Pirates at that time, made up a plaque to celebrate Dock's no-hitter. King is a former Pirate pitcher, and still seems like a young ballplayer, enthusiastic and excitable and partisan. The plaque preserved clippings, under lettering which named the day and the event. When Los Angeles held its testimonial dinner for Chet Brewer, two years later, Dock flew in from Pittsburgh, made a speech, and gave his plaque to Mr. Brewer, who hangs it in his house among a hundred loving cups.

The next time out, Dock pitched four innings no-hit. "Then a single, and then the roof fell in."

In the Championship Series, in October of 1970, Cincinnati beat Pittsburgh three straight games. Dock started the first game, and pitched nine innings shut-out. So did Gary Nolan. In the tenth inning, Ty Cline, who pinch-hit for Nolan, hit a triple. Dock walked two, loading the bases for a possible force-out. But Lee May cleared the bases with a double.

5. Doing Time

In 1970 and 1971, Dock spent the off-season working with black prisoners, in Pennsylvania's Western State Penitentiary and in a rehabilitation center called Grubstake.

When Dock said that baseball saved him from going to prison, he exaggerated his general criminality. Even without baseball, I think he might have turned out to be as careful as Big Daddy. But he had been tried and convicted and put on probation for stealing a car—and some old Neighborhood friends were now in jail for the same crime. He became increasingly aware of the contrast between his own comfort and affluence, and the suffering of his black people. This awareness led Dock to his prison work, and to a variety of largely unpublicized and unknown acts of charity and conscience.

In 1970 Dock fell into casual conversation with a stranger who worked in the Pennsylvania Department of Corrections, and after twenty minutes realized that he had found a job to do. After a series of interviews, Dock began working nine to five, five days a week, at Grubstake. He qualified for the job not by education but by desire combined with street knowledge and street talk.

"I didn't want to get paid, but they gave me some money, about a hundred dollars a week. 'That's cool.' It was something I wanted to be involved with. I was down there Saturdays, Sundays, whenever somebody got in trouble. You had people who had tried just about *everything*, and now they *wanted* to be rehabilitated. I used to go out with them. Several of them I kept with me all the time. I played basketball with them. They tried to get me to play football. I wasn't going to play football! From there, somebody contacted me to go into the penitentiary. I was still in and out of Grubstake all the time, but the second year I went to Western State Penitentiary about fifteen hours a week. I was more or less a troubleshooter. The sociologist went in with me at first. They knew I could relate, because I had the street talk.

"I never had been in a penitentiary. It was new to me. The first day I was there, I said, 'What's happening?' They say, 'Well, what the hell could be happening, in here?' That was my learning, right there! I learned to watch what I say. When I got ready to leave I'd say, 'Well, I'll see you tomorrow.' They say, 'We ain't going nowhere.'

"The first two days, they called me 'the young Duquesne lawyer.' That's what they thought I was. The first day I had a guard taking me around. When they saw me back the third day, fourth day, fifth day, they was no guard, and they began to trust me. Once I told them what I was doing there, I started hearing everything, coming from everywhere. I listened. I observed. I watched. If it was something I thought was important, or could help anyone, I had authority to tell someone who'd tell Shapp"—Milton Shapp, governor of Pennsylvania.

I know Dock no longer works in the prison. "Why did you ever leave the job?"

"I didn't *leave*. Several things happened. There was a lot of guys over there that followed baseball. Guilfoile"—Bill Guilfoile is the publicity man for the Pirates—"gave me two or three hundred yearbooks, and I passed them out to some of the guys, the baseball nuts. Then I brought Charlie Feeney in there." Feeney is one sportswriter Dock trusts. "They didn't like that. The warden didn't like that. He didn't want the press in there. That was the *first* thing."

As usual, Dock acted out of his feelings, and not according to the rules. He began to make friends with the prisoners, to become close, and to listen, especially to those who were educating themselves by consuming the prison library. Certain patches of ignorance, especially among older prisoners who had not walked free for decades, touched him. "There were older brothers in there who didn't know about hair spray for black people's hair. They were still using the old grease my father used. They wanted the grease my father used—they called it Murray's grease—but the prison wouldn't let them have it, because it came in a metal can," and metal could be fashioned into weapons. Dock told them that the grease came in cardboard now. "They didn't know. They're *stuck* over there.

"I went over to the commissary, to see what was there. They didn't have the comb-out *spray*, so later I came with two aerosol cans of spray." The spray makes black hair easier to comb, and leaves it shiny. "It was aerosol cans. It took them two hours to find me. It got back to the warden that I was in there with two aerosol cans. The warden figures that someone is going to take the cans, make bombs out of them. But they know I knew better than that. Sure, there was guys trying to get the cans. I say, 'Man, leave that can alone.'

"I wanted them to see it, to use it. They were going crazy: 'Let me use it! Let me use it!' Before I knew, it was all gone. When they found me, they said, 'You can't bring that stuff in here.' I said, 'Hey, man. It's gone.' "

"So did they tell you not to come back?"

"No, they didn't tell me. The last time I was in there, I took Fuqua in there." Frenchy Fuqua is a running back for the Pittsburgh Steelers. "That was the day before he broke the rushing record. You remember when he did that in Philly, playing the Eagles? I tried to go back in the hole"—solitary confinement—"and this big old brother he said, 'No, you can't go in there.' I wanted to see someone in there. There was a little boy in there. He was about eighteen years old. He and his girlfriend just killed a security guard at a bank in Harrisburg. All he wanted to do was to get out of the cell. He ran track in school, and it was driving him crazy that he couldn't move around. He wanted to see if I could work it where he could get out in the yard. He didn't have to go out with the population. Say, just at two in the morning, all the guards with guns on him. He just wanted to run. They had a little track. "I was going to tell him how I was going to run it on the warden. We had to get our plan together. They stopped me. I knew *then* there was no need of coming back. The following week I took Preston Pearson over"—another Steeler running back now with Dallas—and they wouldn't let me in. They stopped me at the gate."

"Did they give you a reason?"

"I was too mad to sit there and listen to them. Anyway, I was going to spring training that evening. When I got back to Pittsburgh, I received a check for nineteen hundred dollars and three certificates signed by Shapp. I was through. They had written me off."

"Did you try again?"

"I did, before spring training this year. I could tell things were shaky. Used to be I could go right in there. I would just say who I wanted to see. I didn't have to be on business. I named a couple of guys and they said, 'No, you're not on the pass list.' "

Talking with Vaughn Chapel in Los Angeles in 1974, I learn about more visits to prisons.

Vaughn starts by telling me that he and Dock became friends in high school, that they played ball together, and partied. Vaughn is small, and talks rapidly, in little bursts.

"During the off-season, I used to go back east, go to Pittsburgh, five or six years straight. We'd go to New York or D.C. together, when he was working with the Sickle Cell Foundation." Then Vaughn comes to the subject he has been avoiding. "I guess we *really* came close when . . . I done some time in the penitentiary. Something like fifteen months and nine days. This was recently. Last year. Even though we had been close through all these years, I wasn't aware just how close until I had to go away.

"During the time I was away, I found things out about people I thought were friends of mine, but they weren't. There were friends living right here in L.A. that wouldn't take the time to come. Every time Dock came to town, he always made the effort to come and see me. Like the times he did come, he never did say he was coming. I didn't know the Pirates was in town. He would just show. They would call me on the loudspeaker that I had a visitor. I go out there, and I see him. He just threw everything aside when he got to town. A good two-and-a-half, three-hour drive. The dude is a beautiful dude. I didn't get a letter from anybody but him. He used to write me. He cherishes friends. I didn't realize how much, until I took my vacation."

6. *Sickle Cell*

When his work with Pennsylvania prisoners was frustrated, Dock found another way to serve his conscience. In 1971, Willie Stargell, Dock, John Brisker, and twenty-nine other athletes started the Black Athletes Foundation for Sickle Cell Research—an organization to lobby and to raise money for research and treatment, and also to publicize the disease among black people, so that blacks could be tested for the trait and the disease.

Sickle-cell anemia is a fatal disease, which occurs almost exclusively among black people. If you have sickle-cell anemia, you may not hope for a long life. However, the disease can be prevented by education. Sickle-cell anemia is a recessive trait. It is easy enough to identify people who carry the trait by examining their blood. If two trait-carriers reproduce, chances are that they will reproduce doomed children.

Dock carries the sickle-cell trait. Paula does not, and Shangalesa carries only the trait. At the time that they were married, neither Dock nor Paula had been tested.

Although the trait never develops into the disease, and Dock will never have sickle-cell anemia, the trait itself produces some ill effects. Tony Bartirome wonders if the trait is reponsible for Dock tiring in the late innings. "It's possible the tiredness, the trouble in the joints, relate to the trait." Other matters surely do. When Dock is spiked he heals slowly. The leg wound he suffered in Columbus—the time the team petitioned against him—healed slowly because of the trait, before he knew that he was a carrier. Sometimes he passes blood in his urine and undergoes spells of dizziness. "When I start passing blood, it is a form of crisis." He takes iron pills, and feels well again.

In the evolution of black races in Africa, the sickle-cell *trait* leads to survival rather than to death. Sickle cells in the blood suffocate malaria parasites. The person endowed with the trait survives better than the unendowed, in a population exposed to malaria. About eight percent of American blacks have the trait. Sickle-cell anemia itself occurs in three-tenths percent of the black population. If detection can prevent possessors of the trait from procreating, the disease can be eliminated.

The Black Athletes Foundation has had its problems, but it has accomplished prodigies. It has alerted thousands of people to the disease who would otherwise have remained ignorant. And the athletes recruited black musicians to the cause, who carried the message further.

Thirty-two athletes, including Dock, donated a thousand dollars apiece to begin the fund. The foundation sponsored a fair in Pittsburgh to draw people together, so that their blood might be tested. Doctors set up tents wherever black people gathered, at big circuses and big football games. Dock and other athletes traveled around the country, appearing on television or at blood testing sites.

"We did a show with Billye Williams"—Hank Aaron's fiancée, on Atlanta TV. "Doctors were talking about hemoglobin this and hemoglobin that and all this shit. Quite naturally I come right in, I say, 'Hey, you talking to the brothers and sisters in rural areas, don't understand hemoglobins.' I told them to stop there. I started talking the regular talk, breaking it down. I think we got to a lot of people."

When Congress considered a bill appropriating money for sickle-cell research, black leaders and celebrities from all over the country—Dock among them—testified before committees, shook hands, signed autographs, lobbied particular Congressmen. ("They wanted to talk about baseball.") Congress ended by appropriating one hundred and forty-two million dollars for research.

7. The Pittsburgh Brotherhood

Dock has been loved as much in black Pittsburgh as he has been loathed in white Pittsburgh. This love arises partly from *schadenfreude*. (*Schadenfreude* is the delight we take in the discomfiture in others; the black citizenry enjoys it when Dock gives the white folks fits.) But there are nobler sources. With his prison work and his work for the Black Athletes Foundation, Dock has committed himself formally to the brotherhood of blacks who help each other. But his informal commitment is greater.

Dock in Pittsburgh resembles Dock in Los Angeles. He appears unimpressed by his own fame. While old acquaintances in Los Angeles proclaim that he is "just the same," black strangers in Pittsburgh are astonished that he is "just like us." He doesn't let himself be bothered by the tension, the awe, or even the jealousy of others. His friends (black or white) take him home, take him to visit in-laws, take him along to the old folks home to visit Grandma—and Dock is always himself, relaxed and confident, alert and interested, independent and natural.

In the depressed black Pittsburgh culture, he stands out as a model of success who remains natural and human. His best black friend in Pittsburgh, J.W., tells what he does: "Just going out into the community. Going to the playground. Playing ball. Stopping on the streets. Walking around. Rapping with the people. Patronizing stores in the black community. Even Stargell—Stargell is very popular here—they don't see Stargell as much as they see Dock.

"One Sunday we were driving in the street, going to watch a football game, and he decided he wanted to have his hair plaited. We rode up on the Hill"—black Pittsburgh—"and he met these people he met maybe once, a couple of years ago. He stopped the car, got out, asked the girl could she braid his hair." She proceeded to braid it. "He sat down there, bullshitted with her like one of her brothers."

In January of 1971, the winter after Dock's no-hitter, the black community of Pittsburgh gave him a surprise testimonial dinner. J.W. (whose name is William Bauknight), Willie McCray, and Cecil Burt organized it. "We decided"—J.W. tells me—"that he was always so friendly to *kids* in the community—and about that time he was getting a bad press; that can get you down—we decided to have a little banquet for him. He didn't know anything about it. We got a plaque, 'To No-No from the Grass Roots People,' for his no-hitter. We rented a little hall at the University of Pittsburgh, got us some soul food."

John Brisker and other athletes, old and new Pittsburgh friends, all gathered in the rented hall. The press was not invited. The head of NAACP was not invited. No big names, "just people from the black community all over Pittsburgh, from the streets." Dock came along under the impression that a group of athletes were all to be honored. "When he got his plaque, he was in tears."

On an off day in the summer of 1974, while I was visiting Dock in Pittsburgh, he told me he had to go off to a CAP (Community Action Program) banquet honoring O. J. Simpson and Hank Aaron—although he knew that neither would be there. As he sat at his table before the banquet, he began to realize that something strange was happening. He told me the next day:

"I was sitting next to a sister, and I said, 'Who's being honored here tonight?' I knew it was Hank and O.J., but I saw another thing.

"She said, 'You.'

"I said, 'What am I going to be honored for?'

"She said, 'Aw, just be cool.' "

The youth group of CAP gave Dock the award. "It blew my mind." He looked out in the audience, and saw J.W. and Willie McCray. Later, he asked them if they had instigated it again, but they had not. Kids from different sections, from the Hill and from all over Pittsburgh, most of them strangers to Dock, presented him with a plaque, "For being a brother to all."

8. *1971: the All-Star Game*

In 1971, Dock won nineteen and lost nine, with a 3.05 ERA. Out of thirty-one starts, he finished eleven games, struck out a hundred and thirty-seven, and walked only sixty-three.

Dock pitched on opening day, beating the Phillies four to two, and by the All-Star break, halfway through the season, he had won fourteen games.

As the All-Star Game approached, Vida Blue was burning up the American League, and for some reason had touched the national imagination; maybe it was his name, maybe it was Charles Finley's aptitude for public relations. Whenever he pitched, at home or on the road, attendance doubled. After a loss on opening day, Blue had won ten straight games.

Meantime, Dock had won twelve straight.

Sparky Anderson chose the National League All-Star pitchers and of course Dock was among them. Then Dock gave the newspapers a story: They'll never start a brother against a brother, he said. Here's an AP version of the story:

> Dock Ellis leads the National League with fourteen victories, but he says there are two reasons he won't start in the All-Star Game.
> —He's black.
> —Cincinnati Reds manager Sparky Anderson, who'll manage the NL squad, allegedly doesn't like him.

Ellis, fourteen and three, pitched the Pittsburgh Pirates over the Reds Tuesday night for his twelfth straight win. . . .

"I doubt very seriously if they'll start a brother (black man) from the American League and a brother from the National," said Ellis. . . .

Sparky Anderson immediately denied that he disliked Dock Ellis. With apparent bewilderment, he protested, "I don't know where he got that idea. I have never spoken to him and he's never spoken to me." Anderson went on to grumble that if he didn't start him, it would be to protect his arm, and besides, Tom Seaver was ten and three.

All over the country, sports pages erupted in patriotic wrath. Editorials attacked this militant who dared to suggest that preference in this country does not derive directly from merit. How could anyone assert, in this land of freedom and equal opportunity, that organized baseball could differentiate among players according to the color of their skins? At about this time, someone published an article showing that black ballplayers averaged ten points higher batting averages than Latins, who averaged ten points higher than whites.

And indeed, Dock started the All-Star Game. Editorials coast to coast rejoiced that the young militant had been proved wrong. Editorial writers were sold a gross of wolf tickets.

"The only way I could start was to say they wouldn't start me, because I was black. I call it child psychology. I said they wouldn't do it, so they had to."

"Why did you say Sparky didn't like you?"

"To focus attention on Sparky. Now Sparky got to do something! I had the record, but he wasn't going to start me. He was going to start Seaver or Carlton."

"You just made that up, about him not liking you?"

"Oh, yeah. Well, I *told* him that, at the All-Star Game."

The notoriety Dock achieved—mostly by being denounced in pontifical columns—surpassed the fame of the no-hitter. It even surpassed the notoriety of losing the game.

In the first two innings, Dock gave up only one single, and the National League led two to nothing. But in the third inning, Luis Aparicio singled off Dock, and Reggie Jackson—pinch-hitting for Blue who had done his three innings—hit one of the longest home runs in the history of the All-Star Game. It struck the light pole above the third deck in Tiger Stadium, and can still be seen on baseball highlight films. Dock turned around when the ball was hit, but couldn't find it. "I didn't know what was happening. Usually when it's a home run, you see the fans reaching for the ball. I didn't see them."

Jackson's homer tied the game, two-two. Now Rod Carew walked, Bobby Murcer and Carl Yastrzemski both popped out—and Frank Robinson hit a line-drive home run to make the score four to two. The American League finally won the game, for its only victory since 1962.

Dock makes no excuses, talking with me about the All-Star Game. But months later, when we talk about different ball parks and different mounds, he grumbles that the Detroit mound was the *worst* he ever saw.

"Why?" I ask him.

"It was *ridiculous*. It was low, plus it had a big hole in it. They don't have any clay in it. It was just soggy, like sand. You had nothing to *grip*. Evidently those guys over there got *big feet*."

I wonder about the best Detroit pitcher (now with the New York Mets)—and his feet. "Did Micky Lolich pitch that day?"

"I don't know," he says. "I don't know too much about it. When they took me out of the game, I was *gone*. Willie Mays and myself, we were *gone*. I jumped into his limousine."

9. *The Press*

Dock was cynical when he told the press he wouldn't start—if it is cynical to control events by negative predictions. But his statement was probably accurate, as a prediction of what would have happened if he had not predicted it. And why would he not have started the game, when he had the best record in the National League? Well, possibly because somebody didn't want a brother to start against a brother.

Racism so dominates us, becomes so much the air we breathe, that we see it no more than we see the air. Perhaps the sources of athletic racism are relatively innocent—maybe we only like to identify with a hero, and it is difficult to identify with someone whose skin is distinctly different—but when we deny that it exists we are its victims. White players get buildups denied to black players. A black player's prominence is expected of him, admired, but not exclaimed upon; when a white rookie bats .300, watch the coverage in the press. Look at the response to Fred Lynn and Jim Rice, in Boston in 1975.

Hanging around baseball, as I have been doing, I don't see racism in management, in coaching, or in the front office. Reading the newspapers of Detroit and Chicago and Boston and New York, I see it every day.

The list of Most Unpopular Sports Figures, in the last decade or two, is largely black. Muhammad Ali, for a while. Duane Thomas. Dick Allen. Alex Johnson.

Why should this be so?

Reggie Jackson, who does not make the list, talks about his treatment by the press:

"I felt, back in nineteen sixty-nine, when I had a chance at Maris' home-run record, that white pitchers were walking me on purpose because they didn't want to see a black man break the record. I was walking two, three times a game; I never got a good pitch to hit. So when I said something about it to the sportswriters, you know what happened? They went off and wrote that I was a sorehead, a crybaby, a troublemaker.

"I don't think a black writer would have written these things; . . . Why? Because he probably went through something like that himself somewhere.

"No way you can be black in America and not."

When Dock was little, he watched Jackie Robinson play ball on his uncle's television set in Compton. In 1970, Dock met Jackie Robinson at the Apollo Theatre in New York, shook his hand, and talked with him. Just after the All-Star Game, Dock received a letter from Jackie Robinson:

> I read your comments in our paper the last few days and wanted you to know how much I appreciate your courage and honesty. In my opinion progress for today's players will only come from this kind of dedication. I am sure also you know some of the possible consequences. The news media while knowing full well you are right and honest will use every means to get back at you. Blacks should not protest, as you are, even though they know you are right. Honors that should be yours will bypass you and the pressures will be great. When I met you I was left with the feeling that self-respect was very important. There will be times when you will ask yourself if it's worth it all. I can only say, Doc, it is and even though you will want to yield in the long run your own feeling about yourself will be most important. Try not to be left alone, try to get more players to understand your views and you will find great support.

You have made a real contribution. I sincerely hope your great ability continues. That ability will determine the success of your dedication and honesty.

I again appreciate what you are doing—continued success.

Sincerely,

Jackie Robinson

Interviewd by Dave Anderson in *The New York Times*, just a few days later, Robinson said more:

> . . . one guy today who really impresses me is Dock Ellis for what he said at the All-Star Game. . . .
> I wrote him a letter, saying I liked the way he was standing up, but to make some of the other players stand up with him. Don't try to do it alone, because he's young, he doesn't have the strength at this time. I knew what could happen to him. I think baseball is very vindictive. I think very frankly that a black man who was willing to accept their dictates and do what they want him to do can get along beautifully. But if you're a man and you stand on your own two feet, then look out.

In 1971 Pittsburgh papers first suggested that Dock be traded away. The column headed ELLIS PROBABLY MOST UNPOPULAR BUC OF ALL TIME solemnly predicted that Dock would be traded. Like columnists in 1972, 1973, 1974, and 1975, the writer admits that Dock is "personable," and perhaps "one of the best pitchers in baseball," but still presents him like some wrestling villain—Gorgeous George, or The Black Monster, the man you love to hate: Uppity Nigger. Scattered through the story are the revealing phrases: ". . . it sure looks like they'll try to get along without Dock next year." "Joe Brown can be counted on to do the right thing by getting rid of him." " . . . if Ellis remains with the Pirates, he could be the first player ever to keep fans away when it's his turn to work."

Management ignored these directives, for some years.

Baseball—in Joe Garagiola's elegant phrase—is a funny game. At least it's a funny job. If a vice-president of General Motors criticized Chevrolet, or his executive washroom, in the public press, I suppose that he might be asked to resign. On the other hand, the man or woman on the assembly line has freedom of speech, of complaint, and even of work stoppage. The line worker is protected by camaraderie, by the

United Auto Workers, and by his anonymity: nobody puts his complaints in the newspapers, and his work stoppage only becomes news when it becomes collective. As a professor at a university, I can refuse to teach in order to protest a war; I can denounce my dean and my president and my chairman; I can say that my students are illiterate—and nothing happens to me except that I feel a certain chill in the air; I have "tenure."

But if Dock Ellis declines to inhabit an autograph cage, one Sunday afternoon in Pittsburgh, the wire services snap to attention, TV editorialists work up moral dudgeon, and racial stereotypes parade like the Rockettes.

Of course Dock is paid well—better than a factory worker, better than a professor, better than a Rockette—but when we name his salary, do we really think that his wages ought to guarantee his obedience to rules he does not believe in? Does his stipend imply that he should never complain about a short bed? And if he complains about a short bed, why should it make *news* around the country? When Tom Seaver complains that there are no water glasses in his bathroom, does UPI put it on the wire?

Charlie Feeney is a good sportswriter in Pittsburgh. It was he who started the story about the beds, for which Dock bears him no ill will. At the beginning of Dock's career, Feeney was the source of Dock's earliest disaffection with the press.

Dock has always chattered in the clubhouse. In 1969, on the day Ronnie Kline was traded from the Pirates to the San Francisco Giants, Feeney heard Dock teasing Kline about being traded, needling him. I don't know whether Feeney was ingenuous or disingenuous, but he wrote a column in which he appeared to be horrified, and he chastised Dock for his callousness. Dock was hurt and angry. In truth, his needling had been friendly. It took the tone of affected disdain and hostility by which ballplayers indicate affection and acceptance—the language spoken in the country of baseball. If Dock had been silent, or had commiserated with Kline in all seriousness, he would have been proclaiming that the trade was a calamity and an insult. Teasing, he implied that life continued as usual, and that being traded was no big deal. "Man," says Dock five years later, still shaking his head, "Kline *helped* me. We were tight."

Dock's first reaction was not to speak to the press. Then he became more discriminating, and found in Feeney a decent man, without racial axes to grind. A year or two later, Feeney was quoting Dock in *The*

Sporting News: "You misunderstood me once . . . Kline told me that if I ever saw him drinking beer before a game, it would mean he had been traded. When I saw Ronnie drinking a beer before a game in Houston, I knew he had been traded somewhere. I guess it sounded as if I was heckling him. I wasn't."

Really, we don't know if Dock said these words. Once he came to respect Feeney, he gave Feeney permission to quote him whenever Feeney felt like it, even if they hadn't spoken to each other.

10. *Management*

Joe Brown is general manager of the Pirates, a likable albeit dignified man in his fifties, son of the great comedian Joe E. Brown. After apprenticing in minor league management, he became Pirate general manager in 1955, bringing Pirate pennants and world championships. He talks carefully, negotiates well, and generally gets along with his players.

When his ballplayers complain about "management," they must be talking about Joe Brown, and yet they pay him the personal tribute of substituting the abstraction for the name.

(Also the abstratction or euphemism acknowledges that the general manager might be overruled by owners or misrepresented by delegated authority. And, too, it supposes that baseball is run by a gigantic conspiracy, incorporating all owners, general managers, vice-presidents, publicity directors, stockholders, and Bowie Kuhn, an organization as intricate and fiendish as the Red Menace, hiding under the name of Management.)

Joe Brown is an Equal Opportunity Employer. "We've never had less than nine blacks, in the last ten or twelve years. We've had as many as fourteen. I don't think any club in the history of baseball has consistently had as many black players, or as many at one time as fourteen. This is not giving us credit because we don't do it deliberately." The word "blacks" includes Puerto Ricans, Mexicans, and Panamanians—from the dark skin of Manny Sanguillen to the pale tan of Ramon Hernandez.

Talking with Joe Brown, in 1974, I ask him about Dock and the press, Dock and the public.

"Dock's popped off from time to time, and said things which people have objected to more strenuously than I have. He's got sheer immediate intelligence. A lot of people who know him don't get deep enough to realize how smart he is.

"He pops off at times when he's going to get the most publicity. I'm not sure whether it's deliberate or just naïve. For example, in the play-offs about the beds. He comes out on the field at the All-Star Game, and he's surrounded by newspaper reporters." He seems to admire Dock's public relations skill, then qualifies his admiration. "There are times when the public image of the club has not been *improved*."

Joe Brown has received letters telling him to get rid of Dock, because Dock hurts morale. "Well, Dock doesn't. It's just Dock's way. He loves to be the center of attention. He loves to talk. He doesn't disturb the players. They just say, 'Aw, shut up, Ellis.' I think he has a good relationship with most of the players on the team."

I asked Dock about Joe Brown.

"The Pirate organization was my college, from sixty-four to sixty-eight, and Joe Brown was my professor. He was trying to groom me for the world. He's cool. I do a lot of public relations for Joe Brown. A lot of ballplayers, they're always blaming Joe Brown. I say, 'You can't blame Joe Brown. You signed your name on a contract. You're letting them do it. What would you do, if you were Joe Brown?'"

At the beginning, Dock didn't know what to expect of him, and Joe Brown felt that Dock was hostile. But gradually, and with the help of Tom Reich, who negotiates at contract time, they have learned respect for each other.

I ask Dock to talk about baseball management in general, and maybe Joe Brown in particular.

"It's like raising a baby. When some babies cry, they're going to shut up if you *look* at them. That's what Joe Brown'll do, *look hard* at them." Another Pirate told me how he always wore his shades when he negotiated with Joe Brown, so that Joe Brown couldn't fix his eyes on him.

"I learned how to deal with the organization from the older ballplayers, who used to talk about what to do but never did it. Stargell, Clendenon, Jesse Gonder, Maury Wills. They had the right idea, but they never did it. A lot of my moves came from Stargell. He was telling me how he would do it, and then I'd go do it."

"You're talking about negotiating a contract?"

"Right. Willie said, 'Negotiating with Joe Brown, never forget what he says.' I never forget what he says. I bring it right back to him. He said,

'We don't pay you on games you complete, strikeouts . . . I want to pay you for *wins*.' The next year I didn't let him forget it."

Different managements have different ways of controlling different ballplayers. Everybody wants more pay, and everybody has good reasons. What do you do? On some sports teams, the general manager, hearing that his superstar wants another $25,000 next year, shakes his head sadly. Oh, he is sorry to hear that. Gently, gently, he reminds Sammy of the years they nurtured him. He reminds him that the price of tickets rose only fifteen percent last year. He reminds him of fourteen other matters. Then he reminds him of two arrests for drunken driving, the charges dropped in conjunction with political donations by the ball club; and Sammy signs for a $7,500 raise.

On many clubs, management is quick to make loans to ballplayers. "I know a ballplayer with the San Francisco Giants," Dock tells me. "He wanted a home. 'Okay. We'll give you fifteen thousand dollars. Go get the home.' So he has to do anything they say to do. If they say, 'Go to a banquet, *free*,' how can you say I'm not going, and they've given you all this money? Then if you have a good year, they say we'll give you fifteen thousand instead of twenty-five thousand for a raise, because we're lending you all this money."

Dock has never borrowed money from the Pirates.

"Tell me about your college education," I ask Dock.

"When I was younger, a lot of guys on the teams would say, 'Willie, has he graduated yet? Did he get his diploma?' Willie came up to me one time in sixty-nine, and said, 'You got your diploma now.'

"I said, 'I want it in writing.'

"Now some of the guys come up to me and say, 'Does Clines get his diploma now? Does Cash get his diploma now?' I say, 'I'm not giving out diplomas. Stargell gives out diplomas.' He's more tolerant with the younger dudes.

"It's a matter of learning the league, everything as far as the league goes. It would be dealing with management. Dealing with the press. Dealing with the ladies. And the game itself. The game itself has priority over everything."

"Do you have your M.A. now?"

"I have my Ph.D."

"If you were a general manager, how would you handle the players?"

"I think I would handle it the same way Joe Brown handles it, only—I would know more about the individual than he does. When I told him just now that you're here doing a book, and I wanted you to interview him because he was the professor of my college years, Joe Brown chuckled. A chuckle means he understood. If I had said this three years ago, he would have had a blank expression on his face. He wouldn't have known what I was talking about.

"To deal on money, I wouldn't pay them on performance for what they *did*, I would pay them for what *I* thought they would *do*. That's what I would base salary on. That would be motivation to the individual."

"Would you cut them then, next year, if they didn't do what you expected of them?"

"Right. I would tell them: 'Here's the money. Now you earn it!' "

"What's wrong with paying on last year's performance?"

"Management of the Pirates—" Dock shakes his head; this is a real disagreement—"Brown, Murtaugh, Skinner—they spoil them with that *production* thing."

Production for hitters takes account of batting average, home runs, hits, RBIs, runs scored—but it leaves out the ball hit to the wrong field by the right-handed batter, with two runners on base and less than two outs, which records only an out in the batter's statistics—but advances the runners to scoring position. Unselfish baseball doesn't show in statistics of performance. Neither does defensive baseball. The number or percentage of errors shows little; number of chances handled, for an infielder, shows more. For an outfielder, chances handled may simply count the times he pulled up on a fly ball.

On a flight home from Houston, in the bad part of 1974, Al Oliver addressed the team about selfish and unselfish baseball, and on the problems which management made for them, by making their salary dependent on statistical performance. "We do not bunt runners over," Dock remembers him saying, "we do not hit to the other field. Joe Brown ain't going to look back and say, 'Well, Al, you moved that runner over, and we won that game,' or, 'You bunted that runner over,' or this and that."

Dock goes on, "I understand what he says. It's that money thing. You can't get the money for bunting a man over. That's why this team doesn't bunt. That's why they can't bunt."

I ask, "But what about when the coach gives them a bunt sign?"

"When do they get it? I haven't seen a regular bunt sign over four times this season. I don't think there have *been* four times. Maybe just two. Al bunted one time, on his own. Man was on first and second, and he bunted. Somebody got a hit. They scored both runs."

Dock shakes his head. "You drive in so many runs, you hit a certain average, you score this many runs, you get home runs, triples, doubles, and singles—you get so much money. But you come up in the second inning with men on first and second and no outs. 'Hey, man. Move them over!' But then you're just the hitter going up for no at bat. The other fellow has two RBIs instead of you getting the one if you had hit a single. Two if you hit a triple, three if you hit a home run. But thing that's most probable? Bunt? No, you don't do that."

Dock has stated his disagreement with Pirate management. Dock laughs and says, "Maybe when they read this book, they're going to get their shit together."

11. *Umpiring*

In 1971, Dock had his one run-in with umpires—and it failed to surface, and it did not become a newspaper scandal.

On every team in the country of baseball, there are players who believe that the umpires are out to get them: sometimes to get the player himself; sometimes to get the whole team. Umpires provide the perfect material for paranoid fantasies. If they were out to get you, you would only know by bad calls; but everybody makes bad calls, and every team suffers through them; and the umpires would never admit to prejudice; they would conspire; they would cover for each other; *no one would ever know.* Worst of all, if you complained or tried to expose the Conspiracy of the Umpires, nobody would believe you; and then the Conspiracy would *intensify.*

When we use the word paranoia, lest we forget, we do not rule out the possibility that these fantasies might on occasion be accurate hunches. In the words of the poet Delmore Schwartz, "Even paranoids have enemies."

When evidence points to conspiracy, Dock tries to look away. "I don't want to think that way." This habit of mind is only common sense. There's no better way to fail at anything than to walk in a cloak of suspicion, looking for the people who will make you fail. It's much more sensible to put suspicion from your mind—"I don't want to think that way"—and reach back and bring it.

Talking with Gine Clines and Manny Sanguillen, in the summer of 1974, I discover that both of them believe that half of the National League umpires are out to get the Pirates. Manny rattles off examples of games lost, including a World Series game with Baltimore in 1971. Bob Moose was pitching brilliantly, but lost because a National League umpire called balls and strikes. They tell me why: during the umpires' strike in 1970, they tell me, Joe Brown pulled scab umpires up from Triple A.

In 1971, Dock started a historic game.

"The first time they fielded nine black, I was pitching. I pitched maybe one and two-thirds innings. I was throwing that sinker ball. "Ball, ball, ball, ball." And he was telling Sangy, 'Shut up. Set your ass down there and catch the game.' "

Leaving the game because of his alleged wildness, Dock was enraged. He did not leave the game on the field, as he normally does after a bad day.

"I had a feeling that they were out to get me. But I didn't want to think that."

He sat up all night in his Dungeon, the psychedelic room he had made in his apartment. The next morning, an off day, he drove to the airport. "Left the city. Broomed. I just booked California." At the Pittsburgh airport, by weird coincidence, he met the umpiring crew. "Hey, man," said Dock. "Hell of a game you called."

By another coincidence, he bumped into Delores Crawford at the Los Angeles airport—old friend, wife of old friend Willie Crawford who played for the Dodgers then. She had just dropped off a passenger. "She said, 'What's wrong? What are *you* doing here?'

"I just said, 'I can't deal with it. I just wanted to hurt somebody so I left.' And I slept in Willie Crawford's new house from noon until seven o'clock. I didn't want to *think* the umpire was doing that to me."

He talked late with Delores, who calmed him down. (They have made a close friendship out of calming each other down.) In the morning he flew back to Pittsburgh in time to suit up for the night game, and no one on the team, none of his closest friends, knew that he had flown six thousand miles between two games.

"Let me get this straight," I say. "You felt, didn't you, that the umpire

called the balls wrong because the Pirates fielded nine black players?"
"I didn't want to think that."

12. *The Loose Ball Club*

The Pirates are a loose club. In the clubhouse, they use racial epithets on each other: nigger, Dago. When Jerry Reuss came to the Pirates from Houston, he was astonished: "You use the big N," he said. Anybody who said nigger in Houston, he swore, would have gotten himself killed. Of course the epithets, and the continual teasing, show how aggressive people use up their fraternal anger. But when race is talked about openly, the issue festers less. In 1974 Reuss threw a barbecue at his Pittsburgh house and invited only some of the players on the team. A few blacks were invited, but not Al Oliver or Dock. Immediately, they accused him of racial prejudice. Neither of them took their charges seriously, but they made their point: you don't invite *half* the team. Ever.

The notion of friendship on the team intrigues me. "Do you have close friends on the team now?"
"Yeah. Stargell, we roomed together."
"Why don't you have a roommate now?"
"I can't stand it. They just yak-yak-yak-yak. Me and Willie were cool, but they had to break us up. They didn't know what we were doing. They never saw us. We'd get off the bus from the ball park, and they didn't see us again until the bus left for the ball park the next day. They knew we had to be doing something. He would never say nothing, and I would never say nothing."
I'm curious. "How did you meet Willie? Do you remember?"
Dock remembers. "When I came up? In nineteen sixty-five? For the Hype game? *That's* when I met Willie." Willie was in his fourth season. "The first time he ever saw me, he was driving around the corner, here in Pittsburgh. I yelled, 'Stargell! Stargell! Stop the car!' He stopped. I jumped in, I said, 'Let's *go!*'
"He wanted to know, '*Who-are-you?*'
"From then on we were pretty close."
Last night Willie Stargell threw a team party at his luxurious house outside Pittsburgh.

"I wish you could have been there," Dock says. "You could have seen the jealousy among the ballplayers!

"I'm telling you—this arbitration, and this submitting of salaries—! A lot of guys didn't realize, say, what Rennie Stennett was making, or Dave Cash, or Manny Sanguillen, or Al Oliver, or even me. Now you can obtain it."

"I watched people when they came in Willie's house. Oh, buddy! One guy" Dock mimics a man with awe and wonder—"he was looking over a lamp. I ran in the bathroom and got him a napkin. I said, 'Here, check for some dust.' I said, 'Oh, don't worry about a thing. There ain't no dust. Maid coming in four times a week.' "

Manny Sanguillen is Dock's friend from winter ball in the Dominican Republic, and from the minor leagues. "Nobody in this club know Dock like I do," Manny tells me. "Dock tell you that."

Manny is one of the most interesting Pirates. He is interesting for the depth of his passions, his love, and his violence. His smile is almost continual, and his anger is sudden and terrifying. He is a fine mimic, and an entertainer. At a party at Tom Reich's, he jumped around continually, demonstrating stances and dances, and doing a remarkable imitation of his small son, Sangy, Jr. Sangy, Jr., is afraid of spiders; imitating his son, Sangy's body moved like Marcel Marceau, enormously expressive in its twitches and little leaps of terror.

Then he told about his old problem of insomnia. Manny used to wake in the night and read until dawn. Now he was free of that disease, and would sleep all day if his wife did not wake him. Except that on Saturday morning he wakes early—he told me, and his face broke into an astonishing grin—and by 7:30 A.M., no matter how late the night before, he sits at the television set to watch cartoons all morning. "Roadrunner," he said laughing. He has been called Roadrunner for his unorthodox but effective gait. "Roadrunner." His face is contorted with smiling. "Beep. Beep."

Like most of Sangy's friends, Dock is afraid that Sangy might snap out on somebody, some day. Dock remembers Sangy's recent confrontation with Bob Smizik, a Pittsburgh sportswriter who had written, in Sanguillen's opinion, critically and unfairly about Latin and black ballplayers. Smizik tried to reason with Sangy, and over his smile Sangy's eyes were saying *kill*. Dock says, "If Sangy is like that, Smizik better get out of here. He can really be dangerous."

And Manny says of Dock, "I know Dock from deep inside. A looonnnnng time. We be great friends. To me, Dock is a great man. You feel to say something you can't say." One feels the religion, the loyalty, the fierceness, and the goodness all together. Then Sangy begins to be angry at what people have said about Dock. Nixon, he tells me—it is June of 1974—says terrible things and people clap; Dock speaks and they misinterpret him. "Dock is the guy who has great heart." This is not the "heart" of sports pages or of "you gotta have heart," this is the bloody lump of muscle, the sacred heart of Jesus. "But don't try to take advantage of him," Sangy says, and I feel the menace again. "Don't push him around! He know how to deal with that!"

As we leave the party, Tom Reich's house in a suburban town, Sangy expresses concern that we might not be able to find our way back to the Pittsburgh Hilton. We are followed by Sangy until we make the right turn toward the city—halfway there, and out of Sangy's way—when his silver Lincoln Continental leaps past us with a blast on the horn and a long black muscular arm waving.

One morning I suddenly have a thought, and ask Dock, "Do the players ever talk about this book we're doing?"

"They're *scared* of the book," Dock says. "They think it's going to be like Bouton but deep. They know if it's done on me, it's going to *be* me. Nervous people!"

"You like that, huh?"

"*I dig it to death!*"

13. *1971: The Down Slide*

After the All-Star Game in 1971, Dock won five and lost six. A sore arm prevented several starts, and in a number of games he paid his bad-luck dues for his good luck in May and June. Coming to Los Angeles with his midseason record of fourteen and three, Dock assured Ray Jones that he would not win twenty, when twenty wins seemed almost inevitable. Taken out of a Dodger game, leading but with men on base, he listened in the clubhouse as his relief man gave up a home run, and made him losing pitcher.

I ask him if there was anything mental, in going from fourteen and three to five and six.

He nods his head, yes. "After the first half, the season was over really. We had won it. We had it won by the All-Star break. Stargell and I were carrying the team, the first half. Second half, neither of us did anything. The desire was gone. What the hell, who's going to catch us? You *let up*."

As he tells it, I remember the bad second halves of two minor league seasons; you prove something by burning up the league for half a season, and because you have proved yourself, you lose something.

"How does it affect your pitching?" I ask him. "Literally. How are the pitches different?"

He shakes his head. Again, you only know the pitches are different when people start hitting them harder—and then you're not sure. "You go through the motions," he guesses. "Without knowing that you are doing it, you take something off the fastball."

Whatever he lost in the regular season, it didn't come flooding back in the play-offs and the Series. He won the second game of the Championship Series over the Giants in San Francisco, but it was not one of his good days. He pitched five innings, gave up five hits and two earned runs. Pirate hitting saved the day, scoring nine runs to four for the San Francisco Giants.

Taking the pennant three games to one, the Pirates went on to beat Baltimore in a spectacular seven-game series. Dock started the first game, and quickly found himself with a three-run lead. But Frank Robinson, who had homered off him in the All-Star Game, repeated in the second inning of the World Series. In the third inning, Merv Rettenmund hit another homer, with two men on base, and shortly thereafter—he walked Boog Powell—Dock's 1971 season had concluded. Losing pitcher. Kison and Blass were the pitching heroes for the Pirates, in the 1971 World Series.

14. *Making Your Bed*

But if Blass and Kison and Dave McNally and Jim Palmer all pitched better than Dock, on this occasion, they were probably talked about less. The Championship Series and the World Series, in 1971, were notable in the sports pages of the nation for Dock's difficulty in finding a big enough bed.

"Paula and I checked into this hotel in San Francisco, and all the room had was a small queen. Like I'm six feet four and she is almost five feet nine. Her feet were hanging out of the bed and so were mine.

"So I said, 'I would like to have another room, with a bigger bed.' I had stayed in the hotel before—the Jack Tar—and it had a king-size bed. So I went down to the desk, and they said they'd give me another room. They gave me a suite, with four beds—but it was four tiny beds—smaller than the queen! If I could have put them *together*, that would have been *cool*, but they were *stationary*."

So Dock went down to the desk again. "I was going *crazy!*" He found the same clerk. "Now I've got *four* beds that are *all* too small.

"So he said he couldn't do anything about it. I was going *crazy*. So I said, 'Paula, go call a hotel, so we can get *out* of here.' This is when we went to the Hilton. The following day, they had a big article about me in the paper."

Charlie Feeney had been standing at the desk trying to change *his* room, and he had heard the first exchange. When Dock came back the second time, Feeney was reading a paper in the lobby. Feeney jumped up and came over, asking what was wrong, what was the trouble.

Dock was happy to answer.

And in Baltimore for the World Series, Dock stood in a row of twenty people at the Lord Baltimore who were all changing their rooms. "Now I'm a big controversial figure, because I'm in line." And Dock made the papers once more.

It was not much of a tempest, and not much of a teapot. At every World Series, or before every Super Bowl, there are celebrated nonevents. But even nonevents raise passions in frustrated breasts. Dock received telephoned threats, hate letters, and telegrams, like:

Change your rooms one more time and go "drop dead"

and

. . . Come sleep at my house in the box we keep for the cat.

15. *In the Hooches of Vietnam*

After the series, Monte Irvin asked Dock if he would go to Vietnam on a USO tour. Dock was curious. "My friends were coming back from Vietnam, and they were telling me different things. I had a tendency not to believe them. I wanted to see what it was. Willie Stargell and Mudcat had been over there, and they were telling me different things."

He told Irvin, "Hey, if a brother is going, I'll go to Vietnam."

I jump at the notion: "Why with a brother? Wouldn't you be comfortable without a brother?" Working with Dock, I find myself increasingly obsessed by the effects of racial wars.

"I like to cut into different type dudes, but on *that* trip, I wouldn't know anybody. It could have been a white dude that I *knew*."

"Don't you mean that it's easier to get to know a black brother, because you share a culture?"

Dock resists the notion. "Not really. I can imagine a brother that is a brother that is *not* a brother. I can spot the coolness that I dig about a person, whether he's a brother or he's not a brother."

"Anyway," I continue, giving up, "tell me about Vietnam. Who'd you go with?"

"At the beginning, it was supposed to be me, Bobby Bonds, and Reggie Jackson. I knew Bobby Bonds, but I didn't know Reggie. So I asked Bobby about Reggie. "He say, 'Man, if that dude go, I ain't going.'

"I say, 'Well, why? What the fuck? We can all go and have fun.'

" 'I ain't going with him.'

"I say, 'Hey, Bobby. Let's just put our names, and maybe he won't go.'

" 'I'll go if he don't go.'

"Luckily, Reggie scratched.

"So I flew here, to San Francisco, looked at Bobby's house, had dinner, drank. That was the first time I got to meet his wife Pat. We had fun. Pat, she said she hoped the plane go down, because she had my rings.

"When we arrived in Vietnam, it was Bobby Bonds, myself, Nick Colossi the umpire, Jim Enright—a sportswriter whom I didn't know at the time but now we're real close—and Mike Hedlund, he was with Kansas City, and Mike Kilkenny, he was with Detroit. I wanted to be with Bobby, but they split us up into two groups, and they were sending Bobby with somebody, and me with somebody."

I ask, "They were putting one black in each group?"

"Right. I was telling Enright, 'What the fuck is going on?' This is when

I became close to Enright. He said, 'You won nineteen games, and you were with the champs. Bobby Bonds had a hell of a year. The other two guys, they didn't have that good a year.' "

It sounds like the kind of perfectly reasonable explanation which is always incorrect.

"I say, 'Bullshit. Man, I don't want to be fucking around with anybody I don't know; I can't do the things I want to do.' But it was all right. It was cool. Whenever I got to a fire base, I did what I wanted to do anyway. I jumped in the hooch with the brothers.

"They were shooting. It wasn't really wartime, but they were shooting. I said to Bobby, 'Man, this shit ain't real! I'm taking me a quart of gin everywhere I go. When I *go*, I be *high*.'

"Everywhere I went I kept that gin. I had fun, except when they shot at us. We were going down the Cambodian river in a boat, going to see twelve Sea-bees. Then all I saw was bullets ricocheting in the water. Then I realized that my escort officer had never held a gun and fired it in combat, because he was shaking. I grabbed a gun and they told me to put it down.

"All of a sudden I see this big boat—not a *big* boat, but big to be coming down this river. This big redheaded dude—he had hair on his chest sticking out five inches, and he was tattooed—he was *coming*, and he had guns in each hand, and he was coming to rescue us. Evidently there was a sniper."

It occurs to me that I had never heard anybody call Vietnam fun before. "Did you ever take a political stand about Vietnam?"

"Not really. Politically, why should I even deal with it? I know what's going on over there. I jump underground with the brothers in the hooch. When they try to find me, around the fire base, they send an alert out. They have a runner going around, checking all the hooches. 'Dock Ellis in here? Dock Ellis in here?' "

On a respite from their tour, Dock and Bobby Bonds had some free time in Saigon. They decided to do a little shopping, to bring souvenirs back to the United States. They decided to do it with cheap money.

Dock told this story one night in San Francisco, the night after he had pitched and won a game over the Giants, and handled Bobby Bonds with ease. Everyone was high on wine. There were a number of empty Pouilly Fuissé bottles on the windowsill. Every now and then a young waiter brought another bottle.

"Me and Bobby, we're supposed to be the hip brother from L.A. and the hip brother from Frisco, right? We got two hundred dollars apiece in military currency, so we're going to the black market to get some piasters. Our military escort, he knew we were going to do some *wrong*.

"Me and Bobby, we knew the game. Ain't nobody going to gyp us. I've seen this shit done before. We're going to be *on* everything. I said, 'Anybody who fucks with my money, I'm hitting them.' I said, 'If I grab it and they grab it, *you* hit *them*.' He said, 'Everything's cool.'

"So we're walking down the street, waiting on somebody to hit on us about changing some money. We go into this little restaurant. They say, 'You buy five Cokes.' "

Dock mimes bewilderment, looking around the room, counting on his fingers. 'Five Cokes for who?' I say. 'You, me, him, and him? Where's the other one?'

"Then she comes and sits down, and she says, 'I ain't speak good English.'

"She sat down. I said, 'Dig that! What's your name?'

"She gave me her little book, says how many piasters she'll give me for my dollars. I say, 'Come here,' to my military escort. 'Hey, is this cool?' He said, 'Yeah, that's cool.'

"They're going to give us fifty, sixty extra dollars in piasters." Dock was holding the scrip, and one of the men with the woman reached for it. Dock yanked it back. " 'No no no no no,' I said. I counted it right in front of them, where they could see. They had the money in piasters. I said, 'Bobby, get the money, get back in your corner, and count it.' He counted the money in piasters. I peeked too. He said, 'That's it.' Then Bobby went to reach for some more, and she said, 'No no no no no!' He tried to cheat her!"

Dock is walking up and down the hotel room in San Francisco, acting out all the parts, trilling "No no no no no" in the high voice of the streets.

"I got all our money right here in my hand, I got it *locked*." Dock makes a double fist. "I say, 'Bobby, dig this. Lock this money in your hand.' Then the dude with the broad put his hand out. I said, 'Git your hands off of there!' He said, 'I just want to put a rubber band—' I say, 'You can't put no rubber band on there!' "

"Dig this. I said, 'Bobby, keep your hands *locked* on that money.' So I get under the table, to see if they got a hole in the table, to see if they got a little chamber in there. I even took the tablecloth off. They wasn't going to gyp *me*.

"So I counted the piasters. Bobby said, 'Let this dude put the rubber band on it.' I said, 'Bobby, don't let that dude put that rubber band on there.' When he put the rubber band on, I *grab* the money, just like that. I put the piasters right here, in these pockets. Bobby gives them our money. They count it.

"So we're walking down, downtown Saigon. I'm going like this—" Dock mimics a casual amble, cool, only he keeps slapping at his shirt pocket as if he had a virulent twitch. "I'm *petting* my money and my wallet.

"We passed a rug place, and I saw this bad-d-d-d rug. I got to have it. I go in and I say, 'Hey, I want that rug.' You know, I'm taking something back from Nam.

"I pull out my money. Five-hundred-piaster notes, they are orange. That's *all* we counted, five-hundred-piaster notes. I pulled one orange five-hundred-piaster note off the top—and every other thing is *purple*. They're *twenty*-piaster notes, they got a *two* and an *oh* on them! They're worth—all that money's worth—about fifteen dollars!

" 'Bobby,' I say, 'they done fucked us over.' "

Bobby started to scream—in Dock's rendition anyway—and started running back toward the restaurant, knocking people down in his rage. " 'Motherfuckers! I'm going to kick their ass!' Then he slowed down. 'No,' he said, 'I just want to tell them they did a good job.' 'Me too,' I said. 'Let's congratulate them.' I've seen all kinds of games that people run. We were on our job, and they got us. They were *good-d-d-d*.

"Naturally when we got there, they were *gone*."

"Before, when you were talking about Vietnam," I said to Dock, "you said that you knew what was going on over there. I never asked you what you meant."

"When we was leaving, going back, we had a meeting with General Adamson. He was telling us all sorts of shit. He was trying to tell me the way the service was going to be. It's going to be voluntary. I say, 'Wow. That's a trip. Now we're going to be nothing but a military police state.' And it's coming about.

"He also was talking about how there wasn't much drugs over there. I said, 'Bullshit. I'm looking right at it.' I saw the capsules of heroin around. I was offered heroin many times. Several dudes, they got high on heroin in the hooch while I sat there. What the fuck? That's their thing. They were shooting and snorting both. I was even in one place—I forget the fire base—and I walked around the perimeter, and all it was was caps. At night, everyone who was supposed to be on guard was *high*. Caps of heroin. You get it from Mama-san. Mama-san give out *beaucoup*."

"What was it like between the races out there?"

"One time I went out to a lookout post and they had this brother and this little white dude. Both of them were from Mississippi. They got on this story about how they were *close*, how they were not like they used to be. Bullshit. Do they have to tell me they're close? They're protecting each other, in the wartime. They don't have to tell me. I take out my gin. I say, 'Man, I don't even want to hear this bullshit. Let's get high.' "

Back in the United States, army public relations wanted Dock to go on television "with some bullshit. The captain asked me to do the TV. I told him, 'You're pretty cool. In order to protect you, I'm going to tell you what I'm going to say.' I was going to talk about dope. I saw drugs all over Vietnam. And I was going to tell about the black market—soldiers selling jeeps and batteries and things like that. I wasn't going to say what they *wanted* me to say."

The army withdrew its request.

16. *1972*

In 1972 Danny Murtaugh retired again, and Bill Virdon—old Pirate center fielder, Murtaugh's coach and protégé—took over as manager. Dock's record was fifteen and seven, "with a whole bunch of time out for arm trouble." His ERA was 2.71, the lowest since he became a regular, and ninth lowest in the league. He started twenty-five ball games and only finished four, a figure that galls him. "I don't think I was handled right. I was taken out of games where I had no business being taken out."

Murtaugh had removed him from games early also, but not so much as Virdon did. And Virdon left other pitchers in games under conditions which had led to Dock's departure. "Ten times they took *me* out, and let *them* stay in." Dock shakes his head. The same thing happened the next year with Virdon, and continued with Murtaugh when Murtaugh returned. "I try to understand it, to say it's because they think something's wrong with my arm. Maybe they think I'm getting tired."

In spite of the excellent statistics, "Seventy-two was a discouraging season. Murtaugh had a loose team, a loose clubhouse." With Virdon, the club *ambience* shifted a hundred and eighty degrees. The ambience was Boy Scout, to use one of the preferred analogies; it was U. S. Army, and Virdon was general, to use another. When Virdon was top sergeant for Murtaugh, you didn't have to worry about him, because the general himself was loose. When a top sergeant gets promoted to general, watch your ass.

Changes started in spring training. It was a tight camp, on schedule, with stated tasks to perform each day. And it was tight in another sense; the Pirates were saving money on travel. "One time we were going to Miami to play, *on a bus*, and Galbreath invited Giusti, Blass, and Stargell to *fly* with them. I say, 'Hey, man, if you're going to fly, I'm going to fly' (I know why they do it. They knew we were going to strike, so to manipulate their minds, they take them to big parties.) Giusti was player representative, Stargell and Blass unofficial team leaders. "So anyway, I wouldn't ride the bus. Virdon fined me fifty dollars. I said, 'That's cool. It's your fifty dollars.' I flew down there.

In 1972 the Pirates lost a five-game Championship Series with the Cincinnati Reds when Bob Moose threw a wild pitch, relieving Dave Giusti in the fifth game. Dock pitched and lost the fourth game.

"Toward the end of the year my arm went bad, and they got me to miss three starts so I would be ready for the play-offs. Okay, if I'm getting ready for the play-offs, why don't I open the play-offs up? Blass pitches the first game." The first two games were in Pittsburgh. "Why don't I pitch the second game? I tried to tell them, 'This is my ball park. I can pitch my ass off in this ball park.'" Bob Moose started and lost the second game.

Nellie Briles opened the Cincinnati stand, and Bruce Kison got the win as the Pirates went up two to one. Then Dock started in Riverfront Stadium. "I had the best stuff of my career. I was bringing it. If we'd won that game, we would have won everything. I was *into* it.

"But nobody caught the ball. Gene Alley had a bad case of combat shakes. They had Stennett out in left field. That doesn't make any sense. Stennett wasn't used to flipping the glasses down. He couldn't *see*. People were dropping fly balls. And one dude bunted, three and two, and Hebner was back on his heels."

Virdon sent up a pinch hitter for Dock after five innings, and he left the game losing three to nothing. He had given up no earned runs, but he was losing pitcher.

17. *On Being Maced*

In the annals of Dock Ellis, 1972 is the Year of the Mace.

Early in May the Pirates arrived in Cincinnati, with Dock scheduled to pitch the second game of the series. Before walking to the clubhouse, Dock went to a barbershop for a shampoo, and had his hair blown. In the barbershop he met a young black woman, her face swollen and discolored from a beating. Dock—being Dock—asked her who beat her up. She worked in a discotheque, she told Dock, spinning records, and the night before she had left the bar to go out to the parking lot, hearing the sounds of a fight outside. She wanted to protect her car. White cops arrived to break up the fight, and beat her up.

Dock was angry as he walked to the ball park. He persuaded the girl to come with him, promising to get tickets for her. As they approached Riverfront Stadium they bumped into Rennie Stennett and Willie Stargell, all three ballplayers hurrying because they feared that they were late.

A uniformed and armed white security guard stood at the players' entrance. It was his first day on the job. For the first time at any ball park anywhere, in the experience of the Pittsburgh Pirates, the security guard asked for identification from the three ballplayers.

None of them carried a wallet. If you wear tight trousers, if you care, like an eighteenth-century dandy, for the figure you cut, if you attend to the curve of your hip, you do not carry a wallet in your trouser pocket. Nor, if you are a well-dressed ballplayer in May of 1972, do you wear a jacket.

All three wore another sort of identification: World Series rings reading Stennett, Stargell, and Ellis. In addition, Willie Stargell carried a check with his name on it.

"Willie showed him a check as well as the ring," Dock tells me. "Rennie showed him the ring and he let Rennie in. I was walking right by him—they'd never had a guard there before. Then I showed him the ring—" and for no reason that anyone ever supplied, the guard would not let Dock enter without further identification. He had no further identification on his person. Of course Stargell and Stennett identified Dock, but the guard would not accept their guarantees. Dock was furious.

"I m-f'd him to *death*," Dock tells me, lapsing into an unaccustomed euphemism. "Then he put the gun in my face. They shouldn't have guns. I was looking straight down the barrel.

"Stargell and Stennett were *gone*. They never had seen anything like that. I was telling one of them to stay, but they were *gone*. Willie went to get the policeman.

"The gun was shaking. I said, 'Hey, man, let me tell you something: you put that gun *down*. *It makes me nervous.*' "

Dock found himself spread-eagled against the wall of Riverfront Stadium. "While I was on the wall, I was calling him everything I could think of." Then the guard made Dock move from the wall to a car, his hands spread flat along the roof. "Now I'm turning around—'Don't shoot me'—to put my hands up. He moved that gun away from my head. 'You can put it on me,' I told him, 'but put it on my shoulder. Even shoot my shoulder off. But don't kill me.' I could feel the gun when he touched me with it, and it was shaking. He holstered and drew that gun three times. I was saying, 'Hey, man, you better put the handcuffs on me, because I don't want you to shoot me.' "

Then Dock heard a posse of ballplayers approaching. Stargell had not found a policeman, but he had found the Pirates.

"I said, 'Now here come the ballplayers. They're going to kick your ass.' When they started coming, I started sliding around the car. That's when he maced me. He got nervous. He figured if they got to him, I was going to get to him too. They was *coming* too—Virdon leading the parade!

"So he maced me—and I was telling him, right while he was macing me, 'Keep on! Beautiful! This makes me hate better!' "

The posse rescued him, and now the newspapers and the courts began. Dock called Tom Reich, "Tom, they maced me now." The next day he appeared in court, charged by the Cincinnati Reds with assault on their security guard, and won a continuance to June 10. Then he flew back to Pittsburgh for a press conference. In Cincinnati, the guard claimed that Dock had arrived at the ball park drunk, and displayed a half empty bottle of wine as evidence. Dock brought countersuit against the guard and the Cincinnati Reds.

Meantime, Dock's head burned for a few days. "I had just had my hair blown out, and my scalp was open, hot water shampoo. That stuff was burning. It knocked me *down*. I said, 'Man, my head is *burning*.' They couldn't get close to me—that stuff—no one could get close to me."

Before June 10, Dock and Tom Reich found impartial witnesses to the incident—a television crew arriving for the next day's telecast—and the Cincinnati Reds dropped all charges. The Cincinnati ball club wrote Dock a letter of apology—"It blew my mind when I read it; I read it *once a month!*"—and he dropped his lawsuit also.

Joe Brown was true blue, right from the start, at a time when a more cowardly general manager might have adopted a tone of legal neutrality, and might even have suspended Dock while charges were pending. "I called the Cincinnati ball club and told them I stood a hundred percent behind him, and believed what he said." At this time the Cincinnati organization appeared to defend the guard's assertion that Dock was drunk. "Dock is too smart for that," Joe Brown told me.

And Joe Brown issued a statement, Monday, May 8, 1972:

> I think it is important that the position of the Pittsburgh Club in relationship to the unfortunate incident in Cincinnati involving Dock Ellis be stated.
>
> Our players, Wilver Stargell, Rennie Stennett, and Ellis, sought entrance to Riverfront Stadium at the normal time and at the regular gate through which players enter. To my knowledge, no stadium in the National League requires that players produce identification, as the Cincinnati guard did on this occasion for the first time. While statements have emanated from several sources, no allegation can persuade me that Ellis carried a bottle to the stadium or that he was "semi-intoxicated" as charged. My long and close association with Dock gives me the earnest conviction that either action is completely unlike him. While Ellis is certainly an advocate of free speech and there have been occasions when I would have preferred that he remain silent, physical threats and the intemperate use of alcohol are foreign to his nature.
>
> In order that our players will not have to undergo such an unhappy experience again, identification cards bearing individual pictures will be issued to our team tomorrow in Atlanta.

Even the press was not quick to condemn Dock, this time. Though Dock's name made the news—because he had made the news before—most sportswriters realized that Dock would never show up at a ball park drunk and carrying a bottle of wine. Dick Young wrote a column in the *New York Daily News*.

> . . . If you were to meet Dock Ellis for the first time, anytime, you might think he was drunk. He has a wild, babbling way about him, high-strung, has modeled himself, to a large extent, after Ali.

He has an alert mind and loves to show it off.

I must doubt, very seriously, that the wine bottle suddenly produced as evidence belonged to Dock Ellis. He is not a daytime drinker, and much too bright to commit such a patent disciplinary breach.

Later, quoting Dock—"this makes me hate better"—Young ended, "Anyone who must make himself hate has very little true hate in him."

Possibly. *Probably*, but the word "hate," when he said it, meant something for Dock that went beyond rhetoric. While Willie Stargell politely showed a check to confirm his identity, Dock doubtless threw his head back, looked down his nose, put on his haughtiest expression, and took no shit. It was the same expression that enraged assistant principals and coaches at Gardena High and Harbor J. C. The hate that he nurtured while being maced was the hate that was born in Thornburg Park, when the little man in the shed—a functionary like the guard at Riverfront—redrew the boundaries in order to exclude the black boy. When Dock meets white repudiation—you can't come in here, play here, be on my team, hang out on this block, date my sister—Dock's head goes back and his eyes half close, and his pride is exceeded only by his obscenity.

On his next visit to Cincinnati, "I went over early. The clubhouse was locked. I decided to try to get in through the field. I was walking behind home plate, toward where they have the cameras, and this guard hollered, 'Where you going?'

"I say, 'I'm trying to get into the clubhouse.'

"He say, 'Oh, you're Dock Ellis. Thanks for the job.'

"I said, 'What?'

"He said, 'Yeah, they fired that guy.'"

Three years later, in June of 1975, I met Dock in Cincinnati, and went together to a restaurant called Pigall's. I had eaten there the day before—as I am wont to do when I visit Cincinnati—and I had worn a suit but no necktie. Sitting there, I did a survey of the room: every man wore a coat; every man except me wore a tie.

When I picked Dock up at the Stouffer's Cincinnati Inn, he wore splendid light green trousers, a flowered green shirt, green shoes, and his customary rings and pendants. He looked marvelous, pressed and shinning, but he did not look like the Procter & Gamble executives at Pigall's.

The owner, acting as *maître d'*, met us at the door. "I am sorry, but we do not serve gentlemen without coats." Dock's head went back. A quick survey of the restaurant revealed no black faces.

We stepped outside. "You ate there before," Dock said. "Do they make you wear a coat?"

I could say yes. I could also have said, but didn't bother, that Pigall's has catered to black clientele while I have eaten there. Muttering about "this jitterbug restaurant," Dock ran back to the hotel to change. In Manhattan or in San Francisco, in Los Angeles or even in Pittsburgh, a restaurant as good as Pigall's would be too sophisticated to require suit coats. But Cincinnati, hip to food, is square on hair and suit coats.

When Dock returned—and dove into a poached trout, with Pouilly Fuissé, moaning with the excellence of the cuisine—he wore a dark blue suit, tailored to fit him like a sprayed paint, black shoes, white shirt, and a necktie—just acquired in the hotel lobby—which displayed, against a navy background, tiny American flags.

18. *The Death of Clementine*

On New Year's Eve, in 1972, Roberto Clemente died when his airplane crashed into the sea on takeoff from Puerto Rico, a flight Clemente had undertaken in aid of earthquake victims in Nicaragua.

The Pirates wore black armbands in 1973. Gray depression lay over the team. Without Clemente, the ball club lost its style. No one felt this loss, this deprivation, so much as the Pirate ballplayers themselves, each housed in his separate mourning.

"When I first came to the league—"

Dock starts to tell me about Clemente; we have postponed the subject of Clemente many times; it is early in the morning, after a good night's sleep, and he begins with a sense of heaviness; he told me before, "When they try to interview me about Clemente, I say I don't even want to talk about it. I've got it *here*." He points to his head.

"When I first came to the league, that's all you heard of when you heard of the Pirates—Roberto Clemente. To me, the first impression was that he was standoffish. But this was only a manner, how he had to carry himself, because of the superstardom he had reached. Once I broke that wall, he was just like another brother to me."

"How long did it take?"

"About twenty minutes," Dock says. "I looked at him, you know, I *peeked*, and I listened to him talk. I said, 'Aw, man, shut up.' " Imitating himself, Dock's tone of voice is not angry or contemptuous or abrupt, just mildly dismissive—the way you might address your oldest friend if you thought he was being silly.

"And he says, '*Who* is this *rookie?*' " Dock pauses in his story, aware that his imitation is inaccurate. "Let's see. How does he say it? 'Rookie moth-er-fuck-er, *who* are *you?*' " Dock's voice is deliberate, delicately accented, and high pitched; within the high pitch there is vast variety of pitch, a roller coaster on top of a mountain.

"From then on we were friends. That was spring training sixty-six. A lot of people don't know how close we were, because he was always screaming and yelling at me. He used to tell me to shut up. He wanted me to cut into management *then* the way I know how to cut into it *now*. I didn't want to listen. I would always say, 'That's *politicking.*' Basically it's not politicking, it's getting to know the people you're dealing with.

"He made me realize that Joe Brown wasn't a bad dude, that he was just doing a job the best way he knew how. Clemente was the only one to say that he wasn't a bad dude. He always wanted me to get to know, not Joe Brown, but the Galbreaths. I'd say, 'If you didn't do what you had done, you wouldn't know the Galbreaths.' And he said 'No,' and I said, 'Yeah,' and he said 'No,' and I said 'Yeah,' and that's the way it went. We used to argue all the time. We meet and we start arguing, screaming."

"Clementine—that's what I called him—he wanted to know how the other fellows felt about him. He always asked me, 'Why, he never invite me to his parties?'

"I say, 'Man, you in another *world.*' He's not only a superstar, he's *older*. He doesn't want to be like that. He wanted to be one of the fellows. So I'd bring him with me; I say, 'We going to get down together, *everybody.*' And they would do it, they would get down. I think this brought on the paries of the nineteen seventies." It was a new Pirate team, in the seventies. The World Champions of 1960 had dwindled to Roberto Clemente and Bill Mazeroski, and Maz was a pinch hitter and utility man. The young Pirates had grown up reading about Clemente in the sports pages. "It was another thing for the young ballplayers, to see him getting loose and partying. And he liked that."

Then the younger ballplayers like Dock began to give him advice. "Like, he was an older dude, but he didn't know how to chew gum. The way he chewed it, it was like he was trying to be cool." Dock mimics a cool gum chewer, laughing. "And he used to have on like a five-hundred-dollar suit, and a ten-cent pair of socks that didn't even go with the suit! I said, '*Come on!* You making all this money!' Before he died, he had gotten into a very, very hip thing with clothes—bell-bottoms, boots. Oh, he had a *walk*—"Dock stands and struts, awkward and cool and defiant all at once—"and you know how he was broad-shouldered anyway, and he'd be walking—" Dock swings his shoulders from side to side, and Roberto Clemente walks like a Renaissance prince. Dock laughs and laughs, and sits down and becomes quiet. "We talked all the time. We talked about everything. He was one proud individual."

I want to ask more about Clemente. "You told me he helped you in your thinking about management. What else did he help you with? Did he teach you about the game?"

"He was into me and left-handers. When I was pitching, at first, left-handers hit me down into the corner a lot. I was trying to get *in*, and I wasn't getting *in*. He was saying, 'If you can't get *in* there, *hit* them then. Go in there and hit them.'"

"Then I could get my location, he meant." By throwing at the left-handed batters, not worrying about hitting them, Dock with his rising fastball could catch the inside of the plate. "But I couldn't do it at first. I didn't want to hit anyone, just to be throwing strikes. After a while, they started hitting me so hard I threw it in there anyway. I hit a few. I didn't hit as many as he thought I was going to hit.

"He used to quiz me, as if I didn't know what I was doing out there on the mound. I let him know, talking, that I knew what I was doing.

When the newspapers denounced Dock Ellis, Clemente comforted him: "He told me, 'You think you're getting bad publicity. You never had nothing like *this*.' He even sent to Puerto Rico, where he had a collection of clippings, to get some newspapers to show me. They called him 'The Puerto Rican Hot Dog.'"

Of course he *was* a hot dog, as Dock admiringly uses the expression. In an earlier conversation, after Pete Rose had made a spectacular catch off Manny Sanguillen, Dock said to me: "He didn't have to dive that way, he didn't have to jump at the ball like that, but if the man is paying you a hundred thousand dollars a year, you have to be *spectacular*. You are setting the ball up, to make it appear to be a spectacular catch. Sure, Pete does it.

"Clemente, like, Clemente was an *expert* at it. He got *paid* for spectacular play. Clemente used to slide and catch a lot of balls. If he can slide and catch them, he can run and catch them, because as soon as he hits the turf, he slows down. Oh, there are some balls that are diving, and that was his trump suit.

"You have to be *good*, to be a hot dog."

"He never got commercials. They said he had a speech defect, and he couldn't speak proper English. That wasn't true. If he had to do a commercial, he could talk English like I talk English.

"He never got the publicity he should have had. They always said he was jaking." In baseball language, jaking is malingering. "They said he didn't play when he was supposed to be hurt and he wasn't hurt. I've seen him when he couldn't sleep. He couldn't sleep at night because of pain, and they used to write, 'What's hurting Clemente today? What's going to hurt him today?' One time he left here and went down to Puerto Rico to his own doctor, and Murtaugh fined him because he didn't play. Clemente said he was hurt, and Murtaugh said he wasn't. What manager can tell you that you're not hurt—and you're hurt?"

I come back to race again: "I know it's true that black ballplayers do fewer commercials than white ones. How do Latins fit into this? I mean, do they see themselves as blacks or as Latins or what?"

"When I first got here, I used to get into quite a few scuffles about Clementine. I would be in a black neighborhood and they would say Clemente doesn't call himself black. They have a section of town here called the Hill, and it's the black ghetto more or less. The brothers on the Hill say that he didn't consider himself black. They knew him because he used to live there when he first came.

"And I say, 'Well, you don't know Clemente then. He's a black *Puerto Rican*. He's no black *American*. You just don't understand what he's saying. If you can't understand that, I don't even want to talk to you.'

"He was a black *Puerto Rican*. He wasn't an American. I got into a lot of scuffles about that. He was as *black* as you can *get*. He was into it."

"Do many of the Latin ballplayers have problems with ethnic identity? Do some of them feel that they are Latin and not black?"

"They know who to say it around and who not to say it around. They will never say it around me, because I'd jump on their stuff in a hurry.

"I've had to *save* people, because they didn't think they were black and they were black. One time in the minor leagues, in the South, I was with this guy Felix Santana from the Dominican Republic. I was asleep on the bus, and they woke me up. They say, 'They're having some trouble in there.'

"I say, 'What kind of trouble?' I'm tired and sleepy, been riding on the bus about fifteen hours.' I go in the bus stop and the lady is telling him, 'Nigger, get out of here.'

"He says, 'Me no nigger. Me no nigger. Dominican. Dominican.'

"She say, 'You're black. Get out of here.' She didn't know anything about Dominican. Usually, the manager, he'd go and check, but Santana got out so quick. That's the first time that ever happened to me. So I had to grab him.

"La Grange, Georgia."

When Roberto Clemente died, the nature of the Pirates changed. They had been a hitting ball club for many years, perhaps taking on the values of their general manager, but they had in right field a player who did everything. Despite his .317 lifetime batting average, his three thousand hits in eighteen seasons—and all the divisions and subdivisions that statistics can multiply upon his accomplishments as a hitter—many players and fans would remember Roberto Clemente for his arm, or for his immaculate eye in the field, or for his base running.

When he died, the club mourned him by its slowness, its sluggishness, its lethargy, and its depression. Ballplayers who were mostly hitters became ballplayers who were only hitters. Defense, which was never a team accomplishment, became a team failing.

Certain sportswriters alleged that Clemente's absence left the team without a cheerleader, but the Pirates greeted this report with cynicism. "The Pirates never had a leader," Dock says: "When he was in the *lineup*, yeah! That's another good hitter. In the outfield he cut off runs. Shit like that. I hear them running about how he used to come in here sometimes, when we was losing, and say, 'Get them tomorrow, boys! Get them tomorrow!' Fuck that bullshit. Anyone can say, 'Let's get them tomorrow.' In fact he did it; he said it. But I don't think he would really get anybody emotionally *worked up*.

"But he was one proud individual."

19. *1973*

The 1973 season began with the death of Clemente, and ended with the return of Danny Murtaugh—the fourth time raised from the dead—and losing the divisional championship to the New York Mets. It was the year the Pirate defense went crazy. Dock was twelve and fourteen, with an ERA of 3.05.

It was the year of the Dalton Gang. "It consisted of Bob Miller, Bob Moose, Bob Johnson, and Luke Walker. Later on, Rooker joined the crew. He fitted right in. On TV, the Dalton Gang used to wear the trench coats, maxis. They was in*to* it. They bought big old gray cowboy hats and wore cowboy boots. They tried to dress in gray.

"Bob Miller was their leader."

Bob Miller started his big league career in 1957, an eighteen-year-old fireballer with the St. Louis Cardinals. In the expansion draft of 1962 he became an Original Met, and started twenty-one games that year, ending with a record of one and twelve. In 1963 he started for the Dodgers, and went ten and eight, with an ERA of 2.89. As the years went on, his fastball left him, and he threw junk; he started less and relieved more. Minnesota, White Sox, Cubs, Pittsburgh, Detroit, back to the Mets, San Diego. When last heard from, he was pitching in Hawaii, Triple A—an elderly and distinguished citizen of the country of baseball, his hair still blond, his face fleshy, dissipated, and boyish.

"But he wasn't really their leader. He was trying to tell them, 'Hey, don't follow me.' They admired him. I liked him because he was a white dude that could deal *on any level*. He was one of the greatest dudes that I have met, as far as white dudes in baseball go. He's still the same. Nothing bothers Bob Miller. As far as baseball goes, doesn't anything bother him."

Bill Virdon had ended the 1972 season with lineup changes—like Rennie Stennett playing left field. In 1973 there was a sad vacancy in right field. At the same time, the Pirates had two catchers who could hit, young Milt May as well as Manny Sanguillen, and one of them could run better than catchers can normally run. Therefore Manny Sanguillen

started the season in left field. Even without knees, he was better than
"He like to get killed out there," remembers Dock.

During spring training another experiment was tried and failed. Bob
Robertson worked out in left field while Willie Stargell, with game legs,
played first. Stargell plays an adequate first base. Robertson doesn't play
left field at all. This experiment was qickly abandoned, and Stargell
started the season in left field. Even without knees, he was better than
Robertson.

When the season began badly, Virdon gave up on all his experiments.
Manny returned from right field to the plate, and Milt May went to the
bench.

"Seventy-three was a motion year. Going through the motions."

It was also the year of the curlers. Dock has always paid as much
attention to his hair as to his clothes. When he was in high school his Quo
Vadis haircut earned him the nickname of Peanut, soon shortened to
Nut. He has straightened his hair, cornrolled his hair, plaited his hair,
let his hair grow out to a bushy Afro, and clipped it tight. He has even
shaved his head. *Ebony* ran a feature on Dock's various hair-styles.

So when he started wearing curlers to the ball park, in 1973,
Dock-watchers should not have been surprised. In August of that year,
someone photographed Dock hanging around the bullpen, before the
game, with a special size nine baseball cap over his curlers, but with
curlers clearly visible beside his ears.

Dock wore them only during practice. Yet word came down, from on
high, that when he wore curlers he was "out of uniform." He was to
cease and desist.

He did, but not before he spoke his mind. "I know the orders came
from Bowie Kuhn," Dock told Charlie Feeney. "I don't like it. Look
around. There are fellows who wear white shoes in practice. Some wear
jackets. Others don't wear hats. I wasn't going to say anything, but since
they seem to be aiming in my direction, I'm going to say things.

"Only a few years ago, ballplayers weren't allowed to wear mustaches
or goatees, long hair or sideburns. Now all that is okay. Baseball caught
up with the times. Now they're getting behind again. There are many
black men who wear curlers to help their hair. I didn't hear anybody put
out any orders about Joe Pepitone when he wore a hairpiece that went
down to his shoulders."

I find myself curious about the curlers, as if there were more to the
story than meets the eye. For one thing, although I spend a good deal of

time with Dock, I never see him wearing curlers around the house. I
wonder why he wore them just before games. I ask him.

"That's when I was throwing spitballs. When I had the curlers, my
hair would be straight. Down the back. On the ends would be nothing
but balls of sweat."

"Spitballs!" I say. That was one pitch Dock hadn't told me about. "So
you wore curlers for the sake of pitching?"

"Oh, yes! Just one touch at a time. It was something I experimented
with. I do well with them."

"Do you still throw them?"

"No. Every once in a while, I want to load up. I don't fool with it. I
throw it sometimes to left-handed hitters, when I get two strikes on
them, if a man's on first, to get them to hit into a double play."

"When did you start throwing spitters?"

"In nineteen seventy-two, at the end of the year. I threw it four
consecutive games. Natural sweat. When it gets wet, at the end of my
hair there are balls of water. Before every pitch, I would get it." Dock
would reach to the back of his head, and load up his fingertips. "Then I
pick up the resin like this." He looks as if he wipes his fingers on the
resin, but really he keeps his fingertips from touching the bag. Then he
appears to wipe his hand across his shirt. "I go across my chest like this. I
wipe my hat. I get my thumb dry—but I would *have* it. I threw
ninety-nine percent spitballs when I was throwing spitballs, July and
August, nineteen seventy-three."

"What makes a spitball drop? How do you throw it?"

"One of the real heavy spitball dudes broke it down for me. You drop
the ball on the mound, get a rough side on it. You get the spit or sweat or
Vaseline—whatever you use—on the balls of your fingers, and put your
fingers on the fat part of the ball, the rough side for more traction. Then
you release it from the balls of your fingers, and it'll *slow*, it's *got* to go
down, it's the only place it can *go*."

Dock admires the finesse of spitball pitchers, but gave up the spitball
because it was too much of a hassle to acquire the motions of
concealment. "These dudes have all those motions and antics. I couldn't
do it. Right away they'd know I was doing something suspicious. They
can make it do *anything*. They've proven that. They have the judge and
jury out there watching, and they make it do everything, and they don't
see them get it! I admire them."

Even though he has abandoned the spitball, Dock is still accused of throwing it. Jim Lonborg of the Phillies accuses him of it. More importantly, an umpire named Chris Pellakoudas has accused him of it.

"We don't get along too well. He tried to tell me that I throw a spitball. I *did* throw a spitball, in a game that he says I did *not* throw a spitball in. This year I threw a pitch that sank two feet, but it was just a natural sinker. He said it was a spitball. I called him every name outside of God's name that I could call him."

In August of 1973 Dock's arm went sore on him, and he had to stop throwing. For weeks he had felt the sore arm approaching. He was disturbed, but he made jokes about it: he told his teammates that it was nearly time for his vacation. When he negotiated his 1974 conntract with Joe Brown, the next winter, Brown told him that some of the players were annoyed, and that they believed that Dock was really taking a vacation. Jaking.

It wouldn't be the first time, or the last, that Dock and his teammates misunderstood each other, with some people taking wolf tickets for real, and others taking real for wolf tickets.

Six: Two Games in July, and One in August

1. *July 10*

On the tenth of July 1974, I flew to Pittsburgh to see Dock start a game against the Atlanta Braves.

After beating the Giants in Candlestick Park on June 10, Dock had beaten them again in Pittsburgh—going the distance and winning four to two. His record rose to three and five. He lost a game in Chicago. He pitched well but lost in Philadelphia: he left the game in the eighth inning, without having given up a run, but the bases were loaded, and Larry Bowa hit a double off Ramon Hernandez. He pitched to no decision against Philadelphia, lost badly to Houston. On July 10, his record stood at three wins and eight losses. The Pirates remained in last place.

Late in the afternoon, a sudden rain loosed itself on Pittsburgh. Roads flooded and cars stalled. People driving home on the freeways swerved into each other. When I took a taxi from the airport into town, an hour before the game, water had collected in low places on the road, and cars with smashed windshields were pulled up on the median.

At three Rivers Stadium the carpeting was soggy. Two drying machines padded back and forth in the outfield, removing water, groaning and heaving with the indignity of it all. The team had skipped batting practice, and I was late to talk with the ballplayers on the field. I sat back in the stands under the press boxes, hearing the typewriters in the damp night clacking like crickets.

I saw Dock in the distance warming up, down in the bullpen in foul territory next to right field. I wondered how he felt. The Pirates still looked sluggish in the field, with none of the lightness or resiliency that you can see rising like an aura from the bodies of winning ballplayers. From where I sat, I could see Dock's arm reaching back, and then snapping forward, back and then forward, as he threw to Manny Sanguillen in the bullpen. Mike Ryan was on the injured reserve list, now, with a bad back, and for a few days Sangy was the only catcher on the squad.

Dock strolled in from the bullpen, wearing his warm-up jacket, with Don Osborne and Sangy, looking solid and serious as he entered the dugout.

After "The Star-Spangled Banner," and the warm-up pitches, Ralph Garr steps into the box. I settle back for an evening of baseball.

Garr hits a ground ball, fairly sharp, just to Dock's right. Dock is leaning forward with his follow-through, but quickly jumps to his left in order to stop the ball backhanded. The ball touches his glove, and spins away. Base hit.

Craig Robinson comes to bat. Ball one. Ball two. Ball three. When Dock throws a three and one strike, the sparse crowd lifts an ironical cheer. On the next pitch, Robinson hits a soft and easy fly ball to Zisk in right field. Zisk doesn't seem to see the ball, as if he were daydreaming. Belatedly he dashes for it, and falls down as he tries to catch it at the tops of his shoes. The ball bounces past him to the wall, and Robinson pushes on to third base while Garr comes in with the first run of the game. No outs, man on third. The official scorer announces that Robinson has hit a triple.

Then Dock blows a swinging strike past Darrell Evans on a three and two count. One out.

Then Dusty Baker hits a home run over the left-field wall. Three runs in.

Rowland Office hits a line drive to Zisk. Two outs.

Dave Johnson walks on three and two.

Marty Perez singles up the middle.

When Don Osborne walks to the mound, the crowd cheers. The two men speak a few words, and Dock hands him the ball and walks through the dugout and back to the clubhouse. On July 10, he has pitched two-thirds of an inning, and given up three earned runs. His ERA for the day is 40.50.

I sit back in the damp air and listen to the typewriter frogs and the typewriter crickets above me. The Pirates lose. It's a cold night in the country of baseball.

It is next morning before Dock and I get together. By this time I've read the morning newspaper, which says among other things that Dock is worried, even *disturbed*—and that he would now be willing to go to the bullpen. I never heard Dock admit that he was worried about anything. I have *seen* him worried, but I have never heard him admit it: he doesn't like to think that way.

"Did you really say you were worried?" I ask him.

"No. *He* said I was worried. He just never before heard me say that I couldn't figure it out. He asked me what was wrong. 'Ain't nothing *wrong*. I can't figure it out.' Me throwing as I *been* throwing, and them hitting me like that. I don't *know*. My ball is moving just like it used to. Velocity is the same. Everything is the same. They're *hitting* it. They're hitting the fastball, they're hitting the curveball, the change-up. They're hitting everything. It was a fastball Dusty Baker hit out of the park. A fastball, *away*. He just reached out and got it."

"Do you think you'll go to the bullpen?"

"If they want to send me to the bullpen I can't say anything. I don't have anything to my credit."

I ask Dock about the problems he had discovered in his pitching earlier in the year, on his trip to California. Could he be turning his sinking fastball over? Could he be short-arming the curve?

"No," he says. "Sangy tell me I'm doing everything the same now. All you can do is keep firing. You're bound to win sometime." He does not sound convinced.

Going over my game notes, I mention that he almost fielded Ralph Garr's single for an easy out.

"If I hadn't touched it, it would have been a clean base hit. Mario couldn't have got it anyway." Mario Mendoza was playing shortstop.

Then I mention Robinson's triple, courtesy of Richie Zisk.

"But you can't *say* anything like that," says Dock, who never criticizes his teammates' play behind him. "He's the *right fielder*."

I suggest: "Maybe you got upset, after a squib single and a defensive triple, and that's why you threw the home-run ball to Baker."

"No," says Dock firmly. He is proud that he controls his emotions, that he won't let anything upset him and diminish his ability. "That doesn't upset me. You still have eight innings to deal with. The game is nine innings. You can't let one inning mess your concentration up. It has *never* bothered me, even when I was small, coming up through the minor leagues, anything. It never bothered me."

He repeats it so often—that he has never let himself be bothered—that I begin to doubt him. "Don't you ever get mad out there when somebody beats you?"

"I've only gotten mad twice, and that was on purpose. One time in Asheville a guy hit a home run off me in the bottom of the ninth to beat me, and I came off the mound *whistling*. The manager said I should be mad. So I kicked down the door in the clubhouse. Then he said he was going to fine me fifty dollars! So I nailed it back up."

"Was the other time when you flew to California? The time the Pirates fielded a black team?"

"That was different. No, the other time was seventy-two. Virdon took me out of the game, and he tried to tell me how to pitch. How can he tell me how to pitch, I tell him, and he can't even hit? He had no business doing that, especially on the pretense that I was throwing too many curveballs. I just tore off the water cooler, as a *message*."

"But you don't get mad at a fielder who misjudges a ball?"

"As long as you're giving a hundred percent, why should I get mad? I don't care how the breaks go."

I mentioned Ken Brett yelling "motherfucker" at the wall over Murtaugh's head. Dock feels too proud for that. "I just don't fly off like that, not on account of some *baseball* game."

Then I remember a question I have wanted to ask for some time. "You're chewing out there. I never see you chew anything except when you're pitching. What do you chew?"

"Double Bubble."

"You never blow bubbles."

"I don't have time to be blowing no bubbles."

"Do you hear the crowd when things go bad? They gave an ironic cheer when you threw a strike, and they cheered when Osborne came out."

"Not really. Oh, you hear it when you're taken out. You hear that. They used to *boo* me here. For a couple of years they used to boo me all the time, even when I was winning, because of the newspaper articles.

Then it died down, the last couple of years. You hear it and you don't hear it."

"What did you say on the mound with Ozzie?"

"Sangy said, 'Dock, you throwing good.' And he was telling Ozzie I was throwing good. I said to Ozzie, 'Ozzie, *what* are you doing *here?*' He says, 'Giving the guy a chance to warm up.' '*What* do you *mean?*' He says, 'Well, we're going to take you out.' I say, 'Here,' and give him the baseball, and keep on going. I'm not going to stay out there and talk."

2. *The Miseries of Losing*

In Los Angeles, the next morning, Big Daddy was reading the *Los Angeles Times* at the fire station and getting mad. Mr. Brewer was shaking his head and thinking about Dock short-arming the curve. Al Rambo, Ray Jones, Vaughn Chapel, Johnny Wags, Jimmy Grant, Rudy-poo, his sisters Elizabeth and Sandra—well, many of Dock's old friends and family were speculating on what was bugging Nut or Junior.

"When I go to work at the fire station each day," Big Daddy told me when I talked with him, "the first thing I do is turn to the sports page and see if Nut pitched. When he loses I sit there cussing him out. 'Son of a bitch, he ain't been doing his Goddamned job. He's fucking around in the streets!' Or I'm listening to Scully on the radio—the Dodger game—trying to check Pittsburgh out. 'Ellis pitching.' I'm not listening to the Dodgers. I'm just waiting for Scully to give the Pittsburgh score."

Some don't think he really works at it. One old friend told me, "To this day, he's not dedicated to the game. He has the potential to be a twenty-game winner every year, if he applied himself. He could do *with* baseball, or he could do *without* baseball. He's not money-struck. He just takes things *easily.* When he leaves the job he leaves the job. Oh, I don't see him win nineteen games bullshitting, but he could win, shit, twenty-five games if he applied himself."

Others look around for reasons: "It's personal problems. He's confided in me about a few of them. Like his wife. Right now that's what's bothering him. He might not show it but I know it. Once you love a woman like he really loved his wife, once your first love goes apart—it's hard to just wipe it out of your life. The furnace is still there, I believe it.

And he *cares* about his daughter. That bugs him. He can't see his daughter when he wants to see her."

In Pittsburgh when people talk about what's wrong with the Pirates in general—the fans, the ballplayers, the gaggle of associates and hangers-on close to the team—they come up with ideas by the dozen: the Pirates never got over Clemente's death; Murtaugh's too old; they're fat with winning; they're still depressed to have been beaten by the Mets last year; Joe Brown traded away too much, he never should have let Dave Cash go.

Dock himself says, on occasion, "They fucked up when they made all those trades. Joe Brown has a way of saying the Pirates are a family. Well, if we are a family, why trade away your brothers? We sent Cash away. We got rid of Briles. He was an orphan and we brought him in. He wasn't one of the original crew, but he fitted in. He wasn't *the* family man, but he *fitted* in."

The games have been uniformly depressing. One evening Reuss gives up three runs in the first inning, yet he stays in the game. (Dock thinks: why him and not me?) Then Mario fails to cover second base. An inning later, Mario cuts off a ball from the outfield and throws it to third, which is just where he should throw it, but Hebner has forgotten to be there. In another game, Larry Demery warms up throwing beautiful slow curves, and in the game he throws nothing but heat. Boom. Boom.

Relaxing after the game that Demery lost, Dock looks to the good side of losing, the experience a young player needs.

"He'll think about it now," Dock says. "When I came to my first major league spring training, they always told me to throw three and two curveballs, no matter what. From nineteen sixty-five on, I was three and two curve every time. When I got here I had confidence. One day I threw a three and two *change-up*, bases loaded. Two outs. Before the ball even got to the plate, he threw the bat and helmet down. He was looking for *anything* but a change. It was a strike; I just guided it across the plate, not trying to fool him with it. Change-ups you're supposed to throw more or less in the dirt, make them just barely get there. This one, I just *guided* it across the plate."

This is the same change-up that the *Baseball Digest* wrote about, quoting Willie Stargell: "We were in San Diego. The bases are loaded in the bottom of the ninth and we're up by a run. Leron Lee was up and the count went to three and two. Dock throws him the dannedest change-up you ever saw. On three and two, with two outs and the bases full, for cryin' out loud. Lee watches it for strike three. I think it ruined him. He was never the same after that—I mean that was a real chickenshit pitch to throw to a rookie."

Depression affects everyone. The team had never played so badly. They couldn't get used to it. "That's why they are hollering and screaming now. They are dissatisfied with the way things are going. They never had that feeling of losing." Dock is speaking of the younger generation. "I've been with the Pirates when they was losing, but *they've* all been winning, in the minor leagues and everywhere. I've seen this road before."

"Do the players start getting on each other?"

"No squabbling Pirates, no. That's one thing we don't do. We don't say anything we don't always say. We get on each other whether we're winning or losing. We talk about each other *bad.*"

As the morning drags on, the day after Dock's two-thirds of an inning against Atlanta, the air gets heavier and heavier.

"Like I told Rooker," Dock says to me, "I said, 'Man, I don't have no desire to play.' That's the first time I ever *talked* like that."

"Can you say why you don't? I mean, is it just because of losing?"

"This is what Rooker and I were talking about. We talk a lot. It boiled down to one thing. We came to the conclusion that we just had to bust our ass, keep going at them.

"I don't know what's wrong. I'm fighting the lack of desire, this year. Plus I'm not pitching well."

This is the first time that Dock has said that he was not pitching well. "Is it the lack of desire that makes you not pitch well?"

"That's what I don't want to believe! I don't want to believe that. I'm not that type person. That's giving up. I don't want to think like that. They'll tell you I'm not that type person! Nothing bothers me on the field!"

Right now, Dock has to force himself to run between starts.

"And Tony will tell you, when they're worried about guys not getting in shape, my name never comes up. Because I love to run. Even one day this year, about a month ago, I woke up feeling *good*—and I came to the ball park and I told everybody I had *pennant fever.* They had to stop me from running. Pitching coach says, 'You been out there running for an hour and twenty minutes. Why don't you stop?' I say, 'No. I feel too good to stop running.'

"And then, all of a sudden, I lost it. Pennant fever. I got *down.*"

"Is there much of a problem with people keeping in shape now? A lot of people overeat when they're low."

"That's another thing. They don't let us have food after the game anymore. Some of the ballplayers, they blow up so fast. One guy is overweight now but he won't let nobody see him get on the scale." Then we start talking about Willie Stargell's weight. Willie balloons up, over the winter, and struggles in Florida to take it off, running in a rubber suit, doing extra laps. Now he looks in good shape, but when he retires from baseball he will become a very large man. Dock laughs to remember the party at Willie's house last week: "Before I went over to his house, I saw Calvin Hill and Fuqua in a bar. I told them to come over. He was telling them how to lose weight: 'Drink plenty of *wine.*'"

But the laughter is brief, and the bewilderment returns, the unappeasable dis-ease. "It's weird, it's *weird,*" Dock says. "I'm into something I've never been into before. The *rut.*"

The rut for Dock is despair or *accidia,* maybe intensified by the rumors that he will be traded, and exchange the new Pirates for a team of newer strangers. "I keep telling myself that a change would be cool, but I don't want the change. I don't want to change." Dock shakes his head as if he were avoiding a fly. "I feel like the desire, the motivation is *there,* but how can I grasp it, how can I say, 'Let's *go.*' It's getting worse each day. I feel my hamstring muscles tightening. I don't even want to run. I don't want to do anything.

"Being traded is in the back of my head, but I don't want to hear it. It keeps coming out when I talk with you, though. I don't have anybody to talk to about it. I can't do anything about it."

3. *Another Night in July*

On July 14, in the second game of their doubleheader with the Reds, the Pirates' season turned around. Bruce Kison hit some batters, Pirates and Reds encountered each other in the squabble described earlier, and the Pirates won the ball game.

From that day forward, the 1974 Pirates moved rapidly out of last place until they clinched their division with one day left in the regular season. The second half of 1974 was the mirror image of the first half. It fell to Dock to pitch the first game after Kison's Sunday outing.

Houston comes to town on Monday, July 15, bringing a streak of six straight wins. On the infield, the Astros have two games of pepper going, near their own dugout—black pepper and white pepper. There is no BP, and little infield. Tonight the crowd drifts in early, to watch the annual game between the Pirate players and their children.

Mean Mary Jean is in town tonight, having made television commercials all day with Pirate announcer Bob Prince, and she bounces around the infield, kneeling to smile falsely at small children, and her charm is so aggressive that, if translated into Marines, it could take Moscow in twenty minutes. Her deliberate cuteness for a time rubs off on the kids' game, and makes it look shabby. Then Mean Mary Jean retires from the scene, and in a while you begin to realize that the children are real children, and not just short, hoked-up adults.

They are all in uniform, from toddlers who can barely stand to nine-year-olds feeling a little *mature* for this undertaking. Everybody wears the old-fashioned clothes of baseball, carries a bat and a glove, saunters to the plate. In the country of baseball the natives perform a ritual of initiation.

Young Wilver Stargell, number eight, bats left like his daddy; Sangy, Junior, squats for a moment behind the plate; fathers are sons, and sons are fathers, for in this game the three-year-old son may hit the ball only two feet, but—because of the total, insane, dreamlike ineptitude of the fathers—he has hit a home run.

Manny Sanguillen himself has become a pitcher, a *gentle* pitcher, the pitcher of dreams, who underhands a big soft white rubber ball four feet up to home plate. He tries to guess where the bat may be, in order to hit it. Gene Clines starts at third base, Kirkpatrick at shortstop (because neither of the Pirate shortstops has children), Stargell at first, and Patterson catches. If a fielder throws a ball to first, Willie Stargell will drop it.

Young Sangy, after hitting the ball, runs directly to second, seeing no point in going by way of first. Kelly Stargell, another southpaw, hits and Sangy, Junior, scores. Young Wilver hits a line drive that almost reaches the pitcher's mound and drops in for a triple. Paul Popovich, Junior, maybe eighteen months old, touches the ball—Sangy will throw it *until* his bat touches the ball—and comes around to score. Bob Robertson's daughter, Cynthia Giusti—they all score. John Morlan's daughter, when she hits the ball, races like crazy down the third-base line, and falls over third base. Stephanie Rooker hits a home run.

Dock does not appear on the field until after the fathers-children game is done. Shangalesa starred, he tells me, in the 1972 game. "She *got down.*" Instead, Dock plays War in the clubhouse with some of the older children, like Ed Kirkpatrick's sons, too old to hack around with the little kids on the field.

As the game starts, I think that Dock looks grim. Dock pitches to Greg Gross, and on a one and two pitch, Gross singles between short and second. I sink in my seat, convinced that tonight will repeat the fiasco five days back. Then Roger Metzger, with Houston playing hit and run, dribbles an easy comebacker to Dock. One out. Bob Watson hits the first pitch for a double, and scores a run. One out, two hits, one run.

Then Lee May pops to center field and Milt May pops to Sangy.

The Pirates do nothing in their half of the first, and Dock gets Houston out in order at the top of the second. Doug Rader hits a curveball for a pop fly, Bob Gallagher strikes out, and Tommy Helms hits a soft liner to Rennie Stennett at second base.

In the bottom of the second the Pirates get two hits and no runs. They still trail one to nothing.

The Houston pitcher Dave Roberts leads off in the top of the third. He hits an ordinary fly ball to Richie Zisk in right field, who catches it, and then drops it for a two-base error.

It is at moments like this that I am most amazed at the professional athlete. At this moment, even if I possessed his bodily attributes, I would throw my racket in the air, break my putter, chew on the referee's ear, and enlist in the Foreign Legion. But no one acts like this if he wants to play grown-up ball. And this temperament is not genetic but learned. The best athlete is the person who learns not to be deterred from his performance by emotions of disappointment, disgust, or dismay.

Greg Gross is up, who singled to start the game. He flies out to Richie Zisk, who catches it securely. Then Roger Metzger, working the count to three and two, singles; but it is a shallow single, and the base runner is a pitcher, and stays at third. Bob Watson, Dock's "homeboy" who is best hitter on the Astros, and who hit a double off Dock in the first inning, grounds into a double play, and Dock is out of trouble.

As the inning ends, we hear from the loudspeaker that the official scorer has changed Zisk's two-base error into a double for Dave Roberts. Bob Smizik is official scorer.

In the third inning the Pirates go down in order. Lee May grounds out to Frank Taveras to begin the fourth, Taveras moving fast and covering a wide territory. Milt May is at bat again. The first pitch is a ball inside, and then Dock throws two sinking fastballs for strikes. These balls *get down*. Another fastball moves Milt May back; he is set up. The fifth pitch is a beautiful change-up, the strikeout pitch, which floats like a Ping-Pong ball—only it's outside by half an inch. Then the fastball rides too high and Milt May has the first Houston walk.

Doug Rader comes up and Dock throws strikes. At one and two, Rader keeps fouling pitches off. Finally he gets too big a piece, and fouls out to third base. Bob Gallagher grounds out to Taveras, who throws cleanly. I sense *energy* when the team runs off the field.

The Pirates score twice in the fourth and go ahead. In the fifth, Dock stays ahead of everybody, and after an infield hit, Taveras starts a fine double play to end the inning. In the sixth inning, Metzger flies out, Watson grounds out, and Lee May hits a pop fly. Dock looks stronger and stronger. He is not overpowering—he only strikes out four batters in the whole game—but he stays ahead of the batters, and he outthinks them. Pop flies and ground balls, nothing hit hard.

In the seventh, Milt May hits a fly ball which drops in front of Richie Zisk. Dock strikes out Doug Rader in classic fashion: a curveball which Rader fouls; a jammed fastball, fouled again; a fastball wasted outside; then a fastball moving in jams Rader again, and he swings and misses.

Gallagher fouls to Hebner, and Helms takes a called third strike on a fastball. The pitch grazes the outside corner with the delicacy of lovers just touching.

In the eighth inning, Cesar Cedeno leads off by pinch-hitting for Dave Roberts, who has pitched well. Cedeno has been hurt. For this exemplary batter, Dock seems to reach back. He throws a high hard one for a swinging strike. He throws the same pitch again, even harder, and Cedeno swings again and misses again. It is the hardest Dock has thrown all day. Cedeno settles down to foul off the good pitches. Dock wastes one. Another foul or two. Dock's curve stays inside, and the count goes to two and two. Then Dock reaches back for it, and Cedeno swings and misses a third piece of smoke.

Greg Gross sends a slow grounder to Taveras, who charges hard and throws hard across his body to catch him at first base. Roger Metzger hits a wrong field single, and Bob Watson lofts a long high foul which Zisk catches in right field.

In the ninth, Dock starts Lee May with three balls in a row. Then he throws a strike, then another strike, a foul ball—and Lee May hits the ball hard, on the hard surface of the green rug, to Taveras' left. Taveras runs, backhands the ball, straightens, and throws him out. Johnny Edwards, taking over for Milt May as catcher, hits a slow grounder toward first base which hits the zipper and bounces past Kirpatrick. Base hit. Doug Rader and Cliff Johnson, pinch-hitting, both pop out to left field.

The Pirates win, three to one, in two hours and ten minutes, at Three Rivers Stadium, on July 15, 1974, with nine thousand one hundred and twenty-one paid customers in attendance. Winning pitcher, Dock Ellis.

4. The Pleasures of Winning

After the game I go down to the clubhouse. Dock sits in front of his locker, half undressed, while Tony wraps an ice bag around his right elbow. Eight or nine reporters make a semicircle around him, mostly young guys from the suburban papers. Why did he pitch better today? Does he think he's over the hump? Are the Pirates going to win now? He answers laconically, and I can see in his quick eyes that he keeps himself alert and suspicious. After a while I am bored with predictable questions and cautious answers. I go back to the Hilton, order some mixers, and wait for Dock to drop by.

He walks in, splendid in gold, with a fishnet T-shirt. He is high on winning. "Man, we gonna *move*. If I start winning, we gonna *go* somewhere."

We make screwdrivers, relax, and go over the game. I tell him that when Zisk dropped the ball in the first inning, I thought I was watching a rerun. What do you tell yourself, I ask him, when something like that happens?

"Keep *firing!* But sometimes, you try to put too much on the ball, and the ball won't do *anything*."

I tell him, "I thought you got stronger later in the game."

"I just went to the fastball more, that's all. I hung a lot of curveballs, early. I had better stuff when I got knocked out last Wednesday."

"But today you had your location more?" I ask.

Jane Kenyon

Jane Kenyon

Chet Brewer at Dodger Stadium.

The Dockmobile.

With Paula and Shangalesa at the annual fathers-children game in Pittsburgh, 1970.   *Les Banos*

With Shangalesa in 1970.

With Eric, outside Three Rivers Stadium.

With Roberto Clemente before the World Series in 1971. *William Bauknight*

Testifying before the Senate on sickle-cell anemia.

Dock weeps at the presentation from "the Grass Roots People," in Pittsburgh, 1971.

Dock works out in a St. Louis Cardinal uniform at Busch Memorial Stadium in St. Louis.

Dock and his mother.   *Jane Kenyon*

The Ellis house, in the Neighborhood.   *Jane Kenyon*

Author and subject. *Jane Kenyon*

Dock and Renee, 1975, during the suspension. *Jane Kenyon*

"Not really." Dock won't give an inch, about being lifted in the first inning last Wednesday. "I had better *stuff* last Wednesday. If I had got out of the inning, it would have been a different story."

Now the confidence is real. It is not assumed because he wants to think that way.

I tell him he really threw hard when Cedeno pinch-hit.

"Well, I had to. He has the capability of hitting the ball *out*. He was cold. When you come off the bench, you can't hit the gas."

We talk about Taveras, his range and precision tonight at shortstop. I ask Dock what he said to Taveras at the end of the game.

"Way-to-*get-down!*"

In the sixth inning, Dock appeared to shake off a sign from Sangy, with Lee May at bat. Dock has told me that it's usually a decoy, when he shakes off a sign. I ask him if it was real this time.

"No. That was just a thing I was doing go get him to think he was getting the fastball. He *knows* I ain't going to throw him anything but curves. Now he got to think."

I know that Dock and Lee May are friends. I wonder how he does, pitching to his friends.

"Lee May only hurt me once. That was in nineteen seventy, in the play-offs, when he hit a hooking shot to left field. In the dugout, Manny was telling me to throw him the same curve tonight. I said, 'Uh-*uh*.' "

Dock doesn't know how many strikeouts he had. Using my notes, we go over the Ks. He is proudest of how he struck out Doug Rader.

"Rader is a guess hitter. If you stay one step ahead of him, you can get him. If he has men on base, though, forget it—they are coming home, either on a home run or on something deep. That's the way he is. I hate to see him with men on base."

I tell Dock that the team felt vigorous to me tonight as I overheard their chatter, as I saw them practice, as I watched them play.

Dock shakes his head in agreement.

"Like I told you," he says, "I almost lost that desire."

"You seemed to have it tonight."

"As the game progressed. If they'd messed up a couple more balls—and I don't talk like that! I'm starting to talk more and more like that! I don't dig that!"

"Do you pitch differently, depending on who's playing where?"

"Maybe subconsciously I do."

Then I ask him something about his own defense. "Do a lot of people steal on you?"

"Almost at *will*," says Dock. "At *random*. Oh, I used to have a hell of a move, in the minor leagues. That's when I kicked high, higher than Marichal, and then I could swivel my leg and come down toward first. Then they changed my motion."

"Do the hitters act different at the plate, depending on how you've been doing?"

"They're taking more pitches now. The word is out that I don't have my control. That I can't get the corners and have to come up with fat ones."

"When you warm up at the start of an inning, do you throw as hard as you can?"

"I cut loose with at least two pitches."

"What kind of pitches?"

"It depends on who's coming up. Or it might be the second or the third batter I'm thinking about. Or the first."

"Do you get premonitions before you pitch? When you're warming up, do you know whether you have it or not?"

"No. Because you never know until you get out there and fire. You can be in the bullpen and say, 'Oh, no, I don't have *anything* today,' and you can go out there and give up, say, two or three hits. Then some days, in the bullpen, you say, 'Oh, they can't touch me today,' and you might not go two or three innings. You never know. Even when Ricketts was here, I'd be warming up with Ricketts, and he'd say, 'Oh, you'd better watch your head, buddy. Because you don't have shit.' Times when he done that to me, I'd go out there and really pitch. And he'd say, 'Oh, you got away with murder.' "

"Was he psyching you?"

"No. Ricketts tells you like it is."

We pour some more vodka, and Tom Reich comes by, and we go over the game again, and the night waxes onward, rich with the pleasures of winning.

5. *The Second Season*

Dock won eight straight games, and between July 15 and September 6 his record climbed from three and eight to twelve and nine. The only ball game he lost, the rest of the year, was a game against the Dodgers in Los Angeles; and he had always had trouble pitching before the home folks.

On July 21, he beat Atlanta, the team that had knocked him out of the box in the first inning a week before. "I was doing the same things," he told me, "except they were hitting it *at* somebody. In the first inning, Evans hit a home run. It crossed my mind, 'Here we go again.' I didn't have much. I was lucky." On July 26 he shut out Montreal. "At Montreal I was throwing extremely hard. It was moving. I had a hard breaking ball. I *always* throw hard in Montreal. I was telling you about Montreal's high mound. It's even higher now. I wish I could have pitched all three games there."

Then the Pirates—now only three and a half games out of first; seven games behind on July 15—went into New York to play the Mets. The second game, July 31, Dock started against Tom Seaver. "I was selling wolf tickets on the way to the ball park, telling them I was going to *pull* Seaver." Dock did get two hits, though he didn't pull the ball. "Basically, that was to let our team know that he didn't have his good fastball. Not to be looking for it. When he would *show* a good fastball, it would hurt him if he threw it hard. He can't throw the fastball like he used to. I was trying to get a message through. They'll be thinking here *I* am saying I can pull him, what will *they* do to him? They did it to him too."

Dock had to leave the New York game in the eighth inning, exhausted from base running, and the Pirates won eight to three. I asked him if he didn't feel especially confident, pitching against the Mets.

The pitch and roll of winning comes into his voice. "I feel confident pitching against all teams," he says. Then, with the irony that comes to you by the age of twenty-nine: "It's just that I don't beat them all."

Dock runs the bases well. Pirate managers have often used him as a pinch runner. Dick Simpson, who used to play for the California Angels, taught him how to run the bases, when they both played for Mr. Brewer. "I was never *fast*. He taught me how to utilize my legs, as far as gaining momentum, how to *dig*."

Now when he pitches he tries not to run too hard, for fear it will tire him out, as it did in the game with the Mets. "I used to *run*," he says. "When I'd be running, I'd be hatting up. Hat would go off, and I'm gone. Full blast. Now I'll do it up until about the fifth inning."

Tom Reich disapproves of Dock—or any other rotation pitcher—

acting as pinch runner, except in an emergency. Suppose he got hurt, and couldn't pitch?

"But I don't get hurt," Dock argues.

Tom says it could happen to anybody. If he tried to break up a double play, the infielder could come down on top of him and mess up his leg.

"Yes," says Dock, "but he ain't going to have no stomach."

On August 11, Dock beat San Diego. On August 16, he beat Los Angeles in Pittsburgh. On August 21 he beat San Francisco in San Francisco.

"Oh, I was *sick*." He had been troubled with a cold the whole month of August, and had missed a start between the Mets and San Diego. By the end of the month the cold was coming back. "Sangy got mad at me in Frisco, because I was starting to let down. It was nine to two"—the Pirates finally won the game thirteen to two—"and they knew I was sick, and they were supposed to take me out in the fifth or sixth inning. Hey, man, I weighed a hundred and eighty-three pounds when I came to the ball park. I was sick! And it was cold up there. That hurts my arm! So I got pissed off in the seventh inning and started *firing*."

After the series with San Francisco, the Pirates dropped down the coast to Los Angeles. There, I asked him, "Do you feel like you're *in* luck now, as you were *out* of luck before?"

"That's *all*," he said. "I had a bad day in Frisco, day before yesterday. Oh, man! They were hitting *rockets* all over the ball park. Right *at* people. Plus we were *hitting*. The sportswriters, they tried to get me to say I'm doing something different, but, hey, man, I'm doing the same thing."

"Is your location the same? How come you're not throwing home-run balls the way you were?"

Dock speculates that there might be *one* difference, to explain why a winning feeling leads to winning pitching. "When you're losing," he says, "everybody tries to do it by *themselves*."

Today the Pirates are in first place.

6. *Question Period*

For a day or two, before Dock pitches again, we talk and talk and talk.

I have collected a miscellany of topics to ask about—different mounds in different parks, other pitchers, the care of the arm—and this seems like a good time to go over them.

"You like the mound at Montreal, you said. What about others?"

"Montreal and Houston. *High mounds*. You can come *down* off them. Dodger Stadium too—Koufax could kick high and come down."

Like most pitchers and most fans, but unlike ground-ball hitters, Dock dislikes the new parks and the plastic grass. He likes Dodger Stadium because it has grass. "And Forbes Field"—the crazy old Pittsburgh stadium, before they moved to Three Rivers in 1970, which tucked itself into a corner near the University of Pittsburgh—"was a pitcher's paradise. Four hundred and fifty-seven feet to center field. Not many home runs were going to be hit there, unless a left-hander pulled it down the line. But I favored Forbes Field over Three Rivers because of the natural turf, grass. Me being a sinker-ball pitcher. When Maury Wills and Matty Alou were with the Pirates, they had that infield around home plate like *cee*-ment, because they used to hit the ball into the ground to get high hoppers. So me being a sinker-ball pitcher they got hits off me. But when Maury left, they changed the infield to regular dirt. Clay all round home plate. But you get to Three Rivers and the ball is *skipping* through the infield, *jumping*. Plus, from the fans point of view, the fans are not even close to the ballplayers, like they used to be in the old parks. You need binoculars now to see the field."

"What's the park you'd rather go to, of all parks?"

"Montreal. It's the women. It's God gift to earth. I wish I was the color of this thing right here"—Dock slaps the leather cover on the tape recorder, a flat black—"and then go to Montreal." Dock giggles, a sound I'm not used to. "That's a beautiful town. The people are so *understanding* there. For a while there, I thought the Montreal ball club was sending women around, to get the ballplayers tired out. I'm serious. Everyone I talk to, he says, 'You don't get nothing like this in those other cities.'

"The cities are different. But now—" He gets into something else, talking about how the Mets fans bombarded Pete Rose in the outfield last year, and how the Cincinnati wives needed help to get out of the park unharmed. "Willie just told me that's why we got to leave Dodger Stadium on a bus." After they shower and dress, the visiting players used to stroll across the outfield to the parking lot; now their team bus comes right to the dugout, so that they won't be exposed to the violence of lingering fans. "He said that's because of Pete. That doesn't make any sense. That's why some ballplayers don't sign autographs now. They curse a fan out. I noticed Pete running into the dugout one night, and I saw a little kid throw something at him. That doesn't make any sense. That's like being a *gladiator*."

Odd notes.

"Sometimes you throw a ball out when you haven't even pitched with it. Why?"

"*Fat* balls. I got stubby little hands. Some balls are *fatter* than others. I say, 'Here, take this ball back!' "

"Who are the best hitters in the league?"

"I already told you who's the best hitter in baseball. Pete Rose. He can hit. He hits the ball. Contact. Brains have a lot to do with it. He's not a guess hitter. *Reactions!*"

"What do you throw him?"

"Nothing but fastballs. I threw the last change-up to him in Crosley Field. Double. That's when I first came into the league."

"Do other Pirate pitchers pitch him the same way?"

"Well, some of them are left-handers." Dock laughs. "Some of them have sliders. Some throw offspeed stuff. I throw him nothing but fastballs."

"Do some hitters give you special trouble?"

"No one hits me with consistency, and I don't get anyone out with consistency. A swinging bat is a dangerous bat."

"Do you remember many single pitches which you have thrown? I mean particular pitches, like the one you told me about that ended the no-hitter, and like that famous change-up to Leron Lee."

"Yeah. I remember the fastball I threw to Spiezio in the no-hitter. It slid *that* much." Dock's hands are fourteen inches apart. "I remember the first time I threw a strike to a left-hander *inside*. It was to Marshall, with the Mets. I remember throwing spitballs against Philadelphia. I remember seeing spit come off the ball. I remember throwing spitballs in L. A. and Willie Crawford got three base hits. I threw my home boy a spitball, he hit a good pitch. But I got Willie Davis out, who I really wanted to keep off the bases. I remember in Forbes Field, throwing spitballs at Ozzie Virgil, who was going *crazy* trying to tell the umpire I was throwing spitballs. *He's* the one who gave me the *idea*, playing around one year down in the Dominican Republic."

"How does the arm feel, right after pitching?"

"Nothing. I don't feel anything until two days after."

"What about the leg?"

"That'll be sore the next day."

I ask Dock where the arm will hurt, when it hurts, and he points to the muscles in his chest near the collarbone, and in the back under the shoulder blade. "That's from throwing the curveball. And the forearm. Tony will rub the forearm tomorrow."

"Does Tony always put that ice bag on your elbow?"

"Three-quarters of the games, I ask for it. The arm is tired when I finish strong. It's like hanging, barely hanging. They tell me you have small blood vessels in your arm and you break them, you tear them when you throw. The ice clots them and stops them from hemorrhaging. The ice clots them and helps you come back next time."

"What do you do for your arm between starts?"

"After two days you throw. Sometimes between starts I play with the iron ball, walk around holding it, swinging it. Avoid cold air, and throwing unnecessarily." Driving in the car, Dock never wants the air conditioning on, no matter how noxious the freeway air.

"Do you think about your arm all the time?"

"Ever since I was fourteen."

"How much do you throw, when you throw in between starts?"

"Four or five minutes. Just enough to loosen the body. Sometimes you might cut loose accidentally. That's when you're *loose*, so you stop. You don't want to throw hard."

"Do you ever have blisters?" Bruce Kison has to leave a game, from time to time, when a blister pops up on his middle finger.

"Oh, yeah. I used to get the same thing. Feel my finger. Callus on it. See that one too?"

"Do you lose the callus in the off-season?"

"It's like a baby's bootie in the winter. In the spring I have to build it up again. That's when I use the pine tar. I rub the finger in resin to make it hard. The resin is like sand, and it'll make it rough. If you don't rub it it'll never get tough."

I ask Dock about his hitting, and he remembers again how he used to "hit like Clemente" in the Little League, but then was hit on the elbow and became afraid of the ball. Still, he loves to take his turn at the plate, and scorns the idea of the designated hitter. "I dig the challenge!"

I decide to draw him out on his hitting. "Pete Rose was telling me the other day what a good hitter you are." Rose told me how much Dock had improved, how he could bunt now. I think that Dock will say that Pete was conning him.

Dock beams. "That's all I want to hear."

"Do you believe it, when Pete Rose says it?"

"Why don't believe it? I know I'm a good hitter. I'm a Punch and Judy hitter, but I'm a good hitter. I don't hit for power. I even got a hit left-handed the other day. *Pulled* the ball! In San Francisco, he threw me a fastball, a *blazing* fastball. I told the catcher, 'Goddamn, he's really bringing it!' Then he threw me a curveball and I half swung at it. Then I saw him grip the ball and I see he's going to throw me another curveball. I give him my Willie Stargell windup"—Dock stands, and mimes Stargell's left-handed stance, wheeling the bat forward toward the pitcher—"and I swing down like Willie on a ball—base hit!"

"Have you hit any home runs in the major leagues?"

"None. Except in spring training. Billy Champion. I hummed him out. Three and two slider. It took him deep to right field in Bradenton. You know the three-hundred-and-seventy-three mark? Took him over the wall! Three-run home run!"

Talking with Manny Sanguillen, I mention Dock's hitting. Manny grins. "I work with Dock in the Dominican Republic. Dock he no used to hit. He no used to hit the ball. They used to throw him three strikes, right in the middle, and Dock missed it. I teach him how to hit. From then he come in to be *fair* hitter."

I ask Dock, "Are pitchers different from other ballplayers?" I think they are. I tell him, that pitchers seem wittier, more outrageous, and probably more intelligent.

"Some hitters," Dock says, "may have different opinions. And they've got batting averages to prove it."

I had always assumed that pitchers would be the best athletes on the team, but it isn't necessarily so. Some batters assert that pitchers are people with one exaggerated talent, as weird and effective as a giraffe's neck. Pete Rose seems to think that pitchers are weird. "Their environment is different," he told me. "They work once every four or five days. They come to the ball park knowing they're not going to play. They get more sleep the night before they're going to pitch. They probably eat lighter on a pitching day. They do certain repertoires, every day they're going to pitch. They got to put this sock on this way— things like that. Especially if they are on a winning streak. They might *never* change. Pitchers are a different breed, let's face it."

I ask Dock, "Doesn't the pitcher deal with challenges more than hitters do?"

"Well," says Dock, "it's only every four or five days. The hitter, he's out there every day." But he really wants to agree with my assumptions. "The game revolves around *us*," he says. "Pitchers. The game doesn't start until we throw the ball. We're in control."

"What kind of person should you be, to be a pitcher?"

"You got to be *mean*," Dock laughs. "Egotistical! Arrogant! You— King for a Night!"

7. *The Great Pitchers*

Talking about the race with the Mets in '72, Dock mentioned a game Blass started against Tom Seaver. "Oh, I wish I could have pitched that game!" Dock says. "Nancy was so *cocky*." Dock has nicknames for everybody. "She *psyched* all the ballplayers, going over to them before the game, and telling them it was in the bag. I like to pitch against Nancy!"

"Why?"

"*Challenge*. I hook up with her all the time. I *ask* to hook up with her. I always say I get more money beating the best. One year I beat Fergie four times. I beat Gibson three times. Seaver beat me twice but I beat him once. Holtzman once. I was beating the big pitchers."

"Tell me about them. Tell me about Fergie Jenkins for instance."

"He's over in the Little League now," Dock's affectionate name for the American League. "He's thrown a lot of innings for a lot of years. They caught up with him over here. He didn't have a blazing fastball. He never threw strikes—or he only threw strikes when he had to. The ball was so close to being a strike you had to swing at it. And he had the ability to keep the ball low, which comes from pitching in that ball park, in Chicago. When the pitchers throw strikes there, they get killed. Now in Texas, he's gonna win twenty games." (He did, one year; then he didn't; in 1976 he went to Boston.)

"Who are the best pitchers you've ever seen?"

"Oh, Nancy. Nancy is the best motherfucking pitcher I've seen in my life. She can reach back and bring it. Well, Koufax, Gibson, Marichal. They dould *deal*. They could *get down*. They could *do* the *do*.

"I put Nancy and Gibson in the same character, because they are, they were the *overpowering* pitchers. They could blow the fastball by anyone. They didn't *need* finesse. Of course there's nothing wrong with having a couple of more pitches. Seaver throws a hard fastball, a hard slider, no change-up. What he calls a curveball is what I would call a change-up. Just something that takes longer to break.

"Now, he's thrown so many fastballs so many years—I would say six or seven years, with consistency, three hundred innings—no man's arm can take that. It's not his arm, it's his hip. When he's throwing overhand and he drop down, all that weight goes on his hip. He can still rear back and throw, but it hurts his hip." In 1975, Seaver's hip improved, and he pitched with his old skill.

"He's one of the best pitchers to come around, but he's with the wrong team. I call him Nancy. What the hell. He's never bullshitted me. To me he's a good dude, a hell of a dude. We used to play against him when he was at USC. Mr. Brewer will tell you that. We used to stroke him for days, yes, buddy. That was before he learned how to bring it.

"The only one I know that has thrown the hard fastball longer is Bob Gibson, and he's gone now. Age caught up with him. He still threw that ball hard, up until last year. Gibson, he's the guy I told you I used to ask the questions about pitching. He says, 'You can do better than I can, because you got a change-up and a curveball.' Gibson, the best he had was a rising fastball and a hard slider. Every once in a while he'd take something off the slider, and there'd be a little curve—just like Seaver.

"Now they are both throwing different. They are throwing sinkers. They're trying to ride the ball away from the left-hander. They're trying to throw slow curves, change-ups. Gibson even comes from the side sometimes with a curveball. It comes from throwing the ball so hard, so long.

"You take a guy like Marichal, now Marichal, he threw hard, but he threw from so many different positions. Plus he could change speeds in all these positions, and he had pinpoint control. Same with any major league pitcher, he's got to have control to get here anyway. But Marichal was *pinpoint* control. He could put the ball *anywhere* he wanted to put it, and he made it do anything. Screwballs, sinker balls, anything. He probably threw some spitballs.

"Koufax was another. He was the most overpowering pitcher of them all, because he had the big curveball too. The only thing that hurt him was the circulation in his fingers. If he'd kept on being a pitcher, he would have become a junky, the way they were shooting that stuff in his arm. He may have *felt* his arm only twelve to sixteen hours out of four days before he pitched. That's the only time he *felt* his arm, when he pitched. The rest of the time they had that stuff in it. He used to use that—what do they call it?—analgesic balm. I call it atomic balm. Hot ointment. They put it on his arm, to help circulation.

"But he had the big curveball, and the hard, hard fastball, and he gave you the same motion. When he went out, he still had the same things. It's just that he had no feelings in his fingers."

When Dock talks about the great pitchers, he talks about pain, aging, and loss.

"If you had to pick one of them, on his best day, as the best pitcher of all, which one would you pick?"

Dock looks melancholy. Then he recovers his old haughty face: "Dock Ellis."

8. *Homeboys*

At Naomi Ellis Craven's Dock eats nine super tacos at one sitting, and a quart of milk. At Elizabeth's house, Dock eats only eight. ("They were bigger," he apologizes.) Sandra and her husband Clifton and their children come over to both houses. Elizabeth's children—in and out—climb over Dock when he sits still long enough. And Shangalesa runs back and forth—affectionate, strong, athletic, and so active that she gives you a glimpse of the young Dock. Paula—beautiful, reserved—delivers Shangalesa and sits at the edge of the party, leaves, then returns to pick her up again.

Elizabeth and Sandra both had executive jobs before they quit to have children. Dock is proud of them, teases them, and they obviously return the affection. Both of them share the energy and the intelligence, and lack only a little of the dash that their brother wears like a crown.

When Dock pitches in Los Angeles, he is aware that the stands are full of old friends, coaches, and family. At his mother's house, the telephone rings with people asking for tickets. Finally he says that he can get no more. Every night when he goes to the park, whatever city he is in, he must leave a pile of requests for passes. When Dave Parker came back to Cincinnati in 1975, the hottest hitter on the Pirates, he gave out forty-four passes. When Larry Demery started a game in Los Angeles,

August 1974, Dock accused him of giving away the record number of tickets—sixty-three. (He won the game. And he was cool: when Steve Yeager hit a home run off him, he had asked the umpire for a new ball before Yeager's hit had left the park.)

When Dock pitched in Los Angeles, he went against one of his oldest and closest friends, Dodger right-fielder Willie Crawford. I ask Dock if it is difficult to pitch against an old friend like Crawford—or Bobby Watson or Reggie Smith, or another of the many alumni of Mr. Brewer's baseball college. He says it isn't, and I quote Pete Rose, who told me he liked to know the pitchers, because he figured he tried harder against his friends. Dock has to agree. "You have to try hard, else they laugh at you." Just now down in St. Louis, he had been working on his old friend Reggie Smith. "We were on the field, and he was out there running. They didn't want him running while we were on the field. Reggie says, 'Damn that man. Tell him I'm out here getting my leg in shape and go to hell.' First they sent the little equipment man out, then they sent the trainer out. He told the trainer, 'Get out of here.' I said, 'You mean they're bugging you with that trivial stuff?' he said, 'Yeah.' I said, 'Good.' "

9. *Willie Crawford*

Willie speaks slowly, without syntactical sinew, in sentences which wander like the lost tribes of Israel; but Willie's sentences reach the promised land, as his candor makes its direction known.

"I met Dock when I was . . . thirteen or fourteen years old. He was playing . . . for a man named Chet Brewer . . . and I pitched against their team . . . one day at Slauson Playground. About a year later . . . me and a kid named Bobby Tolan . . . was on the team that I was playing for . . . we was playing for the Thompson Tigers . . . we started to play with Mr. Brewer."

Dock had the car, and picked Willie up, and soon they began to party together on weekends after the games, together with Ray Jones and Big Daddy. "Me and Dock became real good personal friends . . . like as we all became professionals, Dock's true character came out . . . his real fight for blacks."

Willie's voice is high, monotonous, steady, as if he were reading badly from a book. He knows he has something to say, and it comes over me that he has rehearsed what he wants to tell me. "He's had opportunities . . . while playing for Pittsburgh, to fight for the black cause . . . across the country. I play for the L.A. Dodgers and it's hard . . . because they control the L.A. press. It's difficult here to make a . . . crusade for blacks. Dock was able to . . . he did prison work in Pennsylvania for blacks . . . I could go into more different things with Dock, but this is what I respect him for. He helped a . . . lot of changes in the Pittsburgh organization . . . probably would never of came about, because there was no one there actually fighting for . . . making it publicly known.

"Dock is the same here as Richie Allen. Because newspapers . . . were trying to make them bad guys in the public's eyes . . . instead of making them heroes . . . like Jackie Robinson. Jackie Robinson didn't fight for blacks . . . until he left baseball. Dock made his fight while he has been in baseball . . . even though he put his job in jeopardy. There should be more black athletes doing this."

Willie pays a momentary tribute to Joe Brown and the Pirate management, for tolerating Dock's activities.

"At an early age I knew he was searching . . . to really leave his mark in life. He found it in his fight for his people. I know somebody said . . . all the trouble he's getting into, it really hurt his mother. His mother would talk to me sometimes . . . and say, 'What's wrong with Dock?' I told her, 'He's fighting for equality for us . . . for all black people, and the kids that come behind us. That they have the opportunity . . . to express themselves freely . . . The whole key . . . to success in anything . . . is self-expression. Freely . . . without strains . . . and agony things to combine in there. I knew Dock was going to . . . use his life wisely . . . because the best knowledge you can realize is in the streets. Education is good foundation for book learning . . . for a businessman or somebody . . . that gives you the foundations for something . . . but street knowledge is the knowledge you really learn . . . and Dock was always out there to learn that. . . .

"You learn more from executing the street than you learn in college. He'd done this all his life. This is why he knows such large numbers of people . . . across the country. This is why he is able to be accepted . . . street knowledge. Dock," says Willie, with an air of summary, "is basically friendly and aggressive."

I ask Willie what it's like to hit against his old friend.

"That's the toughest . . . thing I ever had to do. It's funny . . . he's the only pitcher that . . . ever throwed pitch after pitch . . . after pitch . . . right down the middle of the plate . . . and I never hit a home run off of Dock. Three or four years ago . . . we were playing at Forbes Field . . . Dock used to have a great big breaking curveball . . . and I hit his big breaking curveball off the left center-field fence. . . . It missed going out by maybe five or six inches. I say, 'Why don't you throw the big . . . breaking curveball anymore?' He say, 'Why, so you can hit it?' I say, 'You don't . . . have to throw it to me . . . to the right-handed hitters.' Because I think it's a good pitch for him. He had it . . . when he was young. He learned it from Chet Brewer. . . . Chet Brewer used to have him on the side, teaching him . . . the big breaking curveball. It was a . . . beautiful curveball. The only person whose curveball . . . broke as big as his . . . was Koufax.

"That's the toughest . . . thing I do, from year to year . . . is hit against Dock. Alston . . . knows he's my friend, but I hit Bob Gibson . . . so well, he make sure I have to see . . . Dock. One thing that's fortunate . . . I never had to beat him in a game . . . there's always been someone else . . . I've been able to get hits to keep a rally going . . . but I've had only one extra . . . base hit off him . . . that one in Forbes Field. . . . It's not like I'm not trying. If I hit it out I hit it . . . out. I give a hundred percent."

Willie returns to his subject:
"What made Dock's fight greater . . . was the letter he received . . . from Jackie Robinson. He gave me that letter to read."

We talk about the letter for a minute. Then Willie finishes what he has to say:

"We played so many years together. There are so many of us that are still playing . . . I wish it would come about, while we are still young, young enough . . . we could all play together. . . . I think we'd still win the way we did in those days . . . it's unbelievable how many great ballplayers in baseball played on the same team. Chet Brewer's team.

"I like the sport of baseball, but I do not like . . . the people who run the sport. It provides a decent living . . . if you are willing or able to save for the day when you leave the sport . . . we're not going to get coaches jobs or managers . . . jobs or general managers jobs. All of his life he was searching for . . . that might help other people's life. When he went into baseball he saw the press . . . and at the time of high school

Muhammad Ali was the biggest thing . . . ever hit the sports world. . . . You know, we'd heard about Joe Louis. . . . We heard about how *dumb* Joe Louis was . . . how he lost all his money . . . that was just rapped in our heads, over and over. . . . And how the black man didn't have the opportunity he should have, in baseball . . . baseball did not take the black athlete as soon as the other sports. . . . This was the one thing that kept us going toward baseball . . . because we wanted to go in there and change it."

10. *The End of a Season*

On September 1, Dock started against the Dodgers in Dodger Stadium. The day before, I asked him if he was thinking about the game.

"I'm starting to focus on the lineup now," he said. "What's mainly on my mind now is the *mound*. I know I'm on a streak, and I've never pitched well here. If you don't *pitch* in a park, the mound can confuse you.

"The Dodger mound is like off a mountain. It's as high as Montreal but it's got clay, wet clay. That stuff gets slippery, and it digs a bigger hole. Not a *bigger* hole, but the hole is more firm. Whereas in Pittsburgh, if you get a hole, you can kick the sides down and level it. Here you can't kick the sides down. I'm thinking about the mound now, and I'm visualizing the mound and the plate. Then I'm into the hitters.

"Plus I'm trying to think of the last time I pitched here, what was my best pitch from that mound. About the only thing I can come up with is that I wasn't sleeping, I was partying. *This* Saturday, I'm leaving the game, I'm coming back here to *sleep.*"

Don Sutton will pitch for the Dodgers.

In the first inning, Dock looks strong and confident, chewing his Double Bubble, and raring back to fire. To me—standing behind home plate, behind glass, looking into the ball as it approaches the catcher—the fastball seems to move, but sometimes to veer over the heart of the plate. He is throwing hard, but without location.

With two down he walks Jimmy Wynn, and Steve Garvey singles. Willie Crawford up.

One and two. Then a fastball brushes Willie back. Then Willie

Crawford grounds out to Frank Taveras, and Dock is out of the first inning safely.

In the second inning, Ron Cey hits a ball to Al Oliver, deep in center field, which Oliver first catches and then drops when he slams into the wall. A legitimate double. Then Taveras makes an error on Russell, and base runners occupy first and third. No outs.

Docks bears down, pitching to Yeager. One and two, Yeager hits a pop fly to Taveras. Then Don Sutton strikes out, and Dock is pulling himself out of trouble. Dave Lopes takes Oliver back to the wall again, but Oliver holds on to the ball, and no runs score.

Lucky.

In the third inning, Buckner sends a fly ball into right field for a single. On hit and run, Jimmy Wynn grounds to Stennett. One out, and a man on second. Dock is throwing the fast sinker ball now. Garvey raps the ball on the ground to Taveras, Buckner again running on the pitch, and there are two outs with a man on third. Willie Crawford up.

Willie Crawford hits a double down the left-field line, a classic wrong-field double which raises the chalk on the foul line behind the third baseman's head. It is Willie's second major league extra-base hit against his old friend. Then the Dodgers go out, but they have scored a run.

In the fourth inning Dock holds the line. One-two-three.

In the fifth inning Dock holds the line. One-two-three.

As the sixth inning begins, the Pirates have had five hits, but they have left them all on base. It's one to nothing Dodgers.

Willie Crawford leads off, and flies out. Cey flies out. Russell grounds to Hebner, for what should have been the third out, another one-two-three inning. But the ball trickles under Hebner's glove. Dock looks annoyed, briefly, and then assumes an impassive face. Hebner kicks at the dirt, three times, rapidly. Now Yeager steps in, taking his squat stance. Dock's curve starts out inside but moves—not abruptly, but steadily and predictably—into the middle of the plate, and Yeager times it nicely and lifts it in a long graceful arc into the bleachers in left center.

Now Dock looks truly annoyed, and pitches rapidly to Don Sutton, and walks him. Juan Pizarro begins to warm up in the bullpen. Dave Lopes comes up. On a one strike count, Lopes lifts a fly ball which just climbs over the center-field wall, and Dock is behind five to nothing. Buckner singles to left, and Wynn grounds out to Hebner.

In the top of the seventh, Murtaugh pinch-hits for Dock, and he has lost in his home city once again.

On September 7, Dock beat Montreal two to one. He was pitching the best baseball of his career in the second half of 1974. On September 11, he was beating Philadelphia four to one when Willie Montanez hit a line drive back at him. Dock reached for it with his gloved hand, but the ball knuckled on him. When the ball struck the rear of his pitching hand, it broke the fifth metatarsal, a tiny bone just behind the little finger, and the season was over for Dock.

He didn't want it to be over. He started running five days after the break. A week later he began to throw, gently, unable to hold the ball tight. The hand hurt when it rained, and hurt when he tried to shake hands, but his curveball began to snap as it had not snapped for years. He felt ready to pitch at the end of the season, and eager to pitch in the play-offs. But his hand was not ready. Danny Murtaugh stuck with the pitchers who had been throwing during the last weeks of the season.

When the Pirates won their division, with one day left in the season, an AP photograph showed a hilarious huddle of players hugging each other, with the figure of Dock standing to one side—bemused, benign, pleased, smiling, but distinctly separate.

When the Dodgers took the play-offs, three out of four, from the Pirates, the sputtering season clanked to an abrupt end, and the annaul diaspora sent everyone scattering away, for the four months of exile.

Seven: 1975

1. *Life Without Baseball*

Off-season, Dock has wintered in Pittsburgh, when he wasn't traveling. He tries to stay in shape.

"Do you play basketball?" I ask him.

"Not since I ran into the wall one day, in Pittsburgh in nineteen sixty-nine. I haven't played since." He was playing at the time with a bunch of professional basketball players from the Pittsburgh ABA team. Now he sees more of the Steelers. "Because I train in there, in the winter. Plus I *like* to be in there messing with those football players. I put on a uniform. I'm not going to *hit* anybody, but I put on a uniform and run pass patterns. Say a quarterback wants to go out there and throw early. Then I get *out* of there! Somebody might just want to *play* you know, and they're rough. Break my leg or something."

"Do you get bored in the off-season?"

"I don't get bored until the last two weeks before spring training starts. Then I'm anxious to see how the guys look, how they kept themselves in shape, what the team is going to look like, who they've traded for. You want to cut into the individual and see how he's going to fit into the family."

In the winter of 1973-74, Dock lived in L.A., because he wanted water therapy at the beach, after his knee operation, and he studied real estate while he was recuperating. He would like to work for himself, after baseball. Today, Dock is wearing a button that says, "A Smile a Day Keeps the Boss Thinking."

When he sells real estate, upon his retirement, he plans to base

213

himself in Florida rather than in California. I ask him why.

"It's slow. I like the sound of the wind in the trees there. I like to watch the millionaires walking around. I can't stand L.A.," he tells me. "Smog bothers me. Hurry. It's hit and run. Even when I was there last winter, on a weekend I'd spend the entire time just going to see people. *All* over the freeway."

"Once you told me you wanted to be a disc jockey."

"Disc jockey was just something, you know, to play around with. I still do it, WJOB, my own little station, retired baseball players station. I got some tapes where I'm *screaming*: 'I am the only baseball player to retire at the age of twenty-seven!' That's when I was really into it, two years ago."

"Into retirement?"

"No, disc jockey. That retirement is *psych*. I tell them I'll go back to the post office." Dock worked in the L.A. post office now and then, as a young man. "My *serious* thoughts, for after baseball, were the dry-cleaning business and real estate. I had this fantasy about being a lawyer. But I don't feel like I should go to the bottom. It would be *hard*, first college and then law school." He would be a lawyer in order to work in finance; maybe he can work in finance without a law degree. Tom Reich believes that Dock has a talent for business, and has taken him to business meetings—mergers and other corporate ventures—to give Dock a taste of it.

"Didn't you try to become a movie star one time?"

"I thought I could make it in the movies, but I went at it the wrong way. I got tight with the wrong guy."

In Chicago, when he was being photographed in various hairstyles for Johnson Publications, Dock met the actor Richard Roundtree, who told Dock to look him up in Hollywood. On a visit to L.A. in 1972, Dock decided to make his play for the movies. He found the set where Roundtree was working, and walked into it. "Hey, man. I'm going to talk to Richard," he told the director, who was upset because he was in the process of filming. "I didn't know what was going on," Dock tells me. "It was just a little room."

Dock persisted. "When he asked the director if he could go to lunch with me, then I knew he wasn't a star. He was just upcoming. I thought he could get me into the movies, into a film of my own. I thought he was a star. All I wanted to do was meet somebody I could talk to. Get a screen test or something."

Dock and Ray Jones walked into the dining room of the Beverly Hills

Hotel, dressed to the eyeballs, to wait on Richard Roundtree for lunch. People turned to stare, dropping their olives. Then Roundtree arrived in a black suit and tie. "I didn't think he had to look like that," Dock said. "When I got tired of listening to him talk, I said, 'Hey, man, if you had a brother that wanted to play baseball, I'd take him to Joe Brown.' "

"What about movies now?" I ask. "Do you still think about it?"

"The movies? Now that I don't want to live in L.A., no. And Roundtree was talking about coming onto the set at six o'clock in the morning. I say, 'Hey, man. Uhm-uhm. I don't think I could put up with that breaking-into-the-movies stuff. Just like the minor leagues."

2. *Slowing Down*

On March 11, 1975, Dock turned thirty. Later that season, interviewed by the *New York Daily News,* he revealed that he no longer drank nor smoked. "I came into the game hip, and I'm going out square," he said. "I'm not leading the fast life-style. People like Gibson and Aaron came in square and are going out hip, but I'm different. I knew everything about the outside world when I came in. Tell them I don't mess around. . . ."

Conservatism descended gradually upon Dock. The clothes he wears now—he claims when I challenge him, later that spring—he bought four years ago. "I haven't spent fifty dollars on clothes in the last two years. I've *been* through that phase of the game. I was into it heavy. I wasn't trying to outdress anyone. I was into my *wild* stuff."

I want to hear more about this. "You didn't mind it, though, when heads turned to watch you, when you walked into the Beverly Hills Hotel?"

"Oh, *yeah*! That started in high school, at Cheap Charlie's. I politicked for myself, to be best dressed in the class. I'd tell all the ladies to send my name in. Down in the minor leagues too. I used to wear leather suits. I had three or four of them made. And like the black pants I had on yesterday? I used to buy them by the gross. All colors. That's when they had them with stripes on the side, with tight little tops like James Brown's outfits. Twenty or twenty-five outfits I had. Big gold and silver belts, shiny elastic. And I had a crushed red velvet suit, and a red leather maxicoat."

I ask him where he did his shopping.

"*Anywhere*. I used to just run into shops. Even now, I have the *tendency*. When the want comes, I want to just run in there and check new clothes. But I used to just go into a shop and change clothes. Shoes, socks, underwear, *everything*. Just *change*."

I mention his jewelry, the Pisces pendant he always wears, and the Star of David pendant. "I used to wear everything around my neck. Now I've got things spread out, clothes and jewelry, *all over* the country."

Still, there are the rings—the World Series ring, the ring he made his stepfather give him, a ring that Paula gave him, another that says DOCK, and a slim and elegant gold watch. "My mother bought me this watch, because I can't wear a watch. Too reckless with my arms.

"But I used to wear a ring on every finger, when I first came to the big leagues."

"What slows you down?" (J.W., Dock's Pittsburgh friend, laughs when he hears the question, saying, "Ain't *nobody* as fast as he *used* to be!")

Well, Dock says, he looked at what happened to other ballplayers who didn't slow down. And besides, it just seems to happen, as he gets older. "I was into *everything*, he says. "I was into *every bar*. I used to get high almost every day. Now I'm not so tired of being high, I'm tired of being *around* it."

It was during spring training, 1975, that Dock stopped drinking and smoking. I remembered a conversation from the year before, when we first talked seriously. He told me how much he loved to run. Some pitchers, he said, had to be begged to run. He did it for the love of running.

"Is it that important for a pitcher to run?" I ask.

"I think so," he said in 1974, "because of the life I lead. I lack dedication. If I really dedicated myself to baseball, who knows what I could do? I could run for days and days if I didn't smoke. It's a known fact, smoking is going to stop you."

"What do you mean, you lack dedication?"

"I never really had to *fight* for anything. Everything to me in baseball is *natural*. I never really had to fight for a job. I never really had to *put out* to be *best*. When I said I was going to be a major league ballplayer, I *knew* it. I didn't come in saying, 'Ooh, I'm in the big leagues! Ooh, I'm gonna bust my ass!' I *knew* I had the natural ability to be a professional ballplayer."

"Did you think about becoming the best?"

"That never dawned on me. Because I was full of *play*."

A year later, Dock had changed. In 1974 Murtaugh wanted to send him to the bullpen. In 1974 Dock had been low, and then he had found the joy of winning again. Then he began to feel his body aging. He turned thirty. He told the *New York Daily News* reporter, in the spring of 1975, "I'm *dedicated*."

3. *The Cold Season*

Dock had the best record in the grapefruit league—thirty-seven innings, and only one earned run. I talked to him on the telephone. "I'm going to win twenty-five this year!" he told us, "twenty-two in the season, and one in the play-offs, and two in the World Series!" I had never heard him so optimistic.

Murtaugh decided on Dock to open the season in Chicago. Opening day in Chicago was delayed because of cold weather—snow on the field, as a matter of fact. Then it was delayed again. Again. Finally Dock started, on a cold Thursday, April 10.

With his short fingers, he has trouble throwing the curveball on a cold day. The Pirates won the game, eight to four, but Dock gave up four earned runs and left the game in the fifth inning. In four and a third innings, he gave up four times as many earned runs as he had allowed in thirty-seven innings under the Florida sun.

On April 16 he gave up another four earned runs, in three full innings, while Woody Fryman and the Montreal Expos shut out the Pirates five to nothing. Dock's pitches came in straight and flat, with no movement. On April 22, Dock lost to Montreal again—on that high mound in Jarry Park—and gave up three earned runs.

Then on Sunday, April 27, having compiled a 7.43 ERA in his first three starts, Dock shut out the Phillies, two to nothing, on six hits. "When I felt sweat on my hands I was happy," Dock said after the game. When he warms up, if his hand begins to sweat, he knows he can throw the curveball. And in the game he pitched with care. Even with his bad move to first, he threw there four times when Larry Bowa was on, so that by the time Bowa tried to steal second base, he was half a step late, and Sangy threw him out. Two singles followed, but Dock got the side out without giving up a run. His move to first—bad as it was—had preserved his shutout.

He missed a turn with flu, and then on May 9, Dock was winning pitcher over the Dodgers. He pitched well, but he was lucky to win the game. He was losing three to two—two of the runs earned—when Bob Robertson batted for him in the seventh inning, and hit a bloop single which started a Pirate rally. They scored nine runs off Mike Marshall.

After this game, Dock was two and two on the year. The season appeared to be straightening out. When San Diego followed Los Angeles into Pittsburgh, Dock jumped ahead of Bruce Kison to pitch against Randy Jones on Wednesday, May 14. He left the game in the eighth inning, leading four to three. Ramon Hernandez gave up a single to Willie McCovey, and the fourth run scored, to tie the game. Sam McDowell got the win, when the Pirates scored in the bottom of the eleventh.

Then the Pirates went out to the Coast, to play the same teams over again. On May 20, Dock started the game in San Francisco and gave up five runs in the third inning. "They hit the shit out of me," he told the reporters.

He was scheduled to start again in San Diego on May 26. His lifetime record against the Padres was nine and one. But at the last moment he was scratched, because of a tight shoulder. Bob Moose took his place, and pitched a strong game. The next day in Houston Dock tried to throw, and couldn't throw at all. In earlier years, he had frequently suffered elbow problems in August. A shoulder problem in May was something new. The papers reported his progress. On May 30, "It felt better than it did the first time I threw, but I still feel pain." When the June 2 game with Cincinnati was rained out, a reporter devoted a story to Dock. "I went into the season thinking that if I'd start fifty games I'd win fifty games," Dock told the reporter.

4. A Game in Cincinnati

On June 9 the Pirates flew into Cincinnati and checked into Stouffer's.

Waiting for Dock at the ball park, I walk around on the green carpet and talk to the players who come up the ramp. Bruce Kison, Richie Hebner, Sangy, Ken Brett. A fan leans over the rail—it is early, still quite light in warm and humid Cincinnati; only the truest fans come out this early—and calls to Ken, "Hey, Richie! Richie!" Richie Hebner like Ken Brett is fair, and like Ken Brett is stocky and muscular.

Ken Brett is cool. Ken Brett is fresh. "Richie *who?*" he enunciates, with a fine, lip-curling flair.

We talk about elbows for a few minutes, and Brett goes down to the bullpen to throw. He is on the disabled list, and has told us that he is trying complete rest—but he throws every day for ten minutes. I have difficulty putting these statements together.

Tonight Jerry Reuss is pitching. He comes out early, takes extra BP, and then removes himself to the photographers' cage next to the dugout, where he sits in gloomy isolation, glaring out at the field, as he psychs himself up for the game. I watch him covertly, as his lips snarl in the darkness—he's talking to himself! Then steps out from his eyrie for a moment—a shaggy Byronic figure of isolation—and is addressed immediately from the stands. An old, old man in back of the dugout yells, "Jerry! Jerry!" Reuss looks up, a little irritated, and says, "What?" The old, old man informs him that in Cincinnati you can get a haircut for only three dollars. Reuss is coldly furious. "Thank you," he says. "Thank you very much." He retreats to his dark hole again, his concentration momentarily interrupted, and mutters in our direction, "Old bullshitter! Old bullshitter thinks it's funny!"

Then Dock comes up the walk, and I shake his left hand, and chat, and make plans for later. He will come to my hotel after the game. His shoulder is *fine*, and he will pitch in Houston on Thursday. Kenny Brett is *insane*, to be throwing in the bullpen with a sore elbow. Then Dock goes off to run, and I return to the stands.

The game is a laugher, a nine-two win for the Pirates. Reuss's concentration limits Cincinnati to five hits. But Dave Parker leads the way. He hits a three-run homer in the first inning to give Reuss a five to nothing lead before he starts pitching; then he hits a double and a single. It is his twenty-fourth birthday. He grew up in Cincinnati, and used to sell lemonade and peanuts at Reds' games at old Crosley Field.

5. *The Weird Season*

Back at the hotel, after the game.

He thinks the shoulder injury came from the cold weather, "by me trying to throw the curveball so hard, to get it to *break.*" But the pitching coach told him no, he was the victim of circumstance, waiting six or seven days between starts because of rain and snow. In either case, the weather is to blame for the shoulder.

When it's cold his hand still aches, but when he's pitching he doesn't feel it. They tell him his curveball is still exceptional, but he thinks he's been losing it.

I ask him if he's had any great days so far this year.

"When I beat Philly," he tells me, drinking Scotch, "I was *superb.*" His voice as he pronounces the word becomes snobbish, haughty—and he laughs at the noise he makes. "I felt *good* the second time I pitched against Philly, but I didn't get any decision. They got a lot of hits but I *battled* them. Other than those two times, I haven't felt that good." The ball has been coming in straight, he says, not moving enough. "I beat the Dodgers but I didn't have nothing. I beat them because when they took me out they conmmenced pounding Marshall."

I told him he didn't sound worried. Last year, at least by the start of July, he had begun to start worrying.

"I'm the same now," he tells us, "but I have a year's experience. It doesn't bother me. I've had slow starts the last three or four years."

"Well," I say, thinking of last year, "how's team morale this year?" This year at least the ball club was winning.

"It's been a slow year," Dock says. "It's weird. Morale is a little shaky. There was an article in the paper, where I was relaying a message to the team. They asked me why the fans were not coming to the ball park. So I jumped on that opportunity, and I said, 'Too many black ballplayers.' That gave me the headlines. Then I sent my little message to the team: I used this article to let the orphans know—I use that term referring to guys we have picked up, brought into the family—to be cool, to shut up. I was hearing little things they said, that guys who were part of the family wouldn't say—like, they were saying that Candalaria, even before they were going to bring him up, that he was a smartass. They were saying derogatory things. They said Candalaria couldn't do this and that in another organization. I said, 'Well, this is the *Pirate* organization.' They were name-calling the manager, like him being *dumb.* I say, 'Well, he's the richest dummy I know.' "

When I ask him who is doing the backbiting, he doesn't want to tell me. Hearing him tell what he said in the papers, I wonder if his message was not too subtle, or too cryptic, to deliver itself.

Dock changes the subject to Richie Zisk, team leader in batting the year before, who is not hitting so well, and who is playing without a contract. There are many things that upset him, in this weird season.

"Zisk, he's in a frenzy now," Dock says. "He doesn't know what's happening. It's something like playing out your option. You got guys on the team—orphans—saying, 'Who does he think he is?' " But Dock knows who Richie Zisk is: "He's a *Pirate.*"

How come the Pirates are winning, we ask, with the backbiting and the frenzy?

"Different guys are carrying the team each day. Where last year we were all in a slump together."

Bill Robinson's won some games, I say. Robinson is an outfielder who came over from the Phillies, and one of the new men.

"He surprised me as a ballplayer," Dock says. "I never thought too much of him, playing against him. Coming to our team brings out the best things in guys! Still, he's shocked at the *looseness* on the club. He's like a little kid. He does things that I *know* he didn't do in Philly. He might hit BP, he might not, if he doesn't want to."

It must be difficult, I say, to be treated in the other direction—to go from the Pirates to a tight team.

Dock shakes his head. "I wouldn't know anything about it," he says.

"You were a tight team yourself, this spring," I say. "You gave up drinking and smoking." Dock has just lit up a Kool, to go with his Grant's.

He nods. "I was off until a week and a half ago. June first. I was eating too much."

"Did you feel better, not smoking?" Dock smokes little, and mostly when he has a drink.

"I felt better in spring training, because I was running and nothing was holding me back. Oh, I was training. I was *training.* I was waking in the morning about six-thirty or seven, just wake up automatically, jump in the pool. They tell you don't swim, but I always do. I would swim until I got blasted, couldn't breathe. Then I'd get out of the pool, have me a little cup of coffee or something, then I'd get back in the pool and go underwater for as many times as I could. That's when I stopped smoking. I got all that smoke out of my lungs. I could over-and-back three or four times. Then I'd go down to the camp, run on my own, before anyone gets there, run laps. Every other day I'd run a long sprint. Toward the end, I'd pick a day and I'd run the entire game—two, three hours. I ran so hard my legs were like steel. Then I'd lift weights in the trainer's room. Then I'd go back, and go swimming.

"I weighed in at two hundred and five. I went from two hundred and five to one ninety so quick! I stayed around one eighty-seven all spring. Now I weigh one ninety-eight. But I can lose at least six of that before I pitch."

"Before Thursday?" Today is Monday.

"*Yeah.*"

6. *Dock at Pigall's*

The next day we met at noon to eat at Pigall's. I have already written about how Dock was repulsed at the door for not wearing a jacket, how he made an assessment of the possible racial politics of a dress code, and came back dressed like American royalty.

We order drinks and begin to talk. Drink at lunch before a game—an eight o'clock game—is against a baseball rule, but Dock goes ahead with a clear conscience. He's not pitching—he would never take a drink on a pitching day—and it won't hurt him if he pinch-runs.

Returning to the city of the macing, Dock remembers something to tell me. The man who maced him is dead. He broke his arm in a motorcycle accident, a simple break which formed a blood clot that went to his brain and killed him. "What comes around, comes around," Dock says. An old acquaintance of Dock's told him, and was angry when Dock responded, "Good." Dock looks to be sure we hear him. "I stomped the ground," Dock told me at Pigall's. "*Good.*"

"They're still pitching Stargell on the outside of the plate. They'll give him a single. They just don't want him pulling it out. After he's been pitched to on the outside enough, he'll start slapping those singles out into left field. That's what he did last year. Didn't hit the home runs."

Manny is still doing most of the catching—"I don't see how he does it"—although the Pirates acquired Duffy Dyer from the Mets over the winter. "Dyer caught me one day. The time against Philly when I was battling them. Catched me like I was *Seaver* or somebody. I say, 'Don't be asking me to run that ball *in* on those guys. 'Cause *Seaver* pitches up and in, *I* don't be pitching up and in.' You got to be *quick*, to get up in there. I might go *in* there, but I go *in* there *bad*. *He* wants me to catch some part of the plate. I must have given up fourteen or fifteen hits. I mean they was *hits*. I can't go *in* there. That's the ball they pound between third and short, over the shortstop's head."

I remember last year Dock talking about Seaver's sore hip. "Seaver's back," I say.

But Dock hasn't been following baseball. When he isn't playing, he doesn't want to know about other people playing. "I've been out of socket," he says, and I ask him what he means. "Out of socket," he says. "On the shelf. I haven't been doing anything but running the streets. That's when I started back smoking and drinking."

I think of another topic from last year. "Reuss is doing well. Is he happier?"

"He's one of the boys. I did a lot of work with him. Put in a lot of time. He's one of the boys now."

Then I ask about Bruce Kison. He is pitching well and winning. "What's the difference?" I ask Dock.

"He's changing speeds a lot. He throws a slow curveball now, and a straight change. It seems like he's not afraid to come in on the left-handers. Before, the ball would take off. Now he's learned the rule, to go *in* on left-handers. His little change-up is like a scroogie. It's natural, because he's throwing it from the side. And he throws that hard curve, and the slow curve. I would say it was change of speeds."

A less happy subject is Richie Zisk, and Dock keeps returning to Zisk's problems, like a worried relative.

"He's in a frenzy," he says again. "He's really screwed up. Contract thing is pressing on him."

This year the defense is better all around. The outfield is rational at last. Stargell's move to first base frees left field to Richie Zisk, who was a left fielder all through the minor leagues. Al Oliver plays a fine center field, especially when he feels settled there, secure that he will not be suddenly asked to play first base. In right field, Dave Parker is an inexperienced but talented fielder. He has the wheels to play center field, but is not yet an expert judge of the fly ball. In the winter of 1974-75, the Pirates gave him winter work in center field, in order to improve his outfielding in general. This led to a quarrel with Dock during spring training.

"I got out to the field pretty early," he tells me, eating *pâtisserie* at Pigall's, "and Dave was working out at center field. I said, '—here Dock's voice becomes finicky, pedantic, overrefined—'Dave, *what*—are—you—*do*ing—in center field?' He said, 'This is where I'm going to play.'

"He wasn't *thinking*. Because the club had sent him to winter ball to play center field, he was under the impression that he was going to play center field and Al Oliver was going to play first base.

"I said, 'Hey, if I'm pitching and you're playing center field, I'm going to tell the manager I don't pitch.' He got mad. I told him, I say, 'Well, if you think that, don't ever speak to me again, because I don't talk to dummies.' How could he think he was going to play center field? Take Al Oliver's job? I said, 'You're—out—of—your—mind.' So we didn't speak the entire spring training. Afterward, he found out what I was trying to tell him.

"I run into that problem, with the guys on this team. They don't understand what I'm trying to tell them."

Dock and the rest of the Pirates root for the Reds over the Dodgers—only because they would sooner beat them in the play-offs. We ask Dock if there is still the problem of fraternization, with the Reds.

"Their first trip into Pittsburgh," Dock says, "I still had to throw a ball at Sangy. He was over there chitchatting with Concepcion. That's all I saw. I broke that up."

Suddenly Dock looks across to the front of Pigall's, and exclaims, "Oooh, that's a *bad-d-d-d* hat." A lady entering Pigall's wears a wide floppy white hat. "I got to get my lady one of *them*," says Dock.

I take up an earlier topic. "Do you really think that people stay away from Three Rivers Stadium because the team is so black?"

"Not all that much. Five years ago you could say that, but not now, not really. In Pittsburgh they charge two fifty to park. It's not the *team* that owns the parking lot. The people don't understand. Plus they can't get out of there when the game's over. They can't get in and out of the stadium. And the Pirates don't have anything to do with the parking lot or with the highways. That's the city. They'd have to get tax money to put these roads up. It would be nothing for them to build two or three little off-ramps and on-ramps—but who's gonna pay for it?"

I asked Dock about his social life. Who's the lady for whom he would purchase the bad-d-d-d-d hat? (Later, I discover that he has met Renee, but today he does not mention her name. It is bad luck to expect too much.) "I'm involved with at least three or four women during a season," he shrugs. "I'm looking for *something*. I'm getting *tired*."

"If you settle down again," I ask, "would you have a longer career in baseball?"

"I would say yes."

But, we observe, a baseball career makes it hard to settle down.

"Not really. Because I discipline myself even now. For a week maybe. Then I say, 'Off into the streets again!' I don't *like* to run the streets, but if I'm pushing the corner, I be there."

"Pushing the corner?" we ask.

"Just can't take it anymore. The craving for the streets." There's something melancholy in Dock's tone—the urge toward peace and quiet, the urge the other way. He resolves his melancholy. "I can tell you now," he says gaily, "it's going to be a good year. Maybe not on the field, but off the field. I don't worry about on the field. It's off-the-field that's going to make on-the-field cool."

Still, there's a new component in Dock's talk. He talks about wanting to get over to the Little League. They've got grass on the field, in the Little League. "I'd throw a lot of ground balls." He only gave up one earned run in spring training because he was mostly pitching against American League teams. "I get over there," he says, "I'll make them forget about Cy Young."

Then he mentions that if he retires right now, at the age of forty-five he would draw a thousand dollars a month in pension. When you retire, he says, you can take ten thousand dollars all at once instead of getting your pension. A lot of guys do it.

This suggestion raises my bourgeois hackles: it's spending capital; it's the working-class incapacity to defer reward; it's taking a skateboard now, in lieu of a Rolls-Royce later.

It doesn't bother Dock all that much.

"What they'll do is, they'll get their ten thousand dollars and open a little business. That's what they're doing. If they get their ten thousand dollars, and they've got three partners, that's forty thousand dollars. Now they are *secure*. They have a little business, and they're going to get something every month. Where with baseball, they have to wait until they're forty-five."

"Do many players, while they're playing getting big money, invest their money?"

"A lot of them *talk*. How many do it, I don't know." Then we discuss that attitude, especially common among younger players, that baseball is a golden island in a drab life, that one day they will suddenly find themselves returned to the world their fathers and mother inhabited, the splendor gone. "Tom is getting *me* out of that kind of thinking," Dock says. "Me being a Pisces, I live in a dream world anyway.

"But I *can* go back into dry cleaning," he says abruptly. "I *can* do that. How many people have that opportunity? I can do anything I want to do!"

We talk about McBean again, who has made the Adjustment. "He doesn't like it," Dock says again, "but he made it. I *can* deal with reality."

"What's the adjustment to? Money? Travel?"

"That's it."

"What about adulation?"

"He's still a superstar. He'll always be a superstar in his own surroundings. When I stop, I don't think I'll stop traveling though. I just can't sit still. I'll be doing it wherever I am. I might not go long distances. I would go like to San Diego, San Francisco. I'll be *moving*. Even if I would go across town. Spend a night with someone."

"Now you're talking like L.A. again. What about Florida?"

Dock shrugs the question off. He finds an analogy in Bill Mazeroski, retired now, who never really liked to *travel*. "He says that every now and then he'll go to the golf course"—Mazeroski owns a bar and a golf course, and spends much of his time at the bar—"spend two or three nights there. He says that's his road trip."

I still hear sadness, in this talk of retirement.

"Through all my travels," says Dock, "I have to find me a lady. I'd like to settle down."

Back to baseball, I ask Dock to tell me more about this weird season. Now that they are winning, why isn't morale better?

Dock shakes his head. He is puzzled.

"Baseball is *slow, slow* this year," he says. "I don't know what's wrong. It's weird. It's a *boring* season. I don't think anyone is *interested*. To me, it seems like everyone is waiting for September, for the drive. That's all they talk about."

"Isn't that bad luck?"

Dock is impatient of superstition.

"No. That's all they talk about. 'Wait til September. Wait til September.' " Dock leans back, finishing his coffee. The waiters are standing around. It's almost four o'clock, and only one other party lingers over brandy and coffee. The bus will leave for the ball park in a little over an hour. "I think it's because everybody worked so hard, last year," Dock says. "They worked hard only for one thing. It seems like it would be better if we were *down* now. If we lose six or seven games in a row, that will snap everyone out of it."

7. *The Boring Season*

That night the Pirates beat Cincinnati nine to five, with Willie Stargell hitting three doubles and a single. The Pirates held a one-and-a-half-game lead, in the Eastern Division, over New York and Philadelphia. It was only June 10.

On June 12, Dock pitched five innings in Houston and took the win. "I felt good," Dock said after the game. "I didn't feel nothing." Murtaugh relieved him in the sixth, by prearrangement. He would start work again slowly. But on June 17, when Dock started against the Cardinals in St. Louis, he pitched only four and a third innings, and gave up five runs, four of them earned. In his story on the game, Bob Smizik of the *Pittsburgh Press* called him "the team's major disappointment." Then on June 22 Dock threw a five-hit shutout at the New York Mets, beating them two to nothing. He was throwing heat. The win put Pittsburgh five games on top of its division, while over in the West, Cincinnati was only two games up on the Dodgers.

Then the Pirates lost four games in a row to Philadelphia in Philadelphia.

Dock won his next start, against the Cubs on June 27, by the score of five to one. "I'm doing it without my curve," he told a reporter. "I can't get my curve to break like I want it to." Now he was five and four, with two complete games in a row. Then on July 3 in Montreal, Dock gave up only five singles and one run, and pitched his third straight complete game. Six and four. It seemed as if Dock was finally on the track of the season he predicted in Florida.

On July 8 he was shut out in Pittsburgh by the Dodgers, but he gave up only one run in his seven innings. He allowed three hits, one of them a homer by Jimmy Wynn, which was enough to lose the game. Then at San Diego on July 13, he pitched only four innings, and gave up seven hits and four earned runs. No strikeouts. Then at Los Angeles on July 18 Dock pitched well—in front of the home folks—but ended without a decision. He pitched six full innings and gave up two runs. In San Diego on July 23, Dock gave up only four hits and one run over nine innings.

But his season was inconsistent. In his next start, against Philadelphia in Pittsburgh on July 29, he gave up seven hits and four earned runs in only three and two-thirds innings; losing pitcher. His record had evened up, at seven and seven. ELLIS CONTINUES SLUMP, the *Pittsburgh Press* headlined, and continued:

> *What's happened to Dock Ellis?* How has the man who so baffled National League hitters in the late stages of the 1974 season fallen into a 7-7 record? Where did he leave the talents that enabled him to completely overwhelm every team he faced in spring training? . . .
> Despite such a disappointing season, Ellis will stay in the rotation. Asked if he might replace him with rookie John Candalaria, Murtaugh said, "Not right now. That would give me four left handers and only one rightie and I like more balance than that."

When Dock pitched and won a complete game, the reporter complimented him on "an excellent game" in two lines. When he lost, his "slump" became the focus of the game story. Of course this complaint could be made of sports pages in general.

On August 3, Dock pitched six and a third innings against New York, and gave up three earned runs, a game that Kent Tekulve won for the Pirates in relief. The Pirates were four and a half games in first place, dropped down from the six-and-a-half-game lead they enjoyed at the All-Star break. Then they lost two out of three to the Cardinals. The newspapers started talking slump. By August 8 Smizik was asking in the *Pittsburgh Press* how long Danny Murtaugh would remain patient. He'll make changes, Smizik predicted. "Both John Candelaria . . . and Larry Demery . . . are under consideration for positions in the regular rotation . . . and Bruce Kison and/or Dock Ellis may have bullpen jobs in the future . . . Ellis, the team's part-time sociologist, starts tonight against the Astros, and a repeat of his recent ineffectiveness could put him immediately in the bullpen."

In his next start at Houston, Dock came to the mound three runs ahead, in the first inning—and got only one batter out. He left after giving up four singles and one run, still two runs ahead.

And the Pirates lost, and continued to lose.

No one was hitting. The pitching was less to blame than the hitting, but the team was bad all over; the Pirates were into the losing streak which Dock had foreseen in June—something guaranteed to make the season more interesting.

So the next night they lost again, five to three. Rooker took the loss.

They won a game in Atlanta, and then Bruce Kison lost another game, three to two. Next, Dock started again and gave up four more consecutive singles, leaving the game in the first inning again. He had given up eight hits in a row.

Dock was annoyed that he had been removed from the games. If this sounds ridiculous, there are a few things that should be kept in mind. In the Houston game, Dock was actually leading when he was removed, and none of the hits were hard. Also, it is true that Dock has frequently struggled in the opening inning of a game, and then settled down to pitch a strong game and win. In a follow-up story, after the Atlanta game, Smizik had the headline ELLIS HAS HIS STUFF and the kicker above the headline read, "Or So He Says." In the story he continued to put Dock in the bullpen.

> Though Murtaugh's not saying it, the situation adds up to bullpen duty for Ellis, a status he's said in the past he would not accept.
> . . . The way Dock Ellis has performed lately, his starting and the team winning do not go together.
> As always, Ellis' answer to this dilemma should prove interesting.

The next night in Cincinnati, when the starting pitcher began to give up hits, Murtaugh told Dock to warm up in the bullpen. Dock refused, and Murtaugh said nothing. No one on the team took exception to Dock's refusal: a starting pitcher is not expected to warm up, or to relieve, the day after he started—even if he pitched only part of an inning. A starting pitcher falls into a five- or four-day rhythm, and on the day he pitches, he spends considerable time getting loose. He tends to be stiff the next day.

But the challenge had been made, and the challenge had been acknowledged. It was inevitable that Murtaugh would tell Dock to warm up the next night, in Cincinnati—with the game televised back to Pittsburgh. And it was inevitable that Dock—taking the order as a contest of wills, and not as a genuine request for relief pitching—would refuse the order. Then of course it was inevitable, and understandable, that Murtaugh would suspend his pitcher for refusing to go to the bullpen.

This happened Friday night.

Friday afternoon Dock telephoned me from Cincinnati. Since I had read in the paper that he had refused bullpen duty on Thursday, I was worried for him. He told me not to worry about *him*, but that the Pirates were in bad shape, because Murtaugh was losing his cool. But that wasn't what he was calling me about, he said; he had forgotten the name of that restaurant in Cincinnati.

8. *The Speech*

Saturday morning, Dock received his one-day suspension from Joe Brown, and a two-hundred-dollar fine. It was what he expected to pay in return for asserting his own will against Murtaugh's will. Now he was ready to rejoin the team and go to the bullpen. He telephoned Murtaugh and told him so.

With the matter of the bullpen resolved, as far as he was concerned, Dock started to plan a speech to his teammates.

The day before, he had told me that Murtaugh was losing his cool.

Danny Murtaugh had been the coolest manager Dock had ever known. Harry Walker, Larry Shepherd, and Bill Virdon had been more volatile than Murtaugh, more flappable. Murtaugh was the manager Dock most admired, for his psychological acuity—and for his *cool*.

In an article called "The Bucs Stop Here?" *Sports Illustrated* for August 25 reported, "In the dressing room the usually placid Murtaugh indicates his renewed displeasure by answering reporters' questions loud enough for the offending players to hear. 'We can't get anybody to get a fucking hit,' he fumes." (When I quote newspapers and magazines, I attempt to restore the original speech. *Sports Illustrated* wrote "bleeping hit.") " 'The third and fourth fucking hitters were up there and couldn't do it.' "

In the game just lost, Al Oliver and Dave Parker had left runners on second and third, when they came to bat in the ninth inning. (Dock feels protective, even paternal over Dave Parker; because Al Oliver is an old friend, and a hypersensitive ballplayer, Dock feels protective over him also.) Dave Parker, according to the *Sports Illustrated* reporter, heard Murtaugh in the Atlanta dressing room. "Constructive criticism," he said.

Of course the criticism was not limited to this one occasion, nor to these two ballplayers, nor was it made largely in the presence of reporters. Murtaugh—for Murtaugh—had lost his cool.

As Murtaugh's partisans are quick to point out—and as they are correct to point out—the Pirates were playing horrendous baseball in mid-August of 1975, and Murtaugh was probably cooler than any other major league manager would have been, with the possible exception of Walter Alston. The majors are full of managers who would have been benching people, trading people, waiving people, starting their relievers, relieving their starters—and bringing up an entire Triple A outfield.

Since Murtaugh seldom talked much—Dock felt—when he *did* talk, and *did* criticize his ballplayers, his words had a weight to them. Looking at the bewildered ball club, Dock felt that Murtaugh was undermining the confidence of the ballplayers, and making a bad situation worse. The press was riding Richie Hebner so hard on his fielding, Dock felt, that Hebner was nervous at the plate and wasn't hitting. Richie Zisk had contract problems with Joe Brown, and that's why he wasn't hitting. Dock felt that if the Pirates could just ignore manager and management, and play their own best ball game, that they would pull out of their slump, win their division, and go all the way.

He decided to make his views known. On the bus that carried the team from Stouffer's to Riverfront Stadium, he told player representative Jim Rooker that he wanted to address the team. Rooker told Murtaugh, and Murtaugh called a team meeting, announcing that Dock had a few words to say to his teammates.

Everyone assumed that Dock was going to apologize for not going to the bullpen, and would publicly declare his rededication, and would give the team a fight speech.

"They don't know me then," Dock said afterward. The idea of apologizing had never occurred to him. As far as he was concerned, the bullpen matter had been a private quarrel between him and Murtaugh, and now it was over; now Ramon Hernandez was hurt, and Kent Tekulve was tired, and Dock fully expected to spend the evening in the bullpen at Riverfront Stadium—and quite possibly to face the Reds for the first time since he had hit their first three batters, fifteen months before.

Everything happens, when Cincinnati and the Pirates get together.

No one was carrying a tape recorder that night in the dressing room.

After reading a dozen different accounts of Dock's talk, and after talking with Dock and some of the players about it (I couldn't talk with Murtaugh or Joe Brown; when I got to Pittsburgh a week later, they had agreed to seal lips), I think I know what happened. Approximately. No one who was there will agree with me wholly. No two people, in a room where someone makes a speech, hear exactly the same speech.

Dock began by saying that he would be traded the following winter, and that therefore he would speak his mind openly. (A self-fulfilling prophecy.) This statement of openness implied criticism of others: everything in his speech had been said—continually, widely, and surreptitiously—by other ballplayers behind each other's backs.

He said that he had lost his respect for Murtaugh as a manager, because Murtaugh had panicked and was making stupid moves on the field and criticizing his players unfairly. He said that Joe Brown had messed up Richie Zisk's mind by not settling a contract with him, and that's why Zisk was not hitting. He said panicky pressure from Murtaugh was having the same effect on the hitting of Parker and Oliver. These statements acknowledged that Zisk, Parker, and Oliver were not hitting so well as they might; later, he was accused of attacking his teammates.

But the *Pirates*—Dock insisted—the *teammates*, the *ballplayers* could win despite their manager and their general manager, if they would just ignore management and play as well as they knew how. Warming to another example, he began to say that the team needed Richie Hebner's bat, but that Hebner was so nervous over criticism of his fielding that he couldn't concentrate at the plate.

He had just said, "We all know Hebner's got cement hands" when Danny Murtaugh, his face flaming red, leaped up and interrupted him. First he offered to fight Dock, but Dock refused. Then Don Leppert, with whom Dock had quarreled before, started to take a punch at Dock, but was restrained. Murtaugh told Dock to leave the clubhouse, that he was suspended. Dock took a shower, and emerged to hear a second team meeting—on the subject of the first team meeting—and then walked back to Stouffer's. There, he picked up Renee, who had expected him a few hours later, and they went to Pigall's for dinner.

From coast to coast, newspapers erupted with the latest Dock Ellis scandal. CLOUDS GATHER OVER ELLIS, ran a headline in the *Ann Arbor News*. The AP story which followed said that Dock had delivered "a tirade against his manager and some others." In the *Boston Globe*, another wire service story reported that Dock was "suspended for thirty days without pay—which means that he's out some twelve thousand to fifteen thousand dollars, according to his attorney—and the Pirates cannot replace him on the roster."

Smizik's story, in the *Pittsburgh Press*, was the most colorful:

A furious Danny Murtaugh told Dock Ellis to get out of uniform and leave the clubhouse last night after the problem-child pitcher berated the manager in front of the entire team.

As a result of the incident, Pirate general manager Joe L. Brown suspended Ellis without pay.

Brown said, "I don't care what Ellis is going to do. He has been treated fairly by the Pirate organization and has not reciprocated."

Ellis may remain on the suspended list for no more than thirty days. Asked what would happen after that, Brown said, "We'll leave that to my fertile imagination." . . .

When the Pirates arrived at their clubhouse at Riverfront Stadium at 4:45 for a game with Cincinnati yesterday, Ellis was in the process of getting into uniform and seemed in good spirits.

He conversed freely with his teammates, but had a "no comment" for all questions from reporters.

Player representative Jim Rooker went to Murtaugh telling him that Ellis would like to have a team meeting and wanted the manager present. Murtaugh consented.

"I thought and I think everyone else thought that he wanted to apologize," said Murtaugh.

As events were soon to prove, that was not on the mind of Ellis, who failed to last the first inning in his two previous starts and had been relegated to the bullpen.

"When he started talking I didn't realize what he was saying at first," said Murtaugh. "I wasn't expecting it. When it finally dawned on me I realized it was one of those speeches you hear but you can't believe.

"I can't remember what he said, but it was detrimental to the management, the manager and some of the players."

Murtaugh, an easy-going man who seldom shows anger, was too furious to talk with reporters until some fifteen minutes after the incident.

"I was listening to what he was saying," related the manager, "and I thought, 'Hey, I've got to act.' So I acted." . . .

When it was over, Murtaugh stormed out of the clubhouse. Ellis immediately began dressing and was gone some twenty minutes after the blowup.

Before leaving, he offered a cheery "No comment" to an approaching reporter who asked what he was doing out of uniform. . . .

Dock went back to Pittsburgh.

On Monday in the *New York Daily News*, the story on a Mets victory began, "If the Mets win the pennant, credit the Pirates and Dock Ellis." Jerry Koozman came out of the bullpen to win a game in relief. When his manager had asked him to go to the bullpen, the newspaper said, he responded, " 'Sure, I'll go the bullpen,' and later added, 'I read about Dock Ellis being asked.' "

In *Sports Illustrated*, the reporter wrote:

> . . . Murtaugh assumes Ellis wants to apologize to the team when he requests a meeting before the game. Instead the pitcher begins a loud harangue directed mainly at the bewildered manager, who finally storms over to Ellis and offers to fight him. A coach intervenes and Murtaugh winds up separating coach and player. It may be the only serious exchange that has taken place in the dressing room all week.

Back at the *Pittsburgh Press,* Bob Smizik's prose was dancing:

> The next move is up to Dock Ellis.
> But no matter what baseball's most reluctant reliever does, it probably won't be enough to return him to a Pirate uniform.
> Pirates general manager Joe L. Brown indicated yesterday that Ellis, suspended without pay Saturday after harshly criticizing Manager Danny Murtaugh at a team meeting, would have to go a long way before returning to the Pirates.
> "As of today," said Brown, "I don't know if there's anything he can do to get back in a Pirate uniform."
> Brown, who was seething when he announced Ellis' suspension Saturday before the Pirate-Cincinnati game, added, "I had a close relationship with Dock Ellis. He's injured it rather severely."
> But before Ellis can get to Brown, he must first satisfy Murtaugh, who was expecting an apology rather than an attack when the problem-child pitcher asked for a team meeting. . . .

9. *Exile*

On August 22, I drove to Pittsburgh. Dock was living in a grand apartment on a hill between Pittsburgh and the airport, living with Renee, a beautiful and self-reliant young woman nearly as tall as Dock. In the living room was comfortable new furniture, and an enormous color TV which Dock had bought a few weeks earlier, Renee told me, when he had felt depressed. Pictures of Shangalesa and Roberto Clemente took pride of place in a hallway. In a separate room, the walls were thick with tacked-up snapshots of Dock, of friends, of teammates.

Dock was gone when I arrived, out buying beer. The kitchen was crowded with taco materials. When he entered with an armload of Iron City, we began to talk.

"I believe they took it as a *personal* thing," Dock says. "Which is not what it was intended to *be*. I was telling them how I *felt*. No one can change my feelings."

Dock laughs when he says this, and the laugh is neither humorous nor is it bravado. It protests mildly: *how can anyone expect him to change his feelings? And if he has feelings, is he not free to express them?* I catch a note of appeal in this small laugh. He goes on, and explains, defending himself, and sometimes I hear this appeal again. However much he tells me he was right, this time he *wonders* if he was right. This time he feels dismay.

"They say they're going to keep me suspended for thirty days. You have to pay the price. If you speak your mind you got to pay the price."

I ask him if he sees any of the other ballplayers now.

"No, not outside of Willie. I talked to Parker, to Sanguillen, that's about it. Sangy is telling me it's like a morgue over there. He says, 'No one talk but me.' He says, 'No one talking but me and Parker.' He say everyone say they be talking just because they be hitting the ball."

He gets back to the subject. "I said something you're not supposed to say," he says. "That seems to be the case all the time!" He laughs again.

At this point, all we know is what we read in the newspapers. "Were you trying to help the team?" I ask.

"That's what my intention was. Now Murtaugh took it personally. I didn't say that much *to* him. I just said I had lost respect for him *as a manager*. A lot of stuff was directed at the team."

"Who on the team were you criticizing?" I asked. I believed what I read.

So Dock told me the context in which he had spoken about the players. "I used Parker as an example. How can you single out a twenty-four-year-old *kid* that's carried the team all year?" Ever since Murtaugh singled out Parker, Dock says, Parker stopped hitting. "He singled out Al Oliver too. How are you going to do that and the man's been producing every year he's been here? Plus the dude is temperamental."

I thought Dock was telling me something. "Was he just getting on the black players?"

"No. It didn't have anything to do with that."

Many people have assumed that the quarrel between Murtaugh and

Ellis had something "to do with that," that an unspoken and unacknowledged racial antipathy underlay this conflict. A Boston friend of mine—Boston caught in a racial war between Irish and black—telephoned me, assuming that Murtaugh vs. Ellis was another front of the South Boston wars. But the conflict had nothing to do with race.

"I gave them another example. Richie Zisk. They got his mind all screwed up. He's made statements in the paper now that he would have knocked my block off. But he was one of the first that pulled me over to the side, that night, and told me that everything I said was true. Oh, like I was telling them at the meeting: *Don't let them manipulate your mind.* And take your body and your soul: That's what they've done to him. He pulled me over to the side and tells me one thing, and then contradicts himself in the paper. They got him! I know they got him!"

As we relax on the large soft chairs, the telephone rings and Dock talks with a friend named Sandy. In the course of his chat, I hear Dock explain that apparently he has "hurt their feelings," and mentions that he will meet Murtaugh to set things straight. "They feel like I really *hurt* them," he tells Sandy.

When he hangs up I ask him about this meeting.

"Yeah, I'm calling Murtaugh. I owe the dude—not an *apology*, but to let the dude know that I wasn't directing anything at him personally. I don't have no hard feelings either for him or for Joe Brown. We have always been *friends*. I told him at the meeting, I said, 'I just don't have no respect for you *as a manager.*'"

Dock sprawls on the sofa, Renee beside him. "The point I was trying to get to the team, at the beginning of my little speech, was, 'Let him scream and holler at us and do anything he wants to do—but you just do your thing. *He's* the one who's panicked. It's not the *club. He's* the one who panicked.

"The manager has a right to get mad, but he don't throw the ball and he don't hit the ball. 'It's on you as a ballplayer,' I told them. They didn't hear that. They just heard me when I was saying that he's the one who panicked." Dock was telling them that it was their business to play better ball and win games, whether their manager panicked or not. "He got guys going to the plate *shaking.*"

"When you took your shower," I say, "and came back through, what was going on in the second team meeting?"

"I hear one individual say that 'they—are—the—bosses' "—Dock's voice is precise, sissyish—" 'so—we—are—supposed—to do—what they say.' " He shakes his head. He looks at us to make sure that we have heard him correctly. "When you hear that," he says, "you know just what kind of a ballplayer that's coming from. A ballplayer that all he does is play to the front office. In the long run, they'll come out ahead on their contracts, by siding with management."

We ask him who said it, and he tells us the name of a journeyman ballplayer, older. Then he adds the name of another player with similar toadyish manners. One is black, the other white. "I'm not used to playing with these type ballplayers. They call Murtaugh dummy behind his back. They say Candalaria is a horseshit guy; they don't know him. Outsiders. I'm not used to playing with these type ballplayers. I don't like to be around that environment. No pride! How can they look their sons in the eye and say, 'I am a man.' No pride at all. None at all. None at all."

"Did people speak up at your meeting, when you called the meeting?"

"Only one guy on the team said, 'I don't like it.' That was Rooker, and he said he had lost all respect for me."

"What exactly did you say about Hebner?"

"I told them, I said, 'Now Hebner, they are driving him crazy behind his fielding.' I said, 'But we all know Hebner's got cement hands—' "

I tell Dock I understand how somebody might interpret that metaphor as critical.

"Right!" says Dock. "Nobody knows my head at all. But I was going to tell them, they putting more emphasis on his hands than on his bat. And that's making his bat *weak*, because he's thinking about fielding the ball. See, Hebner's the kind of dude, you've got to leave him alone, let him go ahead.

"But when I said that about hands, that's when he stopped me. He jumped up screaming and cursing. 'You're not going to run my fucking ball club! You're not gonna talk to my ballplayers that way! He called them all assholes for letting me talk to them like that. Which meant he didn't understand what I said either."

"So what did you eat at Pigall's?" I ask Dock.

"I had the lamb," he answered without reflection. "It was out of sight. I ate the *bones*. Renee had something out of sight."

Renee offers from the next room: "Shrimp with mushrooms and cheese sauce."

Dock and Renee show me home movies, from the Pirates' most recent trip to California. Here are Dock and Renee at the beach, at Disneyland with Shangalesa, with Elizabeth, with Sandra and her family, with Momma; the whole family playing cards. Then there is a sequence showing Dock in Dodger Stadium, in Pirate uniform, wandering around before the game, sticking his head out of the dugout, scrutinizing the crowd. All the time he is wearing enormous Elton John sunglasses, with bright-red, heart-shaped rims. As he watches himself moving silently against the white wall of the living room, Dock supplies commentary, his voice rising in pitch to a street voice: "If I was in the crowd," he says, "I would want to cut into that dude. I would think, 'What's going on in his head?' If I saw somebody like that, I would really want to cut into *that* dude!"

Eating tacos at dinner, Dock speculates on the future. The tacos are huge. "I could open a taco stand," he says. "Fifty cents apiece. Not bad. Or I got a job lined up, being a mailman in the Virgin Islands. Yeah, I could walk up and down hills all day, talking shit. Deliver mail. Pay the rent. Buy me a Volkswagen. That's all you can drive over there, streets so small. Out of sight."

The voice is gay. Sadness fills up the room, drifting like snow in North Dakota in February. I want to say something light. "Or you can be a real estate tycoon in Florida," I say.

Dock nods and makes an inclusive gesture. "Something," he says.

10. *The Empty Ball Park*

The next day I go out to the ball park. Before the game, I wander on the turf, feeling alien because Dock sits in his apartment a few miles away, reading hate mail and trying to listen and not to listen to the game on the television. I can't talk to Bruce Kison today, because he's pitching. With most of the other players I feel shy and awkward. They seem to feel shy and awkward when they see me. What can we say to each other? Finally I corner Ken Brett, and he sits down with me in the dugout. He plucks at the white double-knit of his uniform. "I don't think you'll ever see him in one of these again," he says.

First, he gives me the history of Dock in the bullpen, just as I know it. Then he talks about the famous speech. "He said a few things about Richie Zisk, and why he was having an off year perhaps, blaming management mostly. He mentioned some things about Danny putting added pressure on the players. Things were getting a little hairy. All of a sudden, Danny said, 'Hey, that's enough.' He just threw him out of the clubhouse. Next thing we knew, he was going to be suspended for thirty days."

I am hearing a *synoptic* account.

I need more. I want the look and feel of it from other sides. Ken Brett is smart, fresh, tough—a survivor; he played with the Red Sox, on the World Series team of 1967 at the age of eighteen, then with the Phillies, now with the Pirates—with brilliant pitching, amazing hitting, and a recurrent sore elbow. He and Dock have been friendly in the past. Now *Sports Illustrated* has quoted him about Dock's selfishness.

"Did you have any idea of Dock's motives?" I ask. "No. Everybody was like dumbfounded. I really think so. No one said anything. Everybody was looking at each other, until Danny jumped in after about two minutes. We thought, What's *next*? What's going to be *next*?"

A year and a half before, when Dock hit the Cincinnati batters, nobody knew what he was doing; the old pattern was repeating itself. This time, when Dock's action mystified everybody, it came directly after his refusal to go to the bullpen—so that mystification could give way, among some of the players, to anger.

"What's the feeling now?" I ask Ken Brett. "After the suspension?"

"The feeling now is—I think the majority of the team thinks he was wrong. There are a few guys who probably think he was right. Or maybe agree with him for just speaking his mind." Al Oliver was quoted in the press saying that Dock was right to speak up, and to be himself. "Maybe he *was* right in some respects," Brett continues. "I don't think he was. In all respects.

"I don't think his little speech had the effect that he wanted it to have. I think he meant it to be constructive but it didn't come out that way. It came out as an attack on Danny and the management and in the past they've been pretty tolerant. Of everybody, not just Dock. I think that the majority—we didn't really talk about it."

Again I notice the tendency—maybe the necessity—*not* to talk things over.

"He dug himself a hole too deep to get out of, this time. It's unfortunate. He can pitch. I went to the bullpen and I'm a starter. I'm getting paid to start games and I—It's no thrill for me to go to the bullpen. But hell, this is a team. Dock has always said that, and I thought he'd go. I was surprised he didn't go."

I see Joe Brown, and go out to shake his hand. He greets me warmly, or with the appearance of warmth—I'm not positive that you can tell, with a general manager—and we talk for a while about how we cannot talk.

He speaks nonetheless of "our friend." I sense in Joe Brown an exasperated fondness for Dock Ellis.

Then I grab Willie Stargell. He cannot play today, with his fractured ribs, but he suits up and takes BP. Sitting with me in the nearly empty dugout, Willie talks slowly and carefully. I have seen other Willie Stargells—the joking ballplayer, the kind giant among the kids, the sleek and sophisticated bon vivant, dazzling in shades and a dark suit. Today, I see the public Willie, team captain, talking for publication about his old roommate in trouble—and weighing his contrasting obligations to his friend and to his team.

"Knowing Dock as I did—as I do, rather"—Willie begins with a terrible slip of the tongue—"I think that Dock will always try to do something in terms of helping the team sort of weather the particular storm that we were involved in at that time." Public Willie, speaking for print, talks like a Watergate lawyer, with a thousand words too many: "Evidently it just didn't come out right or someone misunderstood him or just what I don't know. I have been getting mixed emotions about the way it was handled. It was done in such a way that people thought it was not done in good taste at all.

"If it was done for the good of the team then I think there was a misunderstanding. I think maybe Dock should let it be known that maybe he just had a short fuse and things were going bad and he's sorry that it came out the way it did. In terms that, if he was stepping on someone's toes, that he didn't intend to—just come out publicly and say that you're sorry."

I think of Dock listening to this. "Have you said these things to Dock?" I ask Willie.

"No. We ate over at a friend's house and had dinner. We talked with the friends and other people, so we didn't get a chance to tear it down and put it back together. I plan to meet with him as soon as possible. I think that whether he plays with the Pirates or not, it's good they know his honest feelings. Dock says a lot of things, and a lot of people take him the wrong way. Like I said, I've known Dock for a number of years. I've seen him when things weren't going so good and when things were going good. Dock has always been a *talker*, and a lot of times people misunderstand him. I know Dock is real, and he's warm. He don't necessarily want people to know about his warmness, but nevertheless he is. If there's ever a situation where he could *help*, or give of his time, he does."

As Willie moves away from the public matter of Dock's necessary apology, and begins to reflect on his friend's character, his language changes.

I ask Willie if he feels though he wasn't there, that he really knows what Dock was up to.

"I think I do. Dock was trying to bring things out into the open. Get everything out into the open and say, 'Look. What happened happened.' I think he was detailing the criticism that—I don't know. Like I say we really haven't talked about the details. I think he should try and get people to understand what he was trying to do. Then let it be said whether he was wrong or right. Then if he felt that what he did was wrong, then apologize. Good people are the ones who can come and say, 'I'm sorry,' or 'I was wrong.' And if you're dealing with good people— which I'm sure that the Pirates are—maybe it would be best for the team if Dock didn't play for the Pirates, but at least they have accomplished something in terms of *rapport*. Then if he leaves there's not that bitter taste."

Through all his talk, I follow the assumption that Dock *was* wrong; although he loves his friend, Willie obviously thinks that Dock's talk was something besides useful criticism. "What was wrong with what Dock did?" I ask him.

He starts again to talk about misunderstanding. But then he allows me to see that he feels that Dock misunderstood his own motives.

"Dock is concerned about his *performance*. Sometimes your fuse is a little short. You start out to say something, and something else comes out."

I change the subject. I tell Willie that it makes me impatient—it even astonishes me—that there has been no word in the newspapers that purports to show Dock's side, Dock's intentions, or even Dock's ideas about his intentions.

"I don't think anyone has been able to get in touch with Dock," Willie says.

This touches on another matter. Everyone I see at the ball park acts astonished that I have been seeing Dock. "Where's he holed up?" they ask me. I tell them that he is in the same apartment he was in last week, and the week before—with the same telephone number, for that matter. I called him. Sandy called him. Anybody can call him who wants to.

Willie ignores what I say, and goes back to my earlier point. "And I don't think things like that should be done in the papers," Willie tells me. "Let the sources get together. What's important is Dock and management now. That's what it's all about. Always go to the source. Then you build from there. I hope it works out. If Dock is back with us, then past is past. If Nixon had said, 'I'm human, I made a mistake. What I've done other Presidents have done before, and I'm sorry,' he would have been given the world."

11. Reading the Mail

After two innings, I feel morose and cannot concentrate on the game. I leave the park and go back to Dock's apartment.

Back on the sofa, Dock and Renee are opening the mail, going through piles of envelopes and postcards delivered to Dock at Three Rivers Stadium. I start by asking him a question about Murtaugh. "Tell me what he did that got you mad, besides getting down at Parker and Oliver. What did he say?"

"Like we all had tight asses. Couldn't get a pin in. Plus he was screaming at Sangy. Like one time he had Sangy bunting. How you going to have the hottest man on the team bunting, and you're down by one run? Robertson and Zisk on the bases. Yeah, he bunted, and they got the man down on second, which is Zisk. *Then* he put in a pinch runner for Robertson at third. Like when he started screaming at Sangy, that's when I started watching the *moves*."

Then Dock talks about Murtaugh's moves with him, taking him out of games. It seems to me I see a connection between these anecdotes. So I quote Willie Stargell about Dock and his own performance, and about

Dock having a short fuse. "Didn't your anger—over how Murtaugh treated you—spill over into your talk?"

Dock is adamant. No, it did not. He does not want to think that way. One subject at a time.

The mail is mostly hate mail. Here's a postcard headed "Denver, Colorado," and dated "August 17, 1975":

> Dear Ellis:
>
> I see where you are pulling a tantrum and refusing to pitch—you black son of a bitch. You are lucky to be able to play ball, when the best you could probably do at any other job would be one hundred dollars a month—but—the league is full of stupid, black bastards trying to show that a nigger is as good as, or better than, anyone else.
> I suppose like all the other niggers you wear those carnival type clothes too—big hats, the whole bit. You must all look like a lot of clowns in the circus! RIGHT ON!
>
> Don Brown
>
> P.S.: I hope Murtaugh runs your black ass right out of the league.

Here's another:

> You were brought up in a TAR PAPER SHACK Now nothing's no' too good for you.
> You're just a STREET NIGGER that never become civilized. Hope they fire your black ass.

Hate mail started when he began professional baseball at Batavia, New York, in 1964, coming from "towns like Geneva, Wellsville—from all the towns I pitched in. It made me *mad*. If I'd had known it was *in* there, I'd never had opened it up."

"Doesn't it still make you mad?"

"I read it to see if I can remember how the people write. The majority usually write them the same way." By stylistic analysis Dock builds up a gallery of his detractors, the men who write with the same outrage year after year.

"Did you ever hear before from Don Brown, of Denver, Colorado?"

Dock laughs. "That's one thing," he says, "you can be sure of. There's no Don Brown, Denver, Colorado."

While there is hate mail there is also support. When the Pirates first returned home, after the suspension, young black kids marched at Three Rivers carrying signs supporting Dock. "Willie saw them," Dock tells me. "The guards took the signs away."

And there are letters, like Jackie Robinson's at the time of the All-Star flap. Today there is a long letter from a black man in Pittsburgh, a casual acquaintance, begging Dock not to shackle "his mind with resentments." He signs his *real* name.

In a normal week, Dock receives thirty or thirty-five letters, mostly requests for autographs. When the newspapers have carried a story, the mail bulges to a hundred, sometimes two hundred. "The majority of the time, Kirkpatrick's son helps me." They read through the mail together, beside Dock's locker at Three Rivers. "He keeps the sweetheart mail and the hate mail."

Continuing through the mail today, Dock finds a letter from Donna, who says that she will soon return from Las Vegas. Donna attributes Dock's problems to bad women, and implies that she will fix everything up.

But most of the letters curse him out as a no-good black bastard nigger who's making more money than he should be.

"One time I got fifty consecutive hate mail letters!" Dock boasts. Not an autograph request or a sweetheart among them. "That was the curlers," he says.

Although he is cool, even amused about the mail, it is not thoroughly funny nor satisfying nor comforting to realize how many maniacs exist out there. A week after I left Pittsburgh, just before Joe Brown reinstated Dock, someone stole Dock's Cadillac—with its DOCK license plate—and burned it to the ground.

Reading the letters, thinking about mail, Dock shows me documents of the current crisis: Joe Brown's two notes of suspension—the bullpen one, and the insubordination one. Then he remembers and finds an earlier and happier letter from Joe Brown. It's dated June 1975:

> Dock—Nice going both on and off the field! I thought you'd like a copy of this nice letter I received about you. Joe.

The nice letter came from Thomas N. Carros, Director of Child Welfare Services for Allegheny County:

> I want to take this opportunity to let you know how much I

appreciate Dock Ellis' splendid cooperation on June 3, when he
was named Honorary Chairman of Foster Parent Recruitment for
Allegheny County Child Welfare Services . . .

Mr. Ellis expressed a sincere interest in our need for foster
parents and was most generous with his time at the stadium. Mr.
Ellis not only gave the children and foster parents his undivided
attention, but also autographed a special Port Authority recruiting
bus.

Autographing a *bus?*

When I have looked over the letters, Dock says, "That hurts me too.
He can't see how I could do something like this, off the field, and then
come down on him so hard; like, represent the team better than anyone
on the team—off the field—and then tell him he's not on his job. He
don't understand me, because he thinks I'm acting *personally.*

"We did a caravan this year and I went on three trips," representing
the Pirates for public relations, visiting children in hospitals. "I've had
kids *standing* and applauding. I say, 'Now, I like to hear *cheers.*' I had
them standing and clapping five or six minutes. I say, 'I played
high-school basketball. I *love* to hear the cheers.' You get attached to the
little babies. There was one little baby—at this place, that wrote the
letter—he didn't even *smile.* He didn't even make an effort to *move.* He
was one of those—they beat him when he was four months old, bad, and
he was like seven months old when I saw him. It was *strange* to hold a
baby, and I couldn't make him laugh! If I tickled him or what. You move
your hand, and he wouldn't follow it with his eyes.

"Then I took him under a tree. He saw the leaves move. I took his
hands and he *felt* the leaves. Then he saw his hands move, and he started
moving his hands. I got him to smile, two or three times. The nurse said
this was the first time he moved his hands or smiled since they brought
him to the hospital. They had broken every bone in his legs. They said
he would never make an effort to stand up, and I had him standing up."

We put the letters away, testimony to hatred and misunderstanding,
testimony to affection and generosity. The letters all confirm Dock's
separation, now, from his team and his profession, his momentary exile
from the country of baseball.

12. *Recall*

At a press conference on August 30, Joe Brown released this statement:

> Dock Ellis has been reinstated today, following his suspension on August 16th after a clubhouse meeting in which he was critical of Danny Murtaugh, his coaches, his teammates and the Pirate front office. This meeting followed an earlier suspension and fine, which resulted from his refusal to comply with his manager's request to go to the bullpen.
>
> The decision to reinstate Dock Ellis is a joint determination on my part and that of Danny Murtaugh after much soul-searching. Both of us feel that morally, it is the proper thing for us to do at this time—just as we both felt that the suspension of Dock was appropriate two weeks ago. It was our firm intention ever since the infractions occurred to suspend him for the maximum period allowable under Baseball rules, and we did not anticipate that Dock would be back in a Pirate uniform in 1975.
>
> However, as time elapsed and as Dock privately indicated his sincere regret over his actions, a desire to apologize and a willingness to return to the team under our conditions, we asked ourselves, "How long should we continue to punish him?" Every religion that I know of teaches that "To err is human to forgive is divine."
>
> Four conditions were imposed on Dock before we would agree to his reinstatement. He has complied with all.
>
> 1) He met with his teammates a short time ago and informed them that he had apologized to Danny Murtaugh. At this meeting, Dock expressed his regret over his statements in Cincinnati and at the embarrassment he had caused his manager. He said he was sorry for bringing the names of his teammates into his conversation, admitted the untimeliness of his remarks and stated that all he wants to do is to help the team win. During the meeting, he further expressed his willingness to pitch whenever and wherever he is asked in the best interests of the team, subordinating his own personal preferences to what his manager feels is best for the Pirates.
>
> 2) He has accepted a substantial fine. Let me clarify this point. He is not being fined in addition to a suspension without pay. His suspension has been lifted retroactive to the date it was imposed, but Ellis is being fined a substantial amount.
>
> 3) The grievance filed through the Players' Association has been withdrawn.

4) The grievance filed through the National Labor Relations Board will be withdrawn.

I would like to make it very clear that our decision to lift the suspension was not affected in any way by the action of the Players' Association. We are not afraid of a fight when we feel we are right. Anyone who knows me and my stubbornness knows that I am not going to back down because of pressure. We are reinstating Dock because we feel it is the right thing to do.

In addition to the moral considerations, we owe it to our players and to our fans to put our best team on the field in our efforts to bring another World Championship to Pittsburgh. Dock *is* a fine pitcher who has proved in the past that he can make major contributions to a winning club. We do not feel that we should penalize the other 24 players by going with anything less than our best when the pennant is at stake. This is particularly true now that Dock has expressed his regret and his willingness to do anything possible to help the team.

It is my hope that with this unfortunate incident behind us, everyone in the Pirate family can now concentrate his time and efforts on the winning of another Championship.

Everybody gave in. Dock apologized and dropped his grievances. Dock received all his back pay, and was fined only $2500.

So what happened?

One observer, quoted by Charlie Feeney, "says that Brown had a good chance to lose the grievance fight, plus possibly losing with the National Labor Relations Board. The Players' Association had filed charges with the NLRB, charging that Murtaugh had disrupted and terminated a duly authorized union meeting on August 16."

So he had.

Maybe both sides had come to feel dismay. Joe Brown's loyalty to Danny Murtaugh is vast and commendable—but a month's suspension could seem an overreaction, two weeks after it was imposed. Or maybe Danny Murtaugh, given a fortnight to think over what had happened, could share with most of his players at least the notion that Dock had intended to act for the good of the team.

Still another possibility is that the suspension had served its purpose. When Dock was suspended on August 16, the Pirates were losing everything. They quickly began to win again, and by the twentieth they were back in first place. On the twenty-second they took both ends of a doubleheader from Cincinnati. By the thirtieth their recovery seemed secure.

Back in 1934, also in August, the Gas House Gang of the St. Louis

Cardinals was struggling toward the National League pennant. Then Dizzy and Paul Dean failed to travel with the team to an exhibition game, and their general manager fined them. When the Deans were fined, they went on strike, and were suspended without pay. The Cardinal ball club, in their absence, began to play better ball. "Football coaches pray for an incident such as this," Branch Rickey said in confidence. "They want something, some development, which can change the direction of a team, fire it up to superhuman effort." The Deans returned and the Cardinals became World Champions.

I don't suggest that Murtaugh was feigning anger in the clubhouse, that Saturday night in Cincinnati. But maybe by August 30, anger had accomplished all that it needed to accomplish.

In *The Sporting News*, back in March 1975, Charlie Feeney wrote about Dock, in his weekly column about the Pirates:

> Somebody accidentally broke a bottle in the trainer's room at Pirate City.
> "Fight . . . fight," Dock Ellis shouted.
> About a dozen Pirates rushed to the door of the trainer's room.
> "The Pirates are fighting again," Willie Stargell shouted. "There's blood all over the place." . . .
> Things became normal again. Ellis shouted at Dave Giusti, who shouted back. It goes on often in the Pirate clubhouse. It goes on in March, in July, in September. . . .
> Ellis is a ring leader of the put-ons. He enjoys riling up teammates in the clubhouse.
> "I wouldn't feel right with another club," said the Pirate pitcher, who often speaks out against the establishment. "First of all, I couldn't get away with my bull with another club. I wouldn't trust the people in the front office or maybe some of the players.
> "Here with the Pirates, I can bull with anybody. I bull with the owner, the general manager, the assistant general manager, the traveling secretary. I'd like to die a Pirate."

An article by John Mehno made the same point later that summer in the weekly Pittsburgh magazine *Score!*:

> "I think Dock's the key to this ballclub," says teammate Al Oliver. "He keeps everybody loose, so if there's any tension at all, it's left in the clubhouse. Dock brings it right out of us."
> Ellis' style is merciless needling, with his put-on insults continually ringing through the clubhouse.
> "That avoids a lot of arguments," Ellis says. "It lets you get rid of all your frustrations. You'll hear guys yellin' and screamin' at each other and it's a good thing."

. . ."Jerry Reuss is an example of a guy who wasn't used to that kind of thing," says Ellis. "He had never heard a white player call a black player 'nigger' until he got here. There was no way anyone could ever have done that on the other clubs he played for."

I think Dock was reinstated, by Joe Brown with Danny Murtaugh's agreement, at least partly because Joe Brown and Danny Murtaugh, like most of the players, liked Dock Ellis and needed what he contributed to the team.

Newspapers were full of quotes from the ballplayers.

Wilver Stargell: "It took a man to do what Dock did. If Nixon had been honest like that, he'd still be President."

Richie Zisk: "We were needling each other. I didn't say it seriously. There were four players that he criticized, and I was mad that he brought me into his problem. That's the only reason I was critical. But if a man's got something to say, he's got a right. He was using other players as an example and it backfired in his face. He started out trying to help the ball club. It came out the wrong way."

Al Oliver: "He was sincere today and he was sincere in Cincinnati too. I know that twenty-two of the ballplayers didn't know what he was talking about that day. He was just trying to state the reasons he felt the team was losing. I think the majority of the ballplayers will accept him. I don't think the fans will."

13. *The End*

So Dock returned to the team, pitched three no-hitters in a row, personally beat Cincinnati in the play-offs, and shut out Boston in the seventh game of the World Series to bring the championship to Pittsburgh. Then, in a special ceremony, he was awarded the Nobel Prizes in Peace, Chemistry, and Literature.

I suppose, however, that I must confine myself to history.

The next day, in a game that Larry Demery started, and in which Bruce Kison picked up the win, Dock made an appearance, pitching one inning in relief. He gave up one hit and one unearned run; there were two errors behind him, neither of them by Richie Hebner's cement hands. The cheers and boos were almost equal.

It was September, the month that the season looked forward to. The Pirates had suffered their worst slump, and were playing decent baseball. On the first day of the month, Tom Seaver shut them out. Then they took two in a row from the Mets, then split a doubleheader. They were holding on to first place, but the starting rotation was in trouble. Only Reuss was pitching well. Rooker was injured, Demery was injured, Kison was wild, and Candalaria was a rookie. "Things are so bad that Dock Ellis"—the *Pittsburgh Press* noted on September 6, exactly a week after reinstatement—"will start Monday."

On Monday, September 8, Dock beat the Cubs three to one, pitching six innings, and giving up five hits and one run. Ramon Hernandez shut them out for the last three innings. "At first the boos may have outnumbered the cheers," said the paper. "But as the game progressed, and Ellis pitched well, the cheers increased. And when he left the game in the seventh inning, some people even rose to their feet in applause. For that, Dock Ellis, the heavy of all heavies, tipped his cap."

On the thirteenth, Dock lost to Montreal, five to one, giving up four earned runs in five innings.

On September 18, Dock started and lost four to one to Philadelphia. BUC FUTURE ROSIER THAN DOCK'S AFTER 4-1 LOSS, said the headline. ". . . there is little likelihood that Dock Ellis will be a Pirate next season," wrote Bob Smizik once again. "Though the problems Ellis caused Pirate management in August may be gone they are not forgotten." The reporter nonetheless quoted Murtaugh as saying that Dock "had bad pitching luck," but "Ellis wasn't prepared to agree. Informed of his manager's opinion, he said, 'They hit the ball hard, nonetheless.' "

Coming back to the clubhouse, Dock found the atmosphere tense and stiff. At his interview with Murtaugh before reinstatement, he felt that Murtaugh still took his remarks personally. Now, his teammates were *weird*, not just with him but with each other. "Everything was false. Even the rah-rah guys, it was *false*."

People were friendly. Richie Hebner, of the maligned hands, drank Scotch with him one long night. At a party where a number of teammates got high, one by one a number of them confided to him that the press had misquoted them, when they were alleged to have judged him harshly.

On September 22, the Pirates beat Philadelphia eleven to three, and clinched their division. In a meaningless game on the twenty-fourth, Dock pitched two innings in relief and gave up one run. His regular season was over.

The Reds beat Pittsburgh three straight for the National League pennant. Dock pitched two innings of relief in the first game in Cincinnati, giving up no runs.

In the seventh inning he retired the Reds in order, striking out two batters. In the eighth, he got Don Gullett to bounce out, and then suffered a single from his old adversary and friend, Pete Rose. It was a fastball that was not quite inside enough, and Pete hit it up the middle, as is his wont. Morgan hit a grounder to Hebner, forcing Rose at second. Then John Bench hit a single to right field off the end of his bat, and Morgan took third. Perez flied out to short center field.

It was Dock's last pitch as a Pittsburgh Pirate.

The vultures were there, perched on a television camera.

When the between-innings commercial faded, the camera centered on Dock taking the last of his warm-ups. There he stood waiting for the ball, his face heavy and somber with intelligence and will. The Cincinnati fans, white and winning, combined boos with ironic cheers. The ball in his glove, leaning forward to stare at the batter, he tipped his cap with slow and hostile dignity, like a Latin translation of a rude gesture.

Oh, in the announcers' booths, wired like space dolls, the chatterers are chattering. Maury Wills, Dock's old teammate, complimented his "good arm," the way you might say, of an ax murderer, that he dressed with good taste. Joe Garagiola marveled how times had changed; why, in *his* day, when *he* was a ballplayer, he used to hope that his manager would like *him!* Nowadays, the manager was supposed to get his players to like him; gee, is that progress?

And all over the country the people who always take no for an answer, who never speak up to anyone in authority, who smile when they are kicked—all the good niggers of all races who shuffle and yassuh the bosses—the army of docile hypocrites nods its head in its armchair. Spokesman Joe, the smiling huckster, who flatters commissioners and networks and products—clever man, witty man, man doubtless cynical about the bosses he flatters and the masses he cajoles—Joe speaks the word: *this man does not play our game.* And Maury Wills, who knows and resents his place, summons the platitudes available, and stops just short of mentioning, by way of summary, that Dock has a Bad Attitude.

People have been trading Dock Ellis from the Pirates since 1971. In 1975, it was serious business.

In fact it might not have happened. It only became necessary when Danny Murtaugh decided to sign for another year as manager. And it was necessary then—as I believe—not because Murtaugh held a grudge or expected further trouble, but because of Pittsburg fans, whipped up by newspapers. If Ellis returned, and Murtaugh were still manager, Murtaugh would have looked irresolute, and Joe Brown desperate. Both of these men, like the ballplayers and anyone close to the club, knew that Dock was a team member, as well as a good right arm. But the public, coached by the press, would not have stood still for it.

After the reinstatement in August, John Mehno had written: "There was a feeling of resentment toward the Pirates by a segment of the community . . ." Dock's unpopularity in Pittsburgh was greater than ever. When *Score!* put Dock on the cover in August, the circulation department had objected in advance. They said that the issue would not sell. The issue was one of the poorest sellers in the history of the magazine.

In the autumn, rumors flew around. Frank Robinson, rumor had it, wouldn't touch him, in a suggested trade for Jim Bibby. Just before the December meetings, Charles Feeney presented an interview with Dock in *The Sporting News,* and it was Dock's farewell to his team:

> Don't look for Dock Ellis to knock the Pirates or their fans. It won't happen.
> When the 1975 season ended, Ellis knew it was his last as a Pirate. He just didn't know where he would be pitching next season.
> Ellis had no choice. If he did, he'd probably select the Yankees because he'd like to play in New York. He thinks that he and Billy Martin could get along because, he said, "We both want to win."
> Ellis has no regrets for anything he did in seven-plus seasons with the Pirates. He knows his run-in with Danny Murtaugh last August was the signal of an ending of his Pirate days. . . .
> Ellis is a Joe Brown man, he said. . . .
> "I can play for Joe Brown," Ellis said. "I've grown to love that man."

On December 11, the Pirates traded Willie Randolph and Ken Brett and Dock Ellis to the New York Yankees for Doc Medich. Doc Medich was finishing medical school at the University of Pittsburgh, which made the trade convenient for him. He is young, he had a poor season in 1975, and obviously Joe Brown was crossing his fingers and counting on years ahead. And Joe Brown bet a hundred dollars, with a Yankee official, that Dock would win at least fifteen games for the Yankees in 1976.

For Dock, it was the best place to go. There were people who shuddered at the thought of Billy Martin and Dock together. Billy Martin loses his cool as often as he keeps it. But when Martin was asked how he felt about Ellis, he said, "The Hall of Fame is full of tough cases."

Meanwhile the tough case, who had lobbied extensively to be traded to the Yankees, was ecstatic. Now he would pitch in the Little League, and throw ground balls on real grass. He would wear pinstripes. He would get the attention that only New York athletes get. In the next *Sporting News*, after the issue which contained Dock's farewell to Pittsburgh, the Yankee writer interviewed Dock, the new Yankee. *Ave atque vale.*

Thinking of Dock when the news reached him, I remembered a night a year and a half earlier, when he had just pulled out of a slump by pitching and winning a complete game against Houston.

Late at the hotel, he sits back in a yellow chair, pulling on a Kool, drinking his orange juice and vodka.

"One year," he says, "I'm going to get my shit together. I'm going to *fuck around*, out there, and win the Cy Young. You'll see. And that's what it'll *be*, just *fucking around*—to see what I can *do*. That's going to be a trip."

He laughs and looks away, twirling the ice in his glass. He laughs again, "You know how Pisces dream," he says.

In the country of baseball, citizens in their prime keep their bags packed, ready to steam from depot to depot, exchanging red and white uniforms for blue and white ones, or occasionally for pinstripes.

Retired citizens keep rows of different uniforms in their closets.

As a ballplayer ages, each move to another team, each spring in the Florida sun again, he moves a little closer to the time when he will retire from the noon of games to the evening porches of memory. And in the meantime, the game becomes more intense and more cherished, each season as the noon declines.